# The
# Wascana
# Poetry Anthology

ഇൗ

# The
# Wascana
# Poetry Anthology

ഇറ

edited by

Richard G. Harvey
English Department, University of Regina

CANADIAN PLAINS RESEARCH CENTER 1996

Canadian Plains Research Center
University of Regina
Regina, Saskatchewan S4S 0A2
Canada

Canadian Cataloguing in Publication Data

Main entry under title:
The Wascana poetry anthology

      Includes index.
      ISBN 0-88977-096-4

1. English poetry.  2. Canadian poetry (English).*
3. American poetry.  4. Poetry - Collections.
I. Harvey, Richard G., 1941-  II. University of Regina.
Canadian Plains Research Center.

PN6101.W383 1996    821    C96-920089-7

Cover Design: Agnes Bray/Donna Achtzehner
Cover Photograph: "Blue Snow" by Bob Howard, courtesy of Bob Howard.

Printed and bound in Canada by
Hignell Printing Limited, Winnipeg, Manitoba

Printed on acid-free paper

# PREFACE

This anthology is the result of a need perceived by a number of my colleagues at the University of Regina for a collection useful in teaching verse to first-year students. Most available such editions are, many have found, simply too large and elaborate for our semester teaching format, or just more advanced than are our students.

The volume's genesis was a survey of our university instructors which asked them to name the ten favorite poems they used in first-year classes. With that list (many repeatedly requested) as a basis, I fleshed out the collection to provide a more rounded survey of English verse from the Middle Ages to recent times, and from both sides of the Atlantic. Special emphasis has been given to poetry by writers of the Great Plains region (both Canadian and American), and by aboriginal poets of the two countries, since the anthology is published by our university's Canadian Plains Research Center, and our Saskatchewan Indian Federated College is the sole such institution at a university in North America. Because of these features, I hope this volume will find a special place among anthologies in an overcrowded field.

Above all, however, I have tried to keep in mind the *teaching* of poetry. Too many works which appear in standard anthologies seem to me unapproachable by the average first-year student; consequently, I have attempted to choose works — not necessarily easy ones — which address experiences and ideas more readily available to beginning university students, and which are more direct and straightforward in expression than many currently anthologized. My own biases will be readily apparent: there is a far higher proportion of comic and satiric verse, of eighteenth-century poems, and of works by women; there are fewer of the standard Romantic and Victorian warhorses. On principle, as well, I have preferred shorter to longer poems, as likely to create better classroom experiences in the time instructors have at their disposal.

Works have also been selected with other aims in mind. Thematic interrelationship is one such criterion. As well as some familiar examples of *carpe diem* poems, for instance, there are less known ones by Gay, Rochester, and Souster; poems by Ralegh, Spenser, and Shakespeare compare human life to theatre; works about poetry itself include examples from Anne Bradstreet to Seamus Heaney. Generic connections have also been considered. Thus there are a number of love complaints — starting with Chaucer's mock one, for example — a group of epigrams and epitaphs, and many sonnets. The even larger collection of elegies (both serious and comic) stretches from Ben Jonson to Robert Kroetsch. Finally, I have tried to provide poems which illustrate most of the poetic techniques defined in the glossary and which are commonly taught in introductory classes in poetry.

Copyright and other problems have prevented inclusion of a few writers (notably T.S. Eliot) which I regret; I hope these omissions may be remedied in future. We have also been restricted by available space and finances. Nonetheless I trust the selection is wide enough to provide for every taste. If your favorite poem is not here, there should be others — especially unfamiliar ones — which will please and challenge.

As for editorial practice: arrangement of authors and works is chronological as much as possible; poems published in the same year are placed alphabetically, as are authors born in the same year. Texts of the poems have been scrutinized carefully and I have generally preferred minimal editorial intrusion. Except in the cases of Smart and Blake, spellings have generally been modernized and standardized to either British or American practice, depending on the nationality of the authors; Canadian poems follow the spellings of original publication. The editor's eclectic Canadian spelling mixture will be readily apparent in the glossary but will not, I hope, prove too objectionable. Punctuation — insofar as is possible — has been left as close to the original printings as can be done without compromising sense or metrics. Contractions have been expanded provided that metrics are not affected. A few readings — such as Suckling's "The Constant Lover" (page 40) — may surprise instructors familiar with the commonly-known versions found elsewhere.

I have attempted to annotate everything which — through years of teaching experience — I know or sense will cause problems for students. If this is either excessive or meagre, I welcome correction from users of the anthology. Other than this, apparatus has been kept to: a glossary of critical terms which should prove useful support for instructors; dates of birth and death; nationality (for aboriginal writers, also tribe); and dates of writing and publication (where known) to the left and right respectively for each poem.

My particular thanks for their assistance goes to Christopher Murray, Ken Mitchell, and my other colleagues in the Department of English, as well as to Brian Mlazgar, Donna Achtzehner, and Agnes Bray of the Canadian Plains Research Center, all at the University of Regina.

Richard G. Harvey

# CONTENTS

# [Sumer is icumen in]¹

| | |
|---|---:|
| Sumer is icumen° in, | *has come* |
| Lhude° sing, cuccu°! | *loudly / cuckoo* |
| Groweth sed° and bloweth° med° | *seed / blooms / meadow* |
| And springth the wude° nu.° | *wood / now* |

5   Sing, cuccu!

| | |
|---|---:|
| Awe° bleteth after lomb, | *ewe* |
| Lhouth° after calve cu,° | *lows / cow* |
| Bulluc sterteth,° bucke verteth.° | *leaps / twists* |
| Murie° sing, cuccu! | *merrily* |

10   Cuccu, cuccu,

Wel singes thu, cuccu.

| | |
|---|---:|
| Ne swik° thu naver° nu! | *cease / never* |

Sing cuccu nu, sing cuccu!
Sing cuccu, sing cuccu nu!

*(ca. 1240-1310)*


# Western Wind

Westron wind, when will thou blow?
The small rain down can rain.
Christ, if my love were in my arms,
And I in my bed again.

*(ca. 1500)*                                    *(1790)*


# The Three Ravens

There were three ravens sat on a tree,
   *Down a down, hay down, hay down,*
There were three ravens sat on a tree,
   *With a down,*

---

1  Compare Ezra Pound's "Ancient Music" (p. 151).

5    There were three ravens sat on a tree,
      They were as black as they might be,
          *With a down, derry, derry, derry, down, down.*[1]

      The one of them said to his mate,
      "Where shall we our breakfast take?"

10    "Down in yonder green field,
      There lies a knight slain under his shield.

      "His hounds they lie down at his feet,
      So well they can their master keep.

      "His hawks they fly so eagerly,°            *fiercely*
15    There's no fowl dare him come nie."°           *near*

      Down there comes a fallow° doe,         *yellow-brown*
      As great with young as she might go.

      She lift up his bloody head,
      And kissed his wounds that were so red.

20    She got him up upon her back,
      And carried him to earthen lake.°        *pit (i.e. grave)*

      She buried him before the prime;°         *[6 a.m.]*
      She was dead herself ere evensong time.°    *[6 p.m.]*

      God send every gentleman
25    Such hawks, such hounds, and such a leman.°    *lover*
*(16th century?)*                      *(1611)*

# Sir Patrick Spens

      The king sits in Dumferling town,
          Drinking the blude-reid° wine:       *blood-red*
      "O whar will I get a guid sailor
          To sail this ship of mine?"

5    Up and spak an eldern° knicht,         *elderly*
          Sat at the king's richt knee:
      "Sir Patrick Spens is the best sailor
          That sails upon the sea."

---

1  The following stanzas repeat the first lines and the refrains.

The king has written a braid° letter,                                          *open*
10    And signed it wi' his hand,
And sent it to Sir Patrick Spens,
    Was walking on the sand.

The first line that Sir Patrick read,
    A loud lauch° lauched he;                                          *laugh*
15  The next line that Sir Patrick read,
    The tear blinded his ee.°                                          *eye*

"O wha° is this has done this deed,                                          *who*
    This ill deed done to me,
To send me out this time o' the year,
20    To sail upon the sea?

"Make haste, make haste, my mirry men all,
    Our guid ship sails the morn:"
"O say na sae, my master dear,
    For I fear a deadly storm.

25  "Late late yestre'en° I saw the new moon,                                          *yesterday eve*
    Wi' the auld° moon in her arm,                                          *old*
And I fear, I fear, my dear master,
    That we will come to harm."

O our Scots nobles were richt laith°                                          *right loath*
30    To weet° their cork-heeled shoon;°                                          *wet / shoes*
But lang owre° a' the play were played,                                          *ere*
    Their hats they swam aboon.°                                          *above*

O lang, lang may their ladies sit,
    Wi' their fans into their hand,
35  Or e'er they see Sir Patrick Spens
    Come sailing to the land.

O lang, lang may the ladies stand,
    Wi' their gold kembs° in their hair,                                          *combs*
Waiting for their ain° dear lords,                                          *own*
40    For they'll see thame na mair.°                                          *more*

Half o'er, half o'er to Aberdour
    It's fifty fadom° deep,                                          *fathoms*
And there lies guid Sir Patrick Spens,
    Wi' the Scots lords at his feet.

*(16th - 18th centuries)*        *(1765)*

# Edward

    "Why does your brand sae drap wi' bluid,
        Edward, Edward?
    Why does your brand sae drap wi' bluid,
        And why sae sad gang° ye, O?"        *go*
5  "O I ha'e killed my hawk sae guid,°        *good*
        Mither, mither,
    O I ha'e killed my hawk sae guid,
        And I had nae mair° but he, O."        *more*

    "Your hawkes bluid was never sae reid,°        *red*
10       Edward, Edward.
    Your hawkes bluid was never sae reid,
        My dear son I tell thee, O."
    "O I ha'e killed my reid-roan° steed,        *chestnut*
        Mither, mither,
15  O I ha'e killed my reid-roan steed,
        That erst° was sae fair and free, O."        *before*

    "Your steed was auld° and ye ha'e gat mair:°        *old / more*
        Edward, Edward.
    Your steed was auld and ye ha'e gat mair:
20       Som other dule° ye dree,° O."        *grief / suffer*
    "O I ha'e killed my fader dear,
        Mither, mither,
    "O I ha'e killed my fader dear,
        Alas and wae° is me, O!"        *woe*

25  "And whatten penance wul ye dree for that,
        Edward, Edward?
    And whatten penance wul ye dree for that,
        My dear son, now tell me, O?"
    "I'll set my feet in yonder boat,
30       Mither, Mither,
    I'll set my feet in yonder boat,
        And I'll fare over the sea, O."

    "And what wul ye do wi' your towers and your ha',°        *hall*
        Edward, Edward?
35  And what wul ye do wi' your towers and your ha',
        That were sae fair to see, O?"
    "I'll let thame stand til they down fa',
        Mither, mither,
    I'll let thame stand til they down fa',
40       For here never mair maun° I be, O."        *must*

"And what wul ye leave to your bairns° and your wife,          *children*
       Edward, Edward,
And what wul ye leave to your bairns and your wife,
       Whan ye gang over the sea, O?"
45  "The warldes room° late them beg thrae° life,          *world's space | through*
       Mither, mither,
The warldes room late them beg thrae life,
       For thame never mair wul I see, O."

"And what wul ye leave to your ain mither dear,
50       Edward, Edward?
And what wul ye leave to your ain mither dear,
       My dear son, now tell me, O?"
"The curse of hell frae° me sal° ye bear,          *from | shall*
       Mither, mither,
55  The curse of hell frae me sal ye bear,
       Sic° counseils ye gave to me, O."          *such*

*(15th - 18th centuries)*

---

GEOFFREY CHAUCER          *English (ca. 1343-1400)*

from *The Canterbury Tales*

# General Prologue

        Whan that Aprill with his° shoures soote°          *its | showers sweet*
   The droghte° of March hath perced° to the roote,          *dryness | pierced*
   And bathed every veyne° in swich licour°          *vein | such liquid*
   Of which vertu° engendred is the flour;°          *power | flower*
5  Whan Zephirus° eek° with his sweete breeth          *west wind | also*
   Inspired hath in every holt and heeth°          *wood and field*
   The tendre croppes,° and the yonge sonne          *new leaves*
   Hath in the Ram his half cours yronne,[1]
   And smale foweles° maken melodye,          *birds*
10 That slepen al the nyght with open ye°          *eye*
   (So priketh hem nature° in hir corages),°          *nature urges them | hearts*
   Thanne longen folk to goon on pilgrimages,
   And palmeres[2] for to seken straunge strondes,°          *foreign shores*
   To ferne halwes,° kowthe° in sondry londes;          *far-away shrines | famed*

---

1  The sun is young because the solar year has just begun with the vernal equinox; it has passed into the second half of the zodiacal sign of Aries (the Ram), in Chaucer's time, March 12-April 11.

2  Pilgrims who had been to the Holy Land carried a palm frond as an emblem.

| | | |
|---|---|---|
| 15 | And specially from every shires ende | |
| | Of Engelond to Caunterbury they wende, | |
| | The hooly blisful martir° for to seke, | *blessed martyr [Thomas à Becket]* |
| | That hem hath holpen° whan that they were seeke.° | *helped / seek* |
| | Bifil° that in that seson on a day, | *it happened* |
| 20 | In Southwerk at the Tabard¹ as I lay | |
| | Redy to wenden on my pilgrymage | |
| | To Caunterbury with ful devout corage,° | *heart, spirit* |
| | At nyght was come into that hostelrye° | *inn* |
| | Wel nyne and twenty in a compaignye | |
| 25 | Of sondry° folk, by aventure yfalle° | *various / chance fallen* |
| | In felaweshipe, and pilgrimes were they alle, | |
| | That toward Caunterbury wolden° ryde. | *wished to* |
| | The chambres° and the stables weren wyde, | *bedchambers* |
| | And wel we weren esed atte beste.° | *best made comfortable* |
| 30 | And shortly,° whan the sonne was to reste, | *briefly* |
| | So hadde I spoken with hem everichon° | *everyone* |
| | That I was of hir felaweshipe anon,° | *immediately* |
| | And made forward° erly for to ryse, | *agreement* |
| | To take oure wey ther as I yow devyse.° | *[will] explain* |
| 35 | But nathelees,° whil I have tyme and space,° | *nonetheless / opportunity* |
| | Er that I ferther in this tale pace,° | *pass, proceed* |
| | Me thynketh it acordaunt to resoun° | *in accord with logic (or propriety)* |
| | To telle yow al the condicioun° | *circumstances* |
| | Of ech° of hem, so as it semed me, | *each* |
| 40 | And whiche they weren, and of what degree, ° | *status, rank* |
| | And eek in what array° that they were inne; | *dress* |
| | And at a knyght than wol I first bigynne. | |
| | | |
| | A Knyght ther was, and that a worthy man, | |
| | That fro the tyme that he first bigan | |
| 45 | To riden out, he loved chivalrie, | |
| | Trouthe° and honour, fredom° and curteisie. | *fidelity / generosity* |
| | Ful worthy was he in his lordes werre,° | *war* |
| | And therto hadde he riden, no man ferre,° | *farther* |
| | As wel in cristendom as in hethenesse,° | *pagan lands* |
| 50 | And evere honoured for his worthynesse; | |
| | At Alisaundre° he was whan it was wonne. | *Alexandria [in 1365)* |
| | Ful ofte tyme he hadde the bord bigonne° | *sat at the head of the table* |
| | Aboven° alle nacions in Pruce;° | *above [knights of] / Prussia* |
| | In Lettow° hadde he reysed° and in Ruce,° | *Lithuania / raided / Russia* |
| 55 | No Cristen man so ofte of his degree. | |
| | In Gernade at the seege° eek hadde he be° | *siege / been* |

---

1 The Tabard Inn in Southwark, across the Thames from London; the road to Canterbury and Dover started there.

Of Algezir, and riden in Belmarye.
At Lyeys was he and at Satalye,[1]
Whan they were wonne, and in the Grete See°     *Mediterranean*
60  At many a noble armee° hadde he be.     *invasion*
At mortal batailles° hadde he been fiftene,     *jousts to the death*
And foughten for oure feith at Tramyssene°     *Tlemcen [Algeria]*
In lystes° thries, and ay° slayn his foo.°     *tournaments | always | foe*
This ilke° worthy knyght hadde been also     *same*
65  Somtyme° with the lord of Palatye°     *formerly | Balat [Turkey]*
Agayn° another hethen in Turkye;     *against*
And everemoore he hadde a sovereyn prys.°     *outstanding reputation*
And though that he were worthy, he was wys,°     *wise, prudent*
And of his port° as meeke as is a mayde.     *manner, behaviour*
70  He nevere yet no vileynye° ne sayde     *rudeness*
In al his lyf unto no maner wight.°     *any sort of person*
He was a verray,° parfit° gentil° knyght.     *true | complete | noble*
But for to tellen yow of his array,°     *dress*
His hors° were goode, but he was nat gay.°     *horses | richly attired*
75  Of fustian° he wered a gypon°     *coarse cloth | tunic*
Al bismotered° with his habergeon,°     *rust-stained | coat of mail*
For he was late ycome from his viage,°     *journey, travel*
And wente for to doon his pilgrymage.

With hym ther was his sone, a yong Squier,°     *knight in service to another*
80  A lovyere and a lusty° bacheler,     *lively*
With lokkes crulle as° they were leyd in presse.°     *curly as if | crimped*
Of twenty yeer of age he was, I gesse.
Of his stature he was of evene lengthe,°     *moderate height*
And wonderly delyvere,° and of greet strengthe.     *agile*
85  And he hadde been somtyme in chyvachie°     *cavalry expeditions*
In Flaundres, in Artoys, and Pycardie,[2]
And born hym weel, as of so litel space,[3]
In hope to stonden° in his lady° grace.     *find favour | lady's*
Embrouded° was he, as it were a meede°     *embroidered | meadow*
90  Al ful of fresshe floures, whyte and reede,°     *red*
Syngynge° he was, or floytynge,° al the day;     *singing | whistling, piping*
He was as fressh as is the month of May.
Short was his gowne, with sleves longe and wyde.
Wel koude° he sitte on hors and faire ryde.     *knew how to*
95  He koude songes make and wel endite,°     *write poetry*

---

1  The Knight has fought the Moors not only at Alexandria in Egypt but in Spain at Grenada and Algeciras [1344 and after], Ben-Marin in Morocco, Ayash in Armenia [1367], and Attalia in Turkey [1361].

2  Flanders, Artois, and Picardy, locations of English-French fighting during the Hundred Years War.

3  Conducted himself well, considering the short time he had been in knightly service.

Juste ° and eek° daunce, and weel purtreye° and write.          *joust | also | draw*
So hoote° he lovede that by nyghtertale°          *passionately | at nighttime*
He sleep° namoore than dooth a nyghtyngale.          *slept*
Curteis° he was, lowely,° and servysable,°          *courteous | modest | attentive*
100     And carf° biforn his fader at the table.          *carved*

        . . . . . . . . . . . . . . . . . . . . . . . . . . . .

        Ther was also a Nonne, a Prioresse,°          *mother superior*
        That of hit smylyng was ful symple and coy;[1]
120     Hire gretteste ooth° was but by Seinte Loy;°          *strongest oath | Eloi [Elegius]*
        And she was cleped° madame Eglentyne.          *called*
        Ful weel she soong the service dyvyne,°          *liturgy*
        Entuned° in hir nose ful semely;°          *intoned | becomingly*
        And Frenssh she spak ful faire and fetisly,°          *elegantly*
125     After the scole of Stratford atte Bowe,[2]
        For Frenssh of Parys was to hire unknowe.
        At mete° wel ytaught was she with alle;°          *meals | moreover*
        She leet° no morsel from hir lippes falle,          *let*
        Ne wette hir fyngres in hir sauce depe;
130     Wel koude° she carie a morsel and wel kepe°          *know how to | take care*
        That no drope ne fille° upon hire brest.          *fell*
        In curteisie° was set° ful muchel hir lest.°          *good manners | fixed | pleasure*
        Hir over-lippe° wyped she so clene          *upper lip*
        That in hir coppe° ther was no ferthyng° sene          *cup | morsel*
135     Of grece,° whan she dronken hadde hir draughte.          *grease*
        Ful semely° after hir mete she raughte.°          *politely | reached for*
        And sikerly° she was of greet desport,°          *certainly | deportment*
        And ful plesaunt, and amyable of port,°          *bearing, manner*
        And peyned hire° to countrefete cheere°          *she took pains | manners*
140     Of court, and to been estatlich of manere,°          *dignified in behaviour*
        And to ben holden digne° of reverence.          *worthy*
        But for to speken of hire conscience,
        She was so charitable and so pitous°          *compassionate*
        She wolde wepe, if that she saugh° a mous          *saw*
145     Kaught in a trappe, if it were deed° or bledde.          *dead*
        Of° smale houndes hadde she that she fedde          *some*
        With rosted flessh,° or milk and wastel-breed.°          *meat | fine white bread*
        But soore wepte she if oon of hem were deed,
        Or if men smoot° it with a yerde smerte;°          *beat | rod painfully*
150     And al was conscience and tendre herte.
        Ful semyly° hir wympul pynched° was,          *elegantly | headdress pleated*
        Hir nose tretys,° hir eyen greye as glas,          *well-made*

---

1   Unaffected and demure, a stock phrase in medieval literature when a lover is praising his mistress.

2   Anglicized French learned at a convent school in a London suburb, rather than at the royal court or in Paris.

Hir mouth ful smal, and therto° softe and reed.°    *also | red*
But sikerly° she hadde a fair forheed;    *certainly*
155 It was almoost a spanne° brood, I trowe;°    *[of a hand] | believe*
For, hardily,° she was nat undergrowe.    *assuredly*
Ful fetys° was hir cloke, as I was war.°    *tasteful | aware*
Of smal° coral aboute hire arm she bar°    *dainty | bore*
A peire of bedes, gauded al with grene,[1]
160 And theron heng° a brooch of gold ful sheene,°    *hung | bright*
On which ther was first write a crowned A,
And after *Amor vincit omnia.*°    *Love conquers all*

. . . . . . . . . . . . . . . . . . . . . . . . . . . . . .

445    A good Wif° was ther of biside° Bathe,    *prosperous woman | from near*
But she was somdel deef,° and that was scathe.°    *somewhat deaf | a pity*
Of clooth-makyng she hadde swich an haunt°    *such a skill*
She passed° hem of Ypres and of Gaunt.°    *surpassed | Ghent [in Flanders]*
In al the parisshe wif ne was ther noon
450 That to the offrynge° bifore hire sholde goon;    *offertory [at Mass]*
And if ther dide, certeyn so wrooth° was she    *angry*
That she was out of alle charitee.
Hir coverchiefs° ful fyne weren of ground;°    *head-coverings | in texture*
I dorste° swere they weyeden° ten pound    *dare | weighed*
455 That on a Sonday weren upon hir heed.
Hir hosen° weren of fyn scarlet reed,    *stockings*
Ful streite yteyd,° and shoes ful moyste° and newe.    *tightly laced | soft*
Boold was hir face, and fair, and reed of hewe.
She was a worthy womman al hir lyve:°    *life*
460 Housbondes at chirche dore she hadde fyve,[2]
Withouten° oother compaignye in youthe —    *not counting*
But thereof nedeth nat to speke as nowthe.°    *right now*
And thries° hadde she been at Jerusalem;    *thrice*
She hadde passed many a straunge strem;°    *foreign sea*
465 At Rome she hadde been, and at Boloigne,
In Galice at Seint Jame, and at Coloigne.[3]
She koude° muchel of wandrynge by the weye.[4]    *knew*
Gat-tothed was she, soothly for to seye.
470 Upon an amblere° esily° she sat,    *pacing horse | comfortably*

---

1  A string of coral prayer beads [i.e. a rosary] divided after every ten with larger green beads (gaudes). This detail, as most of the others in her character description, suggests the Prioress is more of a secular lady from chivalric romance or the court than a spiritually dedicated religious. The motto on her brooch is similarly ambiguous.

2  In the Middle Ages, the marriage service was performed in the porch or outside the church itself, after which a nuptial Mass was celebrated inside.

3  Jerusalem, Rome, Boulogne, St. James of Compostella (in Galicia, Spain) and Cologne were the major pilgrimage sites of Europe.

4  She knew much of travelling on the roads [of pilgrimage], but also "wandered" off the path of virtue. In the next line, the Wife's widely spaced teeth ("gat-tothed") were a sign of the amorousness of the straying woman.

| | |
|---|---|
| Ywympled wel,° and on hir heed an hat | *wearing a large headdress* |
| As brood as is a bokeler° or a targe; | *buckler [both small shields]* |
| A foot-mantel° aboute hir hipes large, | *riding skirt* |
| And on hir feet a paire of spores° sharpe. | *spurs* |
| 475  In felaweshipe wel koude she laughe and carpe.° | *chatter* |
| Of remedies of love she knew per chaunce,° | *as it happened* |
| For she koude of that art the olde daunce.[1] | |

. . . . . . . . . . . . . . . . . . . . . . . . . . . . . .

| | |
|---|---|
| With hym[2] ther rood a gentil Pardoner[3] | |
| 670  Of Rouncivale, his freend and his compeer,° | *comrade* |
| That streight was comen fro the court of Rome.° | *papal court* |
| Ful loude he soong "Com hider, love, to me!" | |
| This Somonour bar to hym a stif burdoun;° | *strong accompaniment* |
| Was nevere trompe° of half so greet a soun. | *trumpet* |
| 675  This Pardoner hadde heer as yelow as wex, | |
| But smothe it heeng° as dooth a strike of flex;° | *hung / hank of flax* |
| By ounces° henge his lokkes that he hadde, | *thin strands* |
| And therwith he his shuldres overspradde;° | *overspread* |
| But thynne it lay, by colpons° oon and oon. | *in "rats'-tails"* |
| 680  But hood, for jolitee,° wered° he noon, | *nonchalance / wore* |
| For it was trussed° up in his walet.° | *packed / knapsack* |
| Hym° thoughte he rood al of the newe jet;° | *he / latest fashion* |
| Dischevelee,° save° his cappe, he rood al bare. | *with loose hair / except for* |
| Swiche glarynge eyen° hadde he as an hare. | *bulging eyes* |
| 685  A vernycle[4] hadde he sowed upon his cappe. | |
| His walet, biforn hym in his lappe, | |
| Bretful° of pardoun comen from Rome al hoot.° | *brimful / hot* |
| A voys° he hadde as smal° as hath a goot.[5] | *voice / high* |
| No berd hadde he, ne nevere sholde have; | |
| 690  As smothe it was as it were late shave. | |
| I trowe° he were a geldyng or a mare.° | *believe / eunuch or homosexual* |
| But of his craft, fro Berwyk into Ware° | *[i.e. the length of England]* |
| Ne was ther swich° another pardoner. | *such* |
| For in his male° he hadde a pilwe-beer,° | *pack / pillow-case* |
| 695  Which that he seyde was Oure Lady veyl;° | *Lady's veil* |

---

1  She knew all the old routines or "tricks of the trade" in relation to unrequited love, including (probably) love potions.

2  The previous character portrait is of the Summoner, whose occupation was to conduct to the ecclesiastical court persons accused of offenses against canon law. The power of the office led to much corruption, and Chaucer's example is an immoral — if likeable — rogue.

3  A Pardoner dispensed papal indulgences, or remittances of penance for sins (especially in Purgatory) in exchange for donations to charitable institutions. This Pardoner purports to represent the hospital of St. Mary Roncevall near London, a branch of an important religious house in Spain. Even more than Summoners, these minor ecclesiastics could be unscrupulous self-seekers — as Chaucer's character openly displays.

4  A souvenir reproduction of St. Veronica's veil, a famous relic in St. Peter's, Rome, bearing the imprint of Christ's face.

5  Like hares (line 684), goats were believed to be lecherous.

|  |  |
|---|---|
| He seyde he hadde a gobet of the seyl° | *piece of the sail* |
| That Seint Peter hadde, whan that he wente | |
| Upon the see,° til Jhesu Crist hym hente.° | *sea | seized, caught* |
| He hadde a croys of latoun° ful of stones, | *cross of brassy alloy* |
| 700 And in a glas he hadde pigges bones. | |
| But with thise relikes,[1] whan that he fond | |
| A povre person° dwellynge upon lond,° | *poor parson | in the countryside* |
| Upon a day he gat hym° moore moneye | *got himself* |
| Than that the person gat in monthes tweye;° | *two* |
| 705 And thus, with feyned° flaterye and japes,° | *false | tricks* |
| He made the person and the peple his apes.° | *tools [made monkeys of them]* |
| But trewely to tellen atte laste,° | *finally* |
| He was in chirche a noble ecclesiaste. | |
| Wel koude he rede a lessoun or a storie,° | *epistle or gospel* |
| 710 But alderbest° he song an offertorie;[2] | *best of all* |
| For wel he wiste,° whan that song was songe, | *knew* |
| He moste preche and wel affile his tonge° | *sharpen his speech* |
| To wynne silver, as he ful wel koude; | |
| Therefore he song the murierly and loude.° | *more merrily and loudly* |

*(ca. 1386-1400)*                              *(1478)*

# The Complaint of Chaucer to His Purse[3]

|  |  |
|---|---|
| To yow, my purse, and to noon other wight° | *person* |
| Complayne I, for ye be my lady dere. | |
| I am so sory, now that ye been lyght;° | *empty, fickle* |
| For certes° but yf° ye make me hevy chere,°[4] | *certainly | unless | appearance* |
| 5 Me were as leef° be layd upon my bere;° | *I would prefer | bier* |
| For which unto your mercy thus I crye, | |
| Beth hevy° ageyn, or elles mot I dye. | *heavy, pregnant* |
| | |
| Now voucheth sauf this day or hyt° be nyght | *it* |
| That I of yow the blisful soun may here° | *hear* |
| 10 Or see your colour lyk the sonne bryght | |
| That of yelownesse hadde never pere.° | *equal* |
| Ye be my lyf, ye be myn hertes stere.° | *rudder* |

---

1  As the Pardoner passes off the alloy as gold, so he claims the stones and pig's bones are genuine saints' relics.

2  Section of the Mass sung before the offering of alms.

3  The *envoy* (*Lenvoy*) — French for "sending" or "dispatch" — is addressed to the newly crowned Henry IV (1399) to continue Chaucer's pension; the rest of the poem (a "ballade") may have been written earlier, and addressed to Henry's predecessor, Richard II, but reused on this occasion (Henry complied). Chaucer mockingly treats his purse as his lover in the language of courtly love complaints (note line 2 and the refrain of each stanza). The *envoy* refers to the legend that England was founded by Brutus, a descendent of Aeneas the Trojan.

4  Chaucer puns on two meanings of "hevy": *weighty* (with gold) and *sorrowful* or *grave* look (on a lady's face).

Quene of comfort and of good companye,
Beth hevy ageyn, or elles moot I dye.

15 Now purse that ben to me my lyves° lyght    *life's*
And saveour° as doun in this world here,    *saviour*
Out of this toune° helpe me thurgh° your myght,    *town / through*
Syn° that ye wole nat ben my tresorere;°    *since / treasurer*
For I am shave° as nye as any frere.°    *bare (i.e. penniless) / friar*
20 But yet I pray unto your curtesye,
Beth hevy agen, or elles moot I dye.

*Lenvoy de Chaucer*

O conquerour of Brutes Albyon,°    *Brutus's Britain*
Which that by lyne and free eleccion
Been verray° kyng, this song to yow I sende,    *very (true)*
25 And ye, that mowen° alle oure harmes amende,    *might*
Have mynde upon my supplicacion.

*(1399, and before?)*      *(1477)*

---

# SIR THOMAS WYATT      *English (1503-1542)*

# [Farewell, Love]

Farewell, Love,° and all thy laws forever,    *Cupid*
   Thy baited hooks shall tangle me no more;
   Senec° and Plato call me from thy lore,    *Seneca [Roman philosopher]*
   To perfect wealth° my wit° for to endeavour.    *well-being / mind*
5 In blind error when I did persever,
   Thy sharp repulse that pricketh aye so sore
   Hath taught me to set in trifles no store
   And scape forth since liberty is lever.°    *perferable*
Therefore farewell; go trouble younger hearts
10    And in me claim no more authority;
   With idle youth go use thy property
   And thereon spend thy many brittle darts:
      For hitherto though I have lost all my time,
      Me lusteth° no longer rotten boughs to climb.    *I desire*

*(1520-30)*      *(MS. ca. 1540)*

# [They flee from me]

They flee from me that sometime did me seek
With naked foot stalking° in my chamber.    *walking quietly*

I have seen them gentle, tame, and meek
That now are wild and do not remember
5   That sometime they put themself in danger°                    *in my debt*
To take bread at my hand; and now they range
Busily seeking with a continual change.¹

Thanked be Fortune it hath been otherwise
Twenty times better, but once in special,°                       *especially*
10  In thin array after a pleasant guise,
When her loose gown from her shoulders did fall
And she me caught in her arms long and small,°                   *slender*
Therewithal sweetly did me kiss
And softly said, "Dear heart, how like you this?"

15  It was no dream: I lay broad waking.
But all is turned thorough° my gentleness                        *through*
Into a strange fashion of forsaking.°                            *abandonment*
And I have leave to go of her goodness
And she also to use newfangleness.°                     *fashionable fickleness*
20  But since that I so kindly° am served,                        *normally*
I would fain know what she hath deserved.

*(1520-30)*                              *(MS. ca. 1540)*

---

# Henry Howard, EARL OF SURREY    *English (1517-1547)*

## [The soote season]

The soote° season, that bud and bloom forth brings,             *sweet*
With green hath clad the hill and eke the vale.
The nightingale with feathers new she sings;
The turtle° to her make° hath told her tale.                    *dove | mate*
5   Summer is come, for every spray now springs.
The hart hath hung his old head on the pale;°                   *enclosure*
The buck in brake° his winter coat he flings;                   *thicket*
The fishes float with new repaired scale;
The adder all her slough away she slings;
10  The swift swallow pursueth the flies small;
The busy bee her honey now she mings;°                          *mixes*
Winter is worn that was the flowers' bale.°                     *harm, death*
        And thus I see among these pleasant things
        Each care decays; and yet my sorrow springs.

*(1557)*

---

1 Wyatt uses hunting terminology here: dogs "range," pursuing ("seeking") game, and may "change" from one quarry to another. Note also the double pun in line 14.

# Sir Walter Ralegh

*English (ca. 1552-1618)*

## The Nymph's Reply to the Shepherd[1]

If all the world and love were young,
And truth in every shepherd's tongue,
These pretty pleasures might me move
To live with thee and be thy love.

5    Time drives the flocks from field to fold,
When rivers rage and rocks grow cold,
And Philomel° becometh dumb;           *the nightingale*
The rest complains of cares to come.

The flowers do fade, and wanton fields
10   To wayward winter reckoning yields;
A honey tongue, a heart of gall,
Is fancy's spring, but sorrow's fall.

Thy gowns, thy shoes, thy beds of roses,
Thy cap, thy kirtle,° and thy posies        *outer petticoat*
15   Soon break, soon wither, soon forgotten,
In folly ripe, in reason rotten.

Thy belt of straw and ivy buds,
Thy coral clasps and amber studs,
All these in me no means can move
20   To come to thee and be thy love.

But could youth last and love still breed,
Had joys no date nor age no need,
Then these delights my mind might move
To live with thee and be thy love.

*(1600)*

## [What is our life?]

What is our life? A play of passion,
Our mirth the music of division.°     *counterpoint, variations*
Our mother's wombs the tiring-houses° be,    *dressing rooms*
Where we are dressed for this short comedy.

---

1  An answer to Christopher Marlowe's "The Passionate Shepherd to his Love" (p. 17). See also John Donne's "The Bait" (p. 26).

5   Heaven the judicious sharp spectator is,
That sits and marks still who doth act amiss.
Our graves that hide us from the searching sun
Are like drawn curtains when the play is done.
Thus march we, playing, to our latest rest,
10  Only we die in earnest, that's no jest.

*(1612)*

---

# EDMUND SPENSER

*English (ca. 1552-1599)*

## from *Amoretti*

### 30

My love is like to ice, and I to fire;
    How comes it then that this her cold so great
    Is not dissolved through my so hot desire,
    But harder grows the more I her entreat?
5  Or how comes that my exceeding heat
    Is not allayed by her heart-frozen cold:
    But that I burn much more in boiling sweat,
    And feel my flames augmented manifold?
What more miraculous thing may be told,
10    That fire, which all things melts, should harden ice,
    And ice, which is congealed with senseless cold,
    Should kindle fire by wonderful device?
Such is the power of love in gentle mind,
    That it can alter all the course of kind.°           *nature*

### 54

Of this world's theatre in which we stay,
    My love like the spectator idly sits
    Beholding me that all the pageants° play,          *roles*
    Disguising diversely my troubled wits.
5  Sometimes I joy when glad occasion fits,
    And mask in mirth like to a comedy:
    Soon after when my joy to sorrow flits,
    I wail and make my woes a tragedy.
Yet she, beholding me with constant eye,
10    Delights not in my mirth nor rues my smart:
    But when I laugh she mocks, and when I cry
    She laughs and hardens evermore her heart.
What then can move her? If nor mirth nor moan,
    She is no woman, but a senseless stone.

One day I wrote her name upon the strand,°          *beach*
    But came the waves, and washèd it away.
    Again I wrote it with a second hand;
    But came the tide, and made my pains his prey.
5  "Vain man," said she, "that dost in vain assay
    A mortal thing so to immortalise;
    For I myself shall like to this decay,
    And eke my name be wiped out likewise."
"Not so," quoth I; "let baser things devise
10    To die in dust, but you shall live by fame:
    My verse your virtues rare shall eternise,
    And in the heavens write your glorious name,
Where whenas death shall all the world subdue,
    Our love shall live, and later life renew."

                *(1595)*

---

# SIR PHILIP SIDNEY          *English (1554-1586)*

## from *Astrophel and Stella*

### 59

Dear, why make you more of a dog than me?
    If he do love, I burn, I burn in love;
    If he wait well, I never thence would move;
If he be fair, yet but a dog can be.
5  Little he is, so little worth is he;
    He barks, my songs thine own voice oft doth prove;°      *test*
    Bidden, perhaps he fetcheth thee a glove;
But I unbid, fetch even my soul to thee.
    Yet while I languish, him that bosom clips,°      *embraces*
10  That lap doth lap, nay lets, in spite of spite,
This sour-breathed mate taste of those sugared lips.
    Alas, if you grant only such delight
        To witless things, then Love, I hope (since wit
        Becomes a clog°) will soon ease me of it.      *hindrance, encumbrance*

*(before 1583)*                 *(1591,1598)*

## Sir John Harington
*English (1560-1612)*

## Of Treason

Treason doth never prosper, what's the reason?
For if it prosper, none dare call it treason.

*(1615)*

## Michael Drayton
*English (1563-1631)*

from *Idea*

### 61

Since there's no help, come let us kiss and part.
Nay, I have done, you get no more of me;
And I am glad, yea, glad with all my heart,
That thus so cleanly I myself can free.
5   Shake hands for ever, cancel all our vows,
And when we meet at any time again,
Be it not seen in either of our brows
That we one jot of former love retain.
Now at the last gasp of Love's latest breath,
10  When, his pulse failing, Passion speechless lies,
When Faith is kneeling by his bed of death,
And Innocence is closing up his eyes,
     Now if thou wouldst, when all have given him over,
     From death to life thou mightst him yet recover.

*(1619)*

## Christopher Marlowe
*English (1564-1593)*

## The Passionate Shepherd to his Love[1]

Come live with me, and be my love,
And we will all the pleasures prove,°                    *test*

---

[1]   See Sir Walter Ralegh's "The Nymph's Reply to the Shepherd" (p. 14) and John Donne's "The Bait" (p. 26).

That valleys, groves, hills, and fields,
Woods, or steepy mountain yields.

5    And we will sit upon the rocks,
Seeing the shepherds feed their flocks,
By shallow rivers, to whose falls
Melodious birds sing madrigals.

And I will make thee beds of roses,
10    And a thousand fragrant posies,
A cap of flowers, and a kirtle,°               *outer petticoat*
Embroidered all with leaves of myrtle.°    *[shrub sacred to Venus]*

A gown made of the finest wool,
Which from our pretty lambs we pull,
15    Fair lined slippers for the cold,
With buckles of the purest gold;

A belt of straw and ivy buds,
With coral clasps and amber studs:
And if these pleasures may thee move,
20    Come live with me, and be my love.

The shepherd swains shall dance and sing
For thy delight each May morning
If these delights thy mind may move,
Then live with me, and be my love.

*(1599)*

---

# WILLIAM SHAKESPEARE         *English (1564-1616)*

## from *Sonnets*

### 18

Shall I compare thee to a summer's day?
Thou art more lovely and more temperate:
Rough winds do shake the darling buds of May,
And summer's lease hath all too short a date:
5    Sometime too hot the eye of heaven shines,
And often is his gold complexion dimmed,
And every fair from fair sometime declines,
By chance or nature's changing course untrimmed;°    *stripped of beauty*
But thy eternal summer shall not fade,
10    Nor lose possession of that fair thou ow'st°               *ownest*
Nor shall Death brag thou wand'rst in his shade
When in eternal lines to time thou grow'st:
      So long as men can breathe or eyes can see,
      So long lives this, and this gives life to thee.

## 29

When in disgrace with Fortune and men's eyes,
I all alone beweep my outcast state,
And trouble deaf heaven with my bootless° cries,  *futile*
And look upon myself and curse my fate,
5 Wishing me like to one more rich in hope,
Featured° like him,° like him with friends possessed, *handsome | another*
Desiring this man's art and that man's scope,
With what I most enjoy contented least;
Yet in these thoughts myself almost despising,
10 Haply I think on thee, and then my state,
(Like to a lark at break of day arising
From sullen° earth) sings hymns at heaven's gate: *gloomy, heavy*
  For thy sweet love remembered such wealth brings,
  That then I scorn to change my state with kings.

## 55

Not marble, nor the gilded monuments
Of princes shall outlive this powerful rhyme;
But you shall shine more bright in these contents
Than unswept stone° besmeared with sluttish° time. *memorial | dirty*
5 When wasteful° war shall statues overturn, *destructive*
And broils° root out the work of masonry, *uprisings, battles*
Nor Mars his sword, nor war's quick fire shall burn
The living record of your memory.
'Gainst death and all oblivious enmity° *forgetful hatred*
10 Shall you pace forth: your praise shall still find room
Even in the eyes of all posterity
That wear this world out to the ending doom.° *doomsday*
  So till the judgment that yourself arise,
  You live in this, and dwell in lovers' eyes.

## 73

That time of year thou mayst in me behold,
When yellow leaves, or none, or few, do hang
Upon those boughs which shake against the cold,
Bare ruined choirs, where late the sweet birds sang.
5 In me thou see'st the twilight of such day
As after sunset fadeth in the west,
Which by and by black night doth take away,
Death's second self, that seals up all in rest.
In me thou see'st the glowing of such fire,
10 That on the ashes of his youth doth lie,
As the deathbed whereon it must expire,
Consumed° with that which it was nourished by. *burnt*
  This thou perceiv'st, which makes thy love more strong,
  To love that well which thou must leave ere long.

## 116

Let me not to the marriage of true minds
Admit impediments:[1] love is not love
Which alters when it alteration finds,
Or bends with the remover to remove.[2]
5  Oh no, it is an ever-fixèd mark°            *seamark, beacon*
That looks on tempests and is never shaken;
It is the star to every wandering bark,
Whose worth's unknown although his height° be taken.    *altitude*
Love's not Time's fool,° though rosy lips and cheeks    *victim*
10  Within his bending° sickle's compass° come;    *curved / sweep*
Love alters not with his brief hours and weeks,
But bears it out° even to the edge of doom.°    *endures / doomsday*
    If this be error and upon me proved,
    I never writ, nor no man ever loved.

## 130

My mistress' eyes are nothing like the sun;
Coral is far more red than her lips' red;
If snow be white, why then her breasts are dun;°    *tan, dark*
If hairs be wires, black wires grow on her head.
5  I have seen roses damasked,° red and white,    *variegated*
But no such roses see I in her cheeks,
And in some perfumes is there more delight
Than in the breath that from my mistress reeks.°    *is exhaled*
I love to hear her speak, yet well I know
10  That music hath a far more pleasing sound;
I grant I never saw a goddess go;°    *walk*
My mistress when she walks treads on the ground.
    And yet by heaven I think my love as rare
    As any she belied° with false compare.°    *misrepresented / comparison*

## 138

When my love swears that she is made of truth,[3]
I do believe her, though I know she lies,
That she might think me some untutored youth,
Unlearnèd in the world's false subtleties.
5  Thus vainly thinking that she thinks me young,
Although she knows my days are past the best,
Simply° I credit her false-speaking tongue:    *straightforwardly, naively*

---

1  An allusion to the marriage service: "if any of you know cause or just impediment why these persons should not be joined together...."

2  Withdraws when its object does.

3  One of several puns throughout this poem; "made of truth" means both "truth-telling" and "faithful to me." "Lies" (2, 3, 14) means "tells lies" and "sleeps with someone else." Other puns include "simply" (7), "habit" (11), and "told" (12).

On both sides thus is simple truth suppressed.
But wherefore says she not she is unjust?°                    *unfaithful*
10   And wherefore say not I that I am old?
Oh, love's best habit° is in seeming trust,                   *dress, procedure*
And age in love, loves not to have years told.°              *counted, divulged*
       Therefore I lie with her, and she with me,
       And in our faults by lies we flattered be.

                                     *(1609)*


from *As You Like It*

# [All the world's a stage]

All the world's a stage,
And all the men and women merely players;
They have their exits and their entrances,
And one man in his time plays many parts,
5    His acts being seven ages. At first the infant,
Mewling° and puking in the nurse's arms.                     *crying*
Then the whining schoolboy, with his satchel
And shining morning face, creeping like snail
Unwillingly to school. And then the lover,
10   Sighing like furnace,° with a woeful ballad              *as a furnace [smokes]*
Made to his mistress' eyebrow. Then a soldier,
Full of strange oaths, and bearded like the pard,°           *leopard*
Jealous in° honor, sudden,° and quick in quarrel,            *of his / rash*
Seeking the bubble reputation
15   Even in the cannon's mouth. And then the justice,
In fair round belly with good capon lin'd,
With eyes severe and beard of formal cut,
Full of wise saws° and modern instances;°                    *sayings / clichéd examples*
And so he plays his part. The sixth age shifts
20   Into the lean and slippered pantaloon,
With spectacles on nose, and pouch on side,
His youthful hose, well saved, a world too wide
For his shrunk shank, and his big manly voice,
Turning again toward childish treble, pipes
25   And whistles in his° sound. Last scene of all,            *its*
That ends this strange eventful history,°                     *chronicle play*
Is second childishness, and mere° oblivion,                   *utter*
Sans° teeth, sans eyes, sans taste, sans every thing.        *without*

*(1599)*                          *(1623)*

Songs from the Plays:

from *Love's Labour's Lost*

# Spring

When daisies pied° and violets blue,     *varicoloured*
 And lady-smocks all silver-white,
And cuckoo-buds of yellow hue,
 Do paint the meadows with delight,
5 The cuckoo then, on every tree,
Mocks married men; for thus sings he,
  Cuckoo,[1]
Cuckoo, cuckoo! O word of fear,
Unpleasing to a married ear!

10 When shepherds pipe on oaten straws,°   *reed pipes*
 And merry larks are ploughmen's clocks,
When turtles tread,° and rooks and daws,  *turtledove's mate*
 And maidens bleach their summer smocks,
The cuckoo then, on every tree,
15 Mocks married men; for thus sings he,
  Cuckoo,
Cuckoo, cuckoo! O word of fear,
Unpleasing to a married ear!

*(1593-95)*        *(1598)*


from *As You Like It*

# [Blow, blow, thou winter wind]

Blow, blow, thou winter wind,
 Thou are not so unkind
  As man's ingratitude;
 Thy tooth is not so keen
5  Because thou art not seen,
  Although thy breath be rude.
Heigh-ho! sing heigh-ho, unto the green holly:
Most friendship is feigning, most loving mere folly:
  Then heigh-ho, the holly!
10   This life is most jolly.

---

1 The bird's call suggests "cuckold" to husbands.

Freeze, freeze, thou bitter sky
That dost not bite so nigh
    As benefits forgot:
Though thou the waters warp,°                                 *freeze*
15     Thy sting is not so sharp
    As friend remembered not.
Heigh-ho! etc.

*(1599)*                                    *(1623)*

from *Twelfth Night*

# [Come away, come away death]

Come away, come away death,
    And in sad cypress let me be laid.
Fly away, fly away breath;
    I am slain by a fair cruel maid.
5   My shroud of white, stuck all with yew,
        O, prepare it.
My part of death, no one so true
        Did share it.

Not a flower, not a flower sweet,
10     On my black coffin let there be strown;
Not a friend, not a friend greet
    My poor corpse, where my bones shall be thrown.
A thousand thousand sighs to save,
        Lay me, O where
15   Sad true lover never find my grave,
        To weep there.

*(1600-01)*                                *(1623)*

from *Cymbeline*

# [Fear no more the heat o' the sun]

Fear no more the heat o' the sun
    Nor the furious winter's rages;
Thou thy worldly task hast done,
    Home art gone, and ta'en thy wages;
5   Golden lads and girls all must,
As chimney-sweepers, come to dust.

Fear no more the frown o' the great,
 Thou art past the tyrant's stroke;
Care no more to clothe and eat,
10  To thee the reed is as the oak:
The sceptre, learning, physic,° must        *medical science*
All follow this and come to dust.

Fear no more the lightning flash,
 Nor the all-dreaded thunder-stone;°      *meteorite*
15 Fear not slander, censure rash;
 Thou hast finished joy and moan:
All lovers young, all lovers must
Consign to thee and come to dust.

No exorciser harm thee.
20 Nor no witchcraft charm thee.
Ghost unlaid forbear thee.
Nothing ill come near thee.
Quiet consummation have,
And renownèd be thy grave.

*(1610-11)*           *(1623)*


from *Two Gentlemen of Verona*

# [Who is Silvia?]

Who is Silvia? what is she,
 That all our swains commend her?
Holy, fair, and wise is she;
 The heaven such grace did lend her,
5 That she might admirèd be.

Is she kind as she is fair?
 For beauty lives with kindness:
Love doth to her eyes repair
 To help him of his blindness,
10 And being helped, inhabits there.

Then to Silvia let us sing
 That Silvia is excelling;
She excels each mortal thing
 Upon the dull earth dwelling.
15 To her let us garlands bring.

*(1592-95)*           *(1623)*

# A Lame Beggar

I am unable, yonder beggar cries,
To stand, or move; if he say true, he *lies*.

(1607)

# A Valediction: Forbidding Mourning

As virtuous men pass mildly away,
    And whisper to their souls, to go,
Whilst some of their sad friends do say
    The breath goes now, and some say, no:

5  So let us melt, and make no noise,
    No tear-floods, nor sigh-tempests move,
'Twere profanation of our joys
    To tell the laity our love.

Moving of th' earth° brings harms and fears,         *earthquakes*
10    Men reckon what it did and meant,
But trepidation of the spheres,[1]
    Though greater far, is innocent.°            *harmless*

Dull sublunary lovers' love
    (Whose soul is sense ) cannot admit
15  Absence, because it doth remove
    Those things which elemented° it.          *composed*

But we by a love, so much refined,
    That our selves know not what it is,
Inter-assurèd of the mind,
20    Care less, eyes, lips, and hands to miss.

Our two souls therefore, which are one,
    Though I must go, endure not yet
A breach, but an expansion,
    Like gold to airy thinness beat.

---

1  Donne alludes to Ptolemy's geocentric model of the cosmos: the earth is surrounded by circling crystal spheres bearing the moon, planets, sun, and fixed stars. Beneath the moon's sphere, all is mundane, changeable, corrupt; beyond it is perfection, despite occasional irregularities of motion ("trepidation").

25   If they be two, they are two so
          As stiff twin compasses are two,
     Thy soul the fixed foot, makes no show
          To move, but doth, if th'other do.

     And though it in the centre sit,
30        Yet when the other far doth roam,
     It leans, and hearkens after it,
          And grows erect, as that comes home.

     Such wilt thou be to me, who must
          Like th'other foot, obliquely run;
35   Thy firmness makes my circle just,°                          *perfect*
          And makes me end, where I begun.

                              *(1633)*


# [Death be not proud]

     Death be not proud, though some have callèd thee
     Mighty and dreadful, for, thou art not so,
     For, those, whom thou think'st, thou dost overthrow,
     Die not, poor death, nor yet canst thou kill me;
5    From rest and sleep, which but thy pictures be,
     Much pleasure, then from thee, much more must flow,
     And soonest our best men with thee do go,
     Rest of their bones, and soul's delivery.°                   *freedom*
     Thou art slave to fate, chance, kings, and desperate men,
10   And dost with poison, war, and sickness dwell,
     And poppy, or charms can make us sleep as well,
     And better than thy stroke; why swell'st thou° then?        *puff yourself up*
     One short sleep past, we wake eternally,
     And death shall be no more, Death thou shalt die.

*(ca. 1609)*                    *(1633)*


# The Bait¹

     Come live with me, and be my love,
     And we will some new pleasures prove
     Of golden sands, and crystal brooks,
     With silken lines, and silver hooks.

---

1   Compare Marlowe's "The Passionate Shepherd to his Love" (p. 17) and Ralegh's "The Nymph's Reply to the Shepherd" (p. 14).

5    There will the river whispering run
     Warmed by thy eyes, more than the sun.
     And there th'enamoured fish will stay,
     Begging themselves they may betray.

     When thou wilt swim in that live bath,
10   Each fish, which every channel hath,
     Will amorously to thee swim,
     Gladder to catch thee, than thou him.

     If thou, to be so seen, be'st loth,
     By sun, or moon, thou dark'nest both,
15   And if myself have leave to see,
     I need not their light, having thee.

     Let others freeze with angling reeds,
     And cut their legs, with shells and weeds,
     Or treacherously poor fish beset,
20   With strangling snare, or windowy net:

     Let coarse bold hands, from slimy nest
     The bedded fish in banks out-wrest,
     Or curious° traitors, sleavesilk° flies             *artful | unravelled silk*
     Bewitch poor fishes' wandering eyes.

25   For thee, thou need'st no such deceit,
     For thou thyself art thine own bait,
     That fish, that is not catched thereby,
     Alas, is wiser far than I.

                    *(1633)*

# The Flea

     Mark but this flea, and mark in this,
     How little that which thou deny'st me is.
     Me it sucked first, and now sucks thee,
     And in this flea, our two bloods mingled be.
5    Confess it, this cannot be said
     A sin, or shame, or loss of maidenhead,
         Yet this enjoys before it woo,
         And pampered swells with one blood made of two,
         And this, alas, is more than we would do.°      *[create pregnancy]*

10   Oh stay, three lives in one flea spare,
     Where we almost, nay more than married are.
     This flea is you and I, and this
     Our marriage bed, and marriage temple is;

Though parents grudge, and you, we'are met,
15 And cloistered in these living walls of jet.
  Though use° make you apt to kill me,                                    *habit*
  Let not to this, self-murder added be,
  And sacrilege, three sins in killing three.

Cruel and sudden, hast thou since
20 Purpled thy nail, in blood of innocence?°                            *[like Herod]*
  In what could this flea guilty be,
  Except in that drop which it sucked from thee?
  Yet thou triumph'st, and say'st that thou
  Find'st not thyself nor me the weaker now.
25   'Tis true, then learn how false, fears be:
    Just so much honour, when thou yield'st to me,
    Will waste, as this flea's death took life from thee.

*(1633)*


# The Sun Rising

    Busy old fool, unruly sun,
      Why dost thou thus,
Through windows, and through curtains call on us?
Must to thy motions lovers' seasons run?
5       Saucy pedantic wretch, go chide
      Late school-boys, and sour prentices,
    Go tell court-huntsmen, that the King will ride,[1]
    Call country ants° to harvest offices;°              *drudges | chores*
Love, all alike,° no season knows, nor clime,                 *unchanging*
10 Nor hours, days, months, which are the rags of time.

    Thy beams, so reverend, and strong
      Why shouldst thou think?
I could eclipse and cloud them with a wink,
But that I would not lose her sight so long:
15      If her eyes have not blinded thine,
      Look, and tomorrow late, tell me,
    Whether both th'Indias° of spice and mine°     *East and West | gold*
    Be where thou leftst them, or lie here with me.
Ask for those kings whom thou saw'st yesterday,
20 And thou shalt hear, All here in one bed lay.

    She is all states, and all princes, I,
      Nothing else is.

---

1 James I was addicted to hunting but Donne also puns on "court-huntsman" to mean "hunt
bureaucratic office."

Princes do but play us; compared to this,
All honour's mimic; all wealth alchemy.°                    *[i.e. fraudulent, fake gold]*
25      Thou sun art half as happy as we,
In that the world's contracted thus;
Thine age asks ease, and since thy duties be
To warm the world, that's done in warming us.
Shine here to us, and thou art everywhere;
30  This bed thy centre is,° these walls, thy sphere.           *[of his cosmos]*

                              *(1633)*

---

## BEN JONSON                                  *English (1572-1637)*

from *Cynthia's Revels*

# Echo's Song

Slow, slow, fresh fount, keep time with my salt tears;
Yet slower yet, o faintly, gentle springs:
List to the heavy part the music bears,
Woe weeps out her division,° when she sings.            *melodic improvisation*
5       Droop, herbs and flowers,
Fall grief in showers;
Our beauties are not ours:
O, I could still,
(Like melting snow upon some craggy hill,)
10      Drop, drop, drop, drop,
Since nature's pride is, now, a withered daffodil.

                              *(1601)*

from *Volpone*

# Song [To Celia]

Come my Celia, let us prove,°                              *experience*
While we may, the sports of love;
Time will not be ours forever:
He, at length, our good will sever.
5  Spend not then his gifts in vain.
Suns that set may rise again:
But if once we lose this light,
'Tis with us perpetual night.
Why should we defer our joys?
10 Fame and rumour are but toys.

Cannot we delude the eyes
Of a few poor household spies?
Or his° easier ears beguile,                                    *[her husband's]*
So removèd by our wile?
15    'Tis no sin love's fruit to steal,
But the sweet theft to reveal:
To be taken, to be seen,
These have crimes accounted been.

*(1606)*


from *Epicoene*

# Clerimont's Song

Still° to be neat, still to be dressed,                          *always*
As° you were going to a feast;                                  *as if*
Still to be powdered, still perfumed:
Lady, it is to be presumed,
5    Though art's hid causes are not found,
All is not sweet, all is not sound.

Give me a look, give me a face,
That makes simplicity a grace;
Robes loosely flowing, hair as free:
10    Such sweet neglect more taketh me
Than all th'adulteries° of art.                                 *adulterations*
They strike mine eyes, but not my heart.

*(1616)*


# Epigram XXII: On My First Daughter

Here lies, to each her parents' ruth,°                          *grief*
Mary, the daughter of their youth:
Yet, all heaven's gifts being heaven's due,
It makes the father less to rue.
5    At six months' end, she parted hence
With safety of her innocence;
Whose soul heaven's queen (whose name she bears),
In comfort of her mother's tears,
Hath placed amongst her virgin train:
10    Where, while that severed doth remain,
This grave partakes the fleshly birth;
Which cover lightly, gentle earth.

*(1616)*

# Epigram XLV: On My First Son

Farewell, thou child of my right hand[1] and joy;
    My sin was too much hope of thee, loved boy.
Seven years thou wert lent to me, and I thee pay,
    Exacted by thy fate, on the just day.
5  O, could I lose all father° now. For why           *paternal feelings*
    Will man lament the state he should envy?
To have so soon 'scaped world's and flesh's rage,
    And, if no other misery, yet age?
Rest in soft peace, and asked, say here doth lie
10    Ben. Jonson his best piece of poetry.
For whose sake, henceforth, all his vows be such,[2]
    As what he loves may never like too much.

*(ca. 1603)*                                     *(1616)*

# Song: To Celia

Drink to me, only, with thine eyes,
    And I will pledge° with mine;                   *toast*
Or leave a kiss but in the cup,
    And I'll not look for wine.
5  The thirst that from the soul doth rise,
    Doth ask a drink divine:
But might I of Jove's nectar sup,
    I would not change° for thine.               *exchange*
I sent thee, late, a rosy wreath,
10    Not so much honouring thee,
As giving it a hope that there
    It could not withered be.
But thou thereon didst only breathe,
    And sent'st it back to me:
15  Since when it grows, and smells, I swear,
    Not of itself, but thee.

*(1616)*

---

1  A literal translation of the Hebrew name *Benjamin*, implying "fortunate" or "dextrous." His son died of plague on his seventh birthday in 1603.

2  i.e. for his son's sake, henceforth, all the speaker's vows be such.

## Delight in Disorder

A sweet disorder in the dress
Kindles in clothes a wantonness:
A lawn° about the shoulders thrown                    *fine linen scarf*
Into a fine distraction:°                                      *confusion*
5   An erring° lace, which here and there         *wandering, floating*
Enthralls the crimson stomacher:°                 *lower bodice piece*
A cuff neglectful, and thereby
Ribbands° to flow confusèdly:                              *ribbons*
A winning wave (deserving note)
10   In the tempestuous petticoat:
A careless shoestring, in whose tie
I see a wild civility:
Do more bewitch me than when art
Is too precise in every part.

*(1648)*

## To the Virgins, To Make Much of Time

Gather ye rosebuds while ye may,
Old time is still a-flying;
And this same flower that smiles today,
Tomorrow will be dying.

5   The glorious lamp of heaven, the sun,
The higher he's a-getting,
The sooner will his race be run,
And nearer he's to setting.

That age is best which is the first,
10   When youth and blood are warmer,
But being spent, the worse, and worst
Times, still succeed the former.

Then be not coy, but use your time,
And while ye may, go marry:
15   For having lost but once your prime,
You may forever tarry.

*(1648)*

# Upon Julia's Clothes

Whenas in silks my Julia goes,
Then, then (methinks) how sweetly flows
That liquefaction of her clothes.
Next, when I cast mine eyes and see
5   That brave° vibration each way free;           *splendid, showy*
O how that glittering taketh me!

*(1648)*

---

## GEORGE HERBERT               *English (1593-1633)*

---

## Love (III)

Love bade me welcome: yet my soul drew back,
    Guilty of dust and sin.
But quick-eyed Love,¹ observing me grow slack°         *hesitant*
    From my first entrance in,
5 Drew nearer to me, sweetly questioning,
    If I lacked any thing.

"A guest," I answered, "worthy to be here:"
    Love said, "You shall be he."
"I the unkind, ungrateful? Ah my dear,
10     I cannot look on thee."
Love took my hand, and smiling did reply,
    "Who made the eyes but I?"

"Truth Lord, but I have marred them: let my shame
    Go where it doth deserve."
15 "And know you not," says Love, "who bore the blame?"
    "My dear, then I will serve."
"You must sit down," says Love, "and taste my meat:"°     *Eucharist*
    So I did sit and eat.

*(1633)*

---

1  "Living"-eyed (that is, Divine) Love.

# The Pulley[1]

When God at first made man,
Having a glass of blessings standing by;
"Let us" (said he) "pour on him all we can:
Let the world's riches, which dispersèd lie,
5        Contract into a span."[2]

So strength first made a way;
Then beauty flowed, then wisdom, honour, pleasure:
When almost all was out, God made a stay,
Perceiving that alone of all his treasure
10        Rest in the bottom lay.

"For if I should" (said he)
"Bestow his jewel also on my creature,
He would adore my gifts instead of me,
And rest in Nature, not the God of Nature:
15        So both should losers be.

"Yet let him keep the rest,
But keep them with repining° restlessness:       *complaining*
Let him be rich and weary, that at least,
If goodness lead him not, yet weariness
20        May toss him to my breast."

           *(1633)*


# The Windows

Lord, how can man preach thy eternal word?
     He is a brittle crazy° glass:       *cracked, distorted*
Yet in thy temple thou dost him afford
       This glorious and transcendent place,
5        To be a window through thy grace.

But when thou dost anneal° in glass thy story,     *fire colours*
       Making thy life to shine within
The holy Preacher's; then the light and glory
       More rev'rend grows, and more doth win:
10       Which else shows wat'rish, bleak, and thin.

---

1 Playing on the classical myth of Pandora's box, Herbert suggests that God withholds the gift of rest in order to "pull" humans to Him. "Rest" puns on the meanings of 1) repose and security, and 2) remainder.

2 Literally, the distance between thumb and little finger of an extended hand. Here it is a metaphor for what is within human control.

Doctrine and life, colours and light, in one
      When they combine and mingle, bring
A strong regard and awe: but speech alone
      Doth vanish like a flaring thing,
15      And in the ear, not conscience ring.

        *(1633)*

## Virtue

Sweet day, so cool, so calm, so bright,
The bridal of the earth and sky:
The dew shall weep thy fall tonight,
      For thou must die.

5  Sweet rose, whose hue angry° and brave°       *red / splendid, showy*
Bids the rash gazer wipe his eye:
Thy root is ever in its grave,
      And thou must die.

Sweet spring, full of sweet days and roses,
10  A box where sweets° compacted lie;       *perfumes*
My music shows ye have your closes,°       *ending cadences*
      And all must die.

Only a sweet and virtuous soul,
Like seasoned timber, never gives:
15  But though the whole world turn to coal,°       *[at Doomsday]*
      Then chiefly lives.

        *(1633)*

---

## JAMES SHIRLEY         *English (1596-1666)*

## [The glories of our blood and state]

The glories of our blood and state
      Are shadows, not substantial things,
There is no armour against fate,
      Death lays his icy hand on Kings:
5        Sceptre and crown,
        Must tumble down
And in the dust be equal made,
With the poor crooked scythe and spade.

Some men with swords may reap the field,
10     And plant fresh laurels where they kill,
But their strong nerves° at last must yield,            *sinews, muscles*
    They tame but one another still:
        Early or late,
        They stoop to fate,
15 And must give up the murmuring breath,
When they, pale captives, creep to death.

The garlands wither on your brow,
    Then boast no more your mighty deeds;
Upon death's purple° altar now,                   *red*
20     See where the victor-victim bleeds:
        Your heads must come,
        To the cold tomb;
Only the actions of the just
Smell sweet, and blossom in their dust.

                *(1659)*

---

## Edmund Waller                           *English (1606-1689)*

# On a Girdle[1]

That which her slender waist confined,
Shall now my joyful temples bind;
No monarch but would give his crown,
His arms might do what this has done.

5 It was my heaven's extremest sphere,°        *[of Ptolemaic cosmos]*
The pale° which held that lovely deer.            *enclosure*
My joy, my grief, my hope, my love,
Did all within this circle move!

A narrow compass! and yet there
10 Dwelt all that's good, and all that's fair;
Give me but what this ribbon bound,
Take all the rest the sun goes round.

                *(1645, 1664)*

---

1  Sash, belt

# Song

     Go, lovely rose!
Tell her that wastes her time and me
     That now she knows,
When I resemble° her to thee,                       *compare*
5      How sweet and fair she seems to be.

     Tell her that's young,
And shuns to have her graces spied,
     That hadst thou sprung
In deserts where no men abide,
10      Thou must have uncommended died.

     Small is the worth
Of beauty from the light retired;
     Bid her come forth,
Suffer herself to be desired,
15      And not blush so to be admired.

     Then die! that she
The common fate of all things rare
     May read in thee;
How small a part of time they share,
20      That are so wondrous sweet and fair!

               *(1645)*

---

## JOHN MILTON                  *English (1608-1674)*

*Sonnet VII*

# [How soon hath Time]

How soon hath Time, the subtle thief of youth,
     Stol'n on his wing my three and twentieth year!
     My hasting days fly on with full career,°          *speed*
     But my late spring no bud or blossom° show'th.    *[i.e. promise]*
5 Perhaps my semblance° might deceive° the truth,   *appearance / misrepresent*
     That I to manhood am arrived so near,
     And inward ripeness doth much less appear,
     That some more timely-happy spirits endu'th.°      *endoweth*
Yet be it less or more, or soon or slow,
10      It shall be still in strictest measure even°        *equal*
     To that same lot, however mean or high,

Toward which Time leads me, and the will of Heav'n;
    All is, if I have grace to use it so,
    As ever° in my great task-Master's eye.               *eternity*

*(1632)*                         *(1645)*

# On the University Carrier

### Who Sickened in the Time of his Vacancy, being Forbid to Go to London, by Reason of the Plague[1]

Here lies old Hobson, Death hath broke his girt,°       *girth*
And here alas hath laid him in the dirt,
Or else, the ways being foul, twenty to one,
He's here stuck in a slough, and overthrown.
5   'Twas such a shifter,° that if truth were known,     *dodger, evader*
Death was half glad when he had got him down;
For he had any time this ten years full,
Dodged with him, betwixt Cambridge and the Bull.°    *inn in London*
And surely, Death could never have prevailed,
10  Had not his weekly course of carriage failed;
But lately finding him so long at home,
And thinking now his journey's end was come,
And that he had ta'en up his latest inn,
In the kind office of a chamberlain°          *inn servant*
15  Showed him his room where he must lodge that night,
Pulled off his boots, and took away the light:
If any ask for him, it shall be said,
Hobson has supped, and 's newly gone to bed.

*(1631)*                         *(1645)*

---

1  Thomas Hobson drove a weekly coach between Cambridge and London from 1564 until shortly before his death on January 1, 1631. Other university students also wrote elegies for him.

*Sonnet XVIII*

# On the Late Massacre in Piedmont[1]

Avenge, O Lord, thy slaughtered saints, whose bones
    Lie scattered on the Alpine mountains cold,
    Even them who kept thy truth so pure of old
    When all our fathers worshipped stocks and stones,
5  Forget not: in thy book record their groans
    Who were thy sheep and in their ancient fold
    Slain by the bloody Piemontese that rolled
    Mother with infant down the rocks. Their moans
  The vales redoubled to the hills, and they
10    To heav'n. Their martyred blood and ashes sow
    O'er all the Italian fields, where still doth sway
  The triple tyrant:° that from these may grow         *the Pope*
    A hundredfold, who having learnt thy way,
    Early may fly the Babylonian° woe.        *Roman [Catholic]*

*(1655)*                    *(1673)*

---

# SIR JOHN SUCKLING        *English (1609-1642)*

# Song

Why so pale, and wan, fond lover?
    Prithee why so pale?
Will, when looking well can't move her,
    Looking ill prevail?
5    Prithee why so pale?

Why so dull and mute, young sinner?
    Prithee, why so mute?
Will, when speaking well can't win her,
    Saying nothing do 't?
10    Prithee, why so mute?

Quit, quit, for shame; this will not move,
    This cannot take her;

---

1  The Waldensians (or Vaudois) were members of an "heretical" sect living in Northwestern Italy (Piedmont) but tolerated by the Roman Catholic rulers of Savoy until Easter Day, 1655, when they were attacked by the current Duke's forces. Over 1700 were killed. Protestants of Northern Europe considered this sect (formed in the twelfth century), which shunned graven images ("stocks and stones"), to be a forerunner of their own later Reformation.

If of herself she will not love,
    Nothing can make her,
15    The devil take her!

*(1638)*

# The Constant Lover

Out upon it, I have loved
    Three whole days together;
And am like to love three more,
    If it hold fair weather.

5   Time shall moult away his wings
    Ere he shall discover
In the whole wide world again
    Such a constant lover.

But pox upon 't, no praise
10   There is due at all to me:
Love with me had made no stay,
    Had it any been but she.

Had it any been but she
    And that very very face,
15  There had been at least ere this
    A dozen dozen in her place.

*(1659)*

---

## ANNE BRADSTREET          *American (1612-1672)*

# Before the Birth of One of Her Children

All things within this fading world hath end,
Adversity doth still our joys attend;
No ties so strong, no friends so dear and sweet,
But with death's parting blow is sure to meet.
5  The sentence past is most irrevocable,
A common thing, yet oh, inevitable.
How soon, my Dear,° death may my steps attend,      *[her husband]*
How soon't may be thy lot to lose thy friend,
We both are ignorant, yet love bids me
10 These farewell lines to recommend to thee,
That when that knot's untied that made us one,

40

I may seem thine, who in effect am none.
And if I see not half my days that's due,
What nature would, God grant to yours and you;
15 The many faults that well you know I have
Let be interred in my oblivious grave;
If any worth or virtue were in me,
Let that live freshly in thy memory
And when thou feel'st no grief, as I no harms,
20 Yet love thy dead, who long lay in thine arms.
And when thy loss shall be repaid with gains
Look to my little babes, my dear remains.
And if chance to thine eyes shall bring this verse,
With some sad sighs honor my absent hearse;
25 And kiss this paper for thy love's dear sake,
Who with salt tears this last farewell did take.

*(1678)*

# The Author to Her Book[1]

Thou ill-formed offspring of my feeble brain,
Who after birth didst by my side remain,
Till snatched from thence by friends, less wise than true,
Who thee abroad, exposed to public view,
5 Made thee in rags, halting to th' press to trudge,
Where errors were not lessened (all may judge).
At thy return my blushing was not small,
My rambling brat° (in print) should mother call,    *insignificant child*
I cast thee by as one unfit for light,
10 Thy visage was so irksome in my sight;
Yet being mine own, at length affection would
Thy blemishes amend, if so I could:
I washed thy face, but more defects I saw,
And rubbing off a spot still made a flaw.
15 I stretched thy joints to make thee even feet,°    *regular metre*
Yet still thou run'st more hobbling than is meet;
In better dress to trim thee was my mind,
But nought save homespun cloth i' th' house I find.
In this array 'mongst vulgars may'st thou roam.
20 In critic's hands beware thou dost not come,
And take thy way where yet thou art not known;
If for thy father asked, say thou hadst none;

---

1 Her book of poems, *The Tenth Muse,* was published in England in 1650 by friends, without the author's knowledge. This poem was apparently written for a proposed authorized edition in 1666, which did not in fact occur until after her death.

And for thy mother, she alas is poor,
Which caused her thus to send thee out of door.

                    *(1678)*

---

## ABRAHAM COWLEY                    *English (1618-1667)*

from *Anacreontics*

# II. Drinking

The thirsty earth soaks up the rain,
And drinks, and gapes for drink again.
The plants suck in the earth, and are
With constant drinking fresh and fair.
5   The sea itself, which one would think
Should have but little need of drink,
Drinks ten thousand rivers up,
So filled that they o'erflow the cup.
The busy sun — and one would guess
10  By his drunken, fiery face no less —
Drinks up the sea, and when he's done,
The moon and stars drink up the sun.
They drink and dance by their own light,
They drink and revel all the night.
15  Nothing in nature's sober found,
But an eternal health goes round.
Fill up the bowl then, fill it high,
Fill all the glasses there, for why
Should every creature drink but I?
20  Why, man of morals, tell me why?

                    *(1656)*

---

## ANDREW MARVELL                    *English (1621-1678)*

# Bermudas

   Where the remote Bermudas ride
In th' ocean's bosom unespied,
From a small boat that rowed along,
The listening winds received this song:

5      "What should we do but sing his praise
       That led us through the wat'ry maze,
       Unto an isle so long unknown,
       And yet far kinder than our own?
       Where he the huge sea monsters wracks,°                          *casts ashore*
10     That lift the deep upon their backs.
       He lands us on a grassy stage,
       Safe from the storms, and prelate's rage.[1]
       He gave us this eternal spring,
       Which here enamels everything,
15     And sends the fowls to us in care,
       On daily visits through the air.
       He hangs in shades the orange bright,
       Like golden lamps in a green night,
       And does in the pomegranates close
20     Jewels more rich than Ormus[2] shows.
       He makes the figs our mouths to meet,
       And throws the melons at our feet.
       But apples° plants of such a price,                              *pineapples*
       No tree could ever bear them twice.
25     With cedars, chosen by his hand,
       From Lebanon, he stores the land.
       And makes the hollow seas, that roar
       Proclaim the ambergris[3] on shore.
       He cast (of which we rather boast)
30     The Gospel's pearl upon our coast.
       And in these rocks for us did frame
       A temple, where to sound his name.
       O let our voice his praise exalt
       Till it arrive at heaven's vault:
35     Which thence (perhaps) rebounding, may
       Echo beyond the Mexique Bay."°                                   *Gulf of Mexico*
          Thus sung they, in the English boat,
       An holy and a cheerful note,
       And all the way, to guide their chime,
40     With falling oars they kept the time.

*(1653)*                          *(1681)*

---

1  Marvell's Non-Conformist sympathies here are clear; the colonists are obviously not Church of England adherents.
2  Hormuz, off Persia, a pearl- and jewel-trading centre.
3  A valuable secretion of sperm whales, used in making perfumes.

# To His Coy Mistress

Had we but world enough, and time,
This coyness, Lady, were no crime.
We would sit down, and think which way
To walk, and pass our long love's day.
5    Thou by the Indian Ganges' side
Shouldst rubies find: I by the tide
Of Humber° would complain. I would             *[Northern English river]*
Love you ten years before the Flood:
And you should, if you please, refuse
10   Till the conversion of the Jews.°                *[just prior to Doomsday]*
My vegetable[1] love should grow
Vaster than empires, and more slow.
An hundred years should go to praise
Thine eyes, and on thy forehead gaze.
15   Two hundred to adore each breast:
But thirty thousand to the rest.
An age at least to every part,
And the last age should show your heart.
For, Lady, you deserve this state,°               *courtly treatment*
20   Nor would I love at lower rate.
      But at my back I always hear
Time's wingèd chariot hurrying near:
And yonder all before us lie
Deserts of vast eternity.
25   Thy beauty shall no more be found,
Nor, in thy marble vault, shall sound
My echoing song: then worms shall try
That long-preserved virginity:
And your quaint° honour turn to dust,         *artificial, fastidious*
30   And into ashes all my lust.
The grave's a fine and private place,
But none I think do there embrace.
      Now therefore, while the youthful hue
Sits on thy skin like morning dew,[2]
35   And while thy willing soul transpires°       *sends off, breathes*
At every pore with instant° fires,             *immediate, urgent*
Now let us sport us while we may;
And now, like amorous birds of prey,
Rather at once our time devour,
40   Than languish in his slow-chapt° power.      *slow-jawed*
Let us roll all our strength, and all

---

1   Like a plant's "soul," growing slowly but without consciousness.

2   The original reading is "glew" which might be a dialectical form of "glow." Most editors, however, accept this simpler emendation.

Our sweetness, up into one ball:
And tear our pleasures with rough strife,
Thorough° the iron gates of life.                                    *through*
45  Thus, though we cannot make our sun
Stand still, yet we will make him run.[1]

*(ca. 1650-58)*                    *(1681)*

---

## JOHN DRYDEN                    *English (1631-1700)*

### Song from *Marriage à la Mode*

# [Why should a foolish marriage vow]

### 1

Why should a foolish marriage vow,
    Which long ago was made,
Oblige us to each other now
    When passion is decayed?
5  We loved, and we loved, as long as we could,
    Till our love was loved out in us both:
But our marriage is dead, when the pleasure is fled:
    'Twas pleasure first made it an oath.

### 2

If I have pleasures for a friend,
10      And farther love in store,
What wrong has he whose joys did end,
    And who could give no more?
'Tis a madness that he should be jealous of me,
    Or that I should bar him of another:
15  For all we can gain, is to give ourselves pain,
    When neither can hinder the other.

*(ca. 1672)*                    *(1672, 1673)*

---

1   See Joshua 10: 12-14.

# To the Memory of Mr. Oldham[1]

Farewell, too little, and too lately known,
Whom I began to think and call my own;
For sure our souls were near allied, and thine
Cast in the same poetic mould with mine.
5    One common note on either lyre did strike,
And knaves and fools we both abhorred alike:
To the same goal did both our studies° drive,       *endeavours*
The last set out the soonest did arrive.
Thus Nisus fell upon the slippery place,
10   While his young friend performed and won the race.[2]
O early ripe! to thy abundant store
What could advancing age have added more?
It might (what nature never gives the young)
Have taught the numbers° of thy native tongue.      *regular metrics*
15   But satire needs not those, and wit will shine
Through the harsh cadence of a rugged line.
A noble error, and but seldom made,
When poets are by too much force betrayed.
Thy generous fruits, though gathered ere their prime,
20   Still showed a quickness;° and maturing time      *pungency, vitality*
But mellows what we write to the dull sweets of rhyme.
Once more, hail and farewell; farewell, thou young,
But ah too short, Marcellus[3] of our tongue;
Thy brows with ivy, and with laurels bound;
25   But fate and gloomy night encompass thee around.

*(1683-84)*                          *(1684)*

# A Song for St. Cecilia's Day, 1687[4]

## I

From harmony, from heav'nly harmony
    This universal frame° began.         *cosmic structure*
   When Nature underneath a heap
    Of jarring atoms lay,

---

1  John Oldham (1652-83) was a promisingly vigorous, if unpolished, young poet who had a considerable success in 1681 with his *Satires Upon the Jesuits*.

2  During *The Aeneid*'s funeral games (V.315-339), Nisus is about to win a footrace but slips in some sacrificial blood; he rolls into the path of another contestant to allow his "young friend" Euryalus to win.

3  Nephew and potential successor of the emperor Augustus who also died, much mourned, at an early age.

4  This ode was written to be set to music for performance at the annual London celebration of the feast day of this patron saint of music and legendary inventor of the organ (November 22).

5       And could not heave her head,
     The tuneful voice was heard from high:
          "Arise, ye more than dead."
     Then cold, and hot, and moist, and dry,°          *[the four elements]*
     In order to their stations leap,
10          And Music's pow'r obey.
     From harmony, from heav'nly harmony
          This universal frame began:
          From harmony to harmony
     Through all the compass of the notes it ran,
15   The diapason¹ closing full in Man.

### II

     What passion cannot Music raise and quell!
          When Jubal struck the corded shell,²
          His list'ning brethren stood around,
          And, wond'ring, on their faces fell
20          To worship that celestial sound.
     Less than a god they thought there could not dwell
          Within the hollow of that shell
          That spoke so sweetly and so well.
     What passion cannot Music raise and quell!

### III

25        The Trumpet's loud clangour
               Excites us to arms
          With shrill notes of anger
               And mortal alarms.
          The double double double beat
30          Of the thund'ring Drum
     Cries: "hark! the foes come;
     Charge, charge, 'tis too late to retreat."

### IV

          The soft complaining Flute
          In dying notes discovers
35        The woes of hopeless lovers,
     Whose dirge is whispered by the warbling Lute.

---

1 The consonance of all the notes of the octave scale. Related also to the Ptolemaic theory of celestial spheres moving in harmony.

2 The first Biblical musician: "the father of all such as handle the harp and organ" (Genesis 4:21).

## V

Sharp Violins proclaim
Their jealous pangs, and desperation,
Fury, frantic indignation,
40   Depth of pains, and height of passion,
For the fair, disdainful dame.

## VI

But Oh! what art can teach,
What human voice can reach,
The sacred Organ's praise?
45   Notes inspiring holy love,
Notes that wing their heav'nly ways
To mend the choirs above.

## VII

Orpheus could lead the savage race;
And trees unrooted left their place,
50   Sequacious of the lyre:[1]
But bright Cecilia raised the wonder high'r;
When to her Organ vocal breath was giv'n,
And angel heard, and straight appeared,
Mistaking earth for heav'n.

GRAND CHORUS
55   *As from the power of sacred lays*
*The spheres began to move*
*And sung the great Creator's praise*
*To all the blest above;*
*So when the last and dreadful hour*
60   *This crumbling pageant shall devour,*
*The Trumpet shall be heard on high,*
*The dead shall live, the living die,*
*And Music shall untune the sky.*

*(1687)*                              *(1687)*

---

1   The prototypical classical musician, his lyre playing drew wild animals, trees, and rocks to follow him.

# L'Amitie: To Mrs M. Awbrey[1]

Soul of my soul! my joy, my crown, my friend!
A name which all the rest doth comprehend;
How happy are we now, whose souls are grown,
By an incomparable mixture, one:
5   Whose well-acquainted minds are now as near
As love, or vows, or secrets can endear.
I have no thought but what's to thee revealed,
Nor thou desire that is from me concealed.
Thy heart locks up my secrets richly set,
10  And my breast is thy private cabinet.°            *treasure chest*
Thou shedst no tear but what my moisture lent,
And if I sigh, it is thy breath is spent.
United thus, what horror can appear
Worthy our sorrow, anger, or our fear?
15  Let the dull world alone to talk and fight,
And with their vast ambitions nature fright;
Let them despise so innocent a flame,
While envy, pride, and faction play their game;
But we by love sublimed so high shall rise,
20  To pity kings, and conquerors despise;
Since we that sacred union have engrossed,
Which they and all the sullen world have lost.

*(1651)*                                      *(1664)*

# On the Death of My First and Dearest Child, Hector Philips

Twice forty months in wedlock I did stay,
    Then had my vows crowned with a lovely boy.
And yet in forty days he dropped away;[2]
    O swift vicissitude of human joy!

---

1  "L'Amitie" is French for friendship; the poem is addressed to Mary Awbrey, a former schoolfriend.

2  Philips married in August 1648; her son was born April 23, 1655 and died May 2 — barely ten days later. Despite her statement in the last line, this was not her final poem. She also had another child, a daughter, a year later, who survived her.

5   I did but see him, and he disappeared,
        I did but touch the rosebud, and it fell;
    A sorrow unforeseen and scarcely feared,
        So ill can mortals their afflictions spell.°            *guess, foretell*

    And now (sweet babe) what can my trembling heart
10      Suggest to right my doleful fate or thee?
    Tears are my muse, and sorrow all my art,
        So piercing groans must be thy elegy.

    Thus whilst no eye is witness of my moan
        I grieve thy loss (Ah, boy too dear to live),
15  And let the unconcernèd world alone,
        Who neither will, nor can, refreshment give.

    An off'ring too for thy sad tomb I have,
        Too just a tribute to thy early hearse.
    Receive these gasping numbers to thy grave,
20      The last of thy unhappy mother's verse.
    *(1655)*                        *(1667)*

---

## APHRA BEHN                                    *English (1640-1689)*

# Song: Love Armed

    Love in fantastic triumph sat,
    Whilst bleeding hearts around him flowed,
    For whom fresh pains he did create,
    And strange tyrannic pow'r he showed;
5   From thy bright eyes he took his fire,
    Which round about in sport he hurled;
    But 'twas from mine he took desire,
    Enough t'undo the amorous world.

    From me he took his sighs and tears,
10  From thee his pride and cruelty;
    From me his languishments and fears, ·
    And ev'ry killing dart from thee.
    Thus thou, and I, the god have armed,
    And set him up a deity;
15  But my poor heart alone is harmed,
    Whilst thine the victor is, and free.

                    *(1684)*

# The Defiance

By Heaven 'tis false, I am not vain;
    And rather would the subject be
Of your indifference, or disdain,
    Than wit or raillery.°                     *banter, teasing*

5   Take back the trifling praise you give,
    And pass it on some other fool,
Who may the injuring wit believe,
    That turns her into ridicule.

Tell her, she's witty, fair, and gay,
10    With all the charms that can subdue:
Perhaps she'll credit what you say;
    But curse me if I do.

If your diversion you design,
    On my good-nature you have pressed:
15  Or if you do intend it mine,
    You have mistook the jest.

*(1684)*


from *A Paraphrase on the Lord's Prayer*

# And forgive us our Trespasses

How prone we are to sin, how sweet were made
The pleasures, our resistless hearts invade!
Of all my crimes, the breach of all thy laws,
Love, soft bewitching love! has been the cause;
5   Of all the paths that vanity has trod,
That sure will soonest be forgiven of God;

If things on earth may be to heaven resembled,
It must be love, pure, constant, undissembled:
But if to sin by chance the charmer press,
10  Forgive, O Lord, forgive our Trespasses.

*(1685)*

# Love and Life: A Song

All my past life is mine no more,
    The flying hours are gone:
Like transitory dreams given o'er,
Whose images are kept in store,
5    By memory alone.

Whatever is to come is not:
    How can it then be mine?
The present moment's all my lot,
And that, as fast as it is got,
10    Phyllis, is wholly thine.

Then talk not of inconstancy,
    False hearts and broken vows;
If I, by miracle, can be
This livelong minute true to thee,
15    'Tis all that heaven allows.

*(1677)*

# Impromptu on Charles II

God bless our good and gracious King,
    Whose promise none relies on;
Who never said a foolish thing,
    Nor ever did a wise one.[1]

*(1707)*

# To the Ladies

Wife and servant are the same,
But only differ in the name:
For when that fatal knot is tied,

---

1 To this famous, supposedly extemporaneous, epigram, the King is said to have replied: "My words are my own; my acts are my ministers'."

Which nothing, nothing can divide,
5   When she the word *Obey* has said,
And man by law supreme has made,
Then all that's kind is laid aside,
And nothing left but state and pride.
Fierce as an eastern prince he grows,
10   And all his innate rigour shows:
Then but to look, to laugh, or speak,
Will the nuptial contract break.
Like mutes, she signs alone must make,
And never any freedom take,
15   But still be governed by a nod,
And fear her husband as her god:
Him still must serve, him still obey,
And nothing act, and nothing say,
But what her haughty lord thinks fit,
20   Who, with the power, has all the wit.
Then shun, oh! shun that wretched state,
And all the fawning flatt'rers hate.
Value yourselves, and men despise:
You must be proud, if you'll be wise.

*(1703)*

---

## ANNE FINCH, COUNTESS OF WINCHELSEA   *English (1661-1720)*

# To the Nightingale

Exert thy voice, sweet harbinger° of spring!                    *herald*
    This moment is thy time to sing,
    This moment I attend to praise,
And set my numbers to thy lays.°                                *songs*
5       Free as thine shall be my song,
    As thy music, short or long.
Poets wild as thou were born,
    Pleasing best when unconfined,
    When to please is least designed,
10   Soothing but their cares to rest.
    Cares do still their thoughts molest,
    And still th' unhappy poet's breast,
Like thine, when best he sings, is placed against a thorn.[1]

---

1   A reference to the legend that nightingales sing most sweetly when they are in pain because wounded by thorns.

She begins. Let all be still!
15      Muse, thy promise now fulfil!
Sweet, oh sweet, still sweeter yet!
Can thy words such accents fit,
Canst thou syllables refine,
Melt a sense that shall retain
20   Still some spirit of the brain,
Till with sounds like these it join?
        'Twill not be! then change thy note;
        Let division° shake thy throat.          *melodic improvisation*
Hark! division now she tries;
25   Yet as far the Muse outflies.
        Cease then, prithee, cease thy tune.
        Trifler, wilt thou sing till June?
Till thy business all lies waste,
And the time of building's past!
30      Thus we poets that have speech,
Unlike what thy forests teach,
        If a fluent vein be shown
        That's transcendent° to our own,          *superior*
Criticise, reform, or preach,
35   Or censure what we cannot reach.

                    *(1713)*


# A Letter to Daphnis,¹ April 2, 1685

This to the crown and blessing of my life,
The much loved husband of a happy wife.
To him whose constant passion found the art
To win a stubborn and ungrateful heart;
5    And to the world, by tend'rest proof discovers,
They err, who say that husbands can't be lovers.
With such return of passion as is due,
Daphnis I love, Daphnis my thoughts pursue;
Daphnis, my hopes, my joys, are bounded all in you:
10   Even I, for Daphnis' and my promise' sake,
What I in women censure, undertake.
But this from love, not vanity, proceeds;
You know who writes, and I who 'tis that reads.
Judge not my passion by my want of skill:
15   Many love well, though they express it ill;
And I your censure could with pleasure bear,
Would you but soon return, and speak it here.

*(ca. 1685)*                    *(1903)*

---

1   Lady Winchelsea's poetic name for her husband; elsewhere she calls herself *Ardelia*.

# A Reasonable Affliction

On his death-bed poor Lubin lies:
    His spouse is in despair;
With frequent sobs and mutual cries,
    They both express their care.

5  A diff'rent cause, says parson Sly,
    The same effect may give:
Poor Lubin fears that he shall die;
    His wife, that he may live.

*(1718)*

# A True Maid

"No, no; for my virginity,
    When I lose that," says Rose, "I'll die":
"Behind the elms last night," cried Dick,
    "Rose, were you not extremely sick?"

*(1718)*

# An Epitaph

    Interred beneath this marble stone
Lie saunt'ring Jack, and idle Joan.
While rolling threescore years and one
Did round this globe their courses run;
5  If human things went ill or well;
If changing empires rose or fell;
The morning past, the evening came,
And found this couple still the same.
They walked and eat, good folks: What then?
10  Why then they walked and eat again:
They soundly slept the night away:
They did just nothing all the day:
And having buried children four,
Would not take pains to try for more.
15  Nor sister either had, nor brother:
They seemed just tallied° for each other.          *matched*

Their moral° and economy°　　　　　　*morality / household expenditure*
Most perfectly they made agree:
Each virtue kept its proper bound,
20　Nor trespassed on the other's ground.
Nor fame, nor censure they regarded:
They neither punished, nor rewarded.
He cared not what the footmen did:
Her maids she neither praised, nor chid:°　　　　　*criticized*
25　So every servant took his course;
And bad at first, they all grew worse.
Slothful disorder filled his stable;
And sluttish plenty decked her table.
Their beer was strong; their wine was port;
30　Their meal was large; their grace was short.
They gave the poor the remnant-meat,
Just when it grew not fit to eat.

　　　They paid the church and parish rate;°　　　　　*tax*
And took, but read not the receipt:
35　For which they claimed their Sunday's due
Of slumb'ring in an upper pew.

　　　No man's defects sought they to know;
So never made themselves a foe.
No man's good deeds did they commend;
40　So never raised themselves a friend.
Nor cherished they relations poor:
That might decrease their present store:
Nor barn nor house did they repair:
That might oblige their future heir.

45　　　They neither added, nor confounded;°　　　　　*wasted*
They neither wanted, nor abounded.
Each Christmas they accompts° did clear;　　　　　*accounts*
And wound their bottom° round the year.　　*thread [i.e. settled finances]*
Nor tear, nor smile did they employ
50　At news of public grief, or joy.
When bells were rung, and bonfires made,
If asked, they ne'er denied their aid:
Their jug was to the ringers° carried,　　　　　*bell-ringers*
Whoever either died, or married.
55　Their billet° at the fire was found,　　　　　*firewood donation*
Whoever was deposed, or crowned.

　　　Nor good, nor bad, nor fools, nor wise;
They would not learn, nor could advise:
Without love, hatred, joy, or fear,
60　They led — a kind of — as it were:
Nor wished, nor cared, nor laughed, nor cried:
And so they lived; and so they died.

*(1718)*

# A Description of the Morning

Now hardly here and there a hackney coach
Appearing, showed the ruddy morn's approach.
Now Betty from her master's bed has flown,
And softly stole to discompose her own.
5    The slipshod 'prentice from his master's door
Had pared the dirt, and sprinkled round the floor.
Now Moll had whirled her mop with dext'rous airs,
Prepared to scrub the entry and the stairs.
The youth with broomy stumps° began to trace       *worn-out broom*
10   The kennel-edge,[1] where wheels had worn the place.
The smallcoat man° was heard with cadence deep;    *charcoal seller*
Till drowned in shriller notes of *chimney-sweep.*
Duns° at his Lordship's gate began to meet,       *bill collectors*
And Brickdust Moll° had screamed through half a street.  *scouring powder seller*
15   The turnkey° now his flock returning sees,         *jailer*
Duly let out a-nights to steal for fees.
The watchful bailiffs take their silent stands;
And schoolboys lag with satchels in their hands.[2]

*(1709)*

# Stella's Birthday

### Written in the year 1718[3]

Stella this day is thirty-four,
(We shan't dispute a year or more:)
However Stella, be not troubled,
Although thy size and years are doubled,
5    Since first I saw thee at sixteen,
The brightest virgin on the green.
So little is thy form declined,
Made up so largely in thy mind.

---

1  The gutter running down the centre of the street, "to find old Nails" (Swift's original note).
2  Cf. Shakespeare's "All the World's a Stage," lines 7-9 (p. 21).
3  "Stella" was Swift's pet name for Miss Hester Johnson (1681-1728), a dear friend since the time he was her tutor in the 1690s. From 1719 until the year of her death, he sent an annual birthday poem —often playfully lessening her true age or alluding to her plumpness. Until the change to the Gregorian Calendar in the mid-eighteenth century, the new year began at the end of March. Stella's birthday fell on March 13, and was therefore in the year we now call 1719.

Oh, would it please the gods to *split*
10    Thy beauty, size, and years, and wit,
No age could furnish out a pair
Of nymphs so graceful, wise and fair:
With half the lustre of your eyes,
With half your wit, your years, and size:
15    And then before it grew too late,
How should I beg of gentle fate,
(That either nymph might have her swain,)
To split my worship too in twain.

*(1719)*                              *(1727)*

# On Stella's Birthday

### *Written in the Year 1720-21*

All travellers at first incline
Where'er they see the fairest sign;°              *inn sign*
And if they find the chamber neat,
And like the liquor, and the meat,
5    Will call again, and recommend
The Angel Inn to every friend:
What though the painting grows decayed,
The house will never lose its trade;
Nay, though the treach'rous tapster Thomas
10    Hangs a new angel two doors from us,
As fine as dauber's° hands can make it,        *painter's*
In hopes that strangers may mistake it;
We think it both a shame and sin
To quit the true old Angel Inn.

15    Now, this is Stella's case in fact,
An angel's face, a little cracked;
(Could poets, or could painters fix
How angels look at thirty-six:)
This drew us in at first, to find
20    In such a form an angel's mind:
And every virtue now supplies°           *compensates for*
The fainting rays of Stella's eyes.
See, at her levee° crowding swains,      *morning reception*
Whom Stella freely entertains
25    With breeding, humour, wit, and sense;
And puts them to so small expense:
Their mind so plentifully fills,
And makes such reasonable bills;
So little gets for what she gives,
30    We really wonder how she lives!

And had her stock been less, no doubt
She must have long ago run out.

    Then who can think we'll quit the place
When Doll hangs out her newer face;°               *inn sign*
35  Nailed to her window full in sight
All Christian people to invite;
Or stop and light at Chloe's head°         *another inn sign*
With scraps and leavings to be fed.

    Then Chloe, still go on to prate
40  Of thirty-six, and thirty-eight;
Pursue your trade of scandal-picking,
Your hints that Stella is no chicken;
Your innuendos, when you tell us
That Stella loves to talk with fellows:
45  But let me warn you to believe
A truth, for which your soul should grieve;
That, should you live to see the day
When Stella's locks must all be grey;
When age must print a furrowed trace
50  On every feature of her face;
Though you and all your senseless tribe,
Could art, or time, or nature bribe,
To make you look like beauty's queen,
And hold forever at fifteen:
55  No bloom of youth can ever blind
The cracks and wrinkles of your mind,
All men of sense will pass your door,
And crowd to Stella's at fourscore.°         *eighty*

*(1721)*                           *(1727)*

# A Satirical Elegy on the Death of a Late Famous General[1]

His Grace! impossible! what, dead!
Of old age too, and in his bed!
And could that Mighty Warrior fall?
And so inglorious, after all!
5  Well, since he's gone, no matter how,
The last loud trump must wake him now:

---

[1] John Churchill, first Duke of Marlborough, was the brilliant Whig general of British and Allied forces against the French in the War of the Spanish Succession (1702-1713), victor at Blenheim and many other battles. He was, however, an old ideological foe of the Tory and High Church Swift.

And, trust me, as the noise grows stronger,
He'd wish to sleep a little longer.
And could he be indeed so old
10  As by the newspapers we're told?
Threescore, I think, is pretty high;
'Twas time in conscience he should die.
This world he cumbered long enough;
He burnt his candle to the snuff;[1]
15  And that's the reason, some folks think,
He left behind *so great a stink.*
Behold his funeral appears,
Nor widow's sighs, nor orphan's tears,
Wont at such times each heart to pierce,
20  Attend the progress of his hearse.
But what of that, his friends may say,
He had those honours in his day.
True to his profit and his pride,
He made them weep before he died.

25  Come hither, all ye empty things,
Ye bubbles° raised by breath of kings;           *fools, dupes*
Who float upon the tide of state,
Come hither, and behold your fate.
Let pride be taught by this rebuke,
30  How very mean a thing's a Duke;
From all his ill-got honours flung,
Turned to that dirt from whence he sprung.

*(1722)*                              *(1764)*


# On the Day of Judgement

With a whirl of thought oppressed,
I sink from reverie to rest.
An horrid vision seized my head,
I saw the graves give up their dead.
5  Jove, armed with terrors, burst the skies,
And thunder roars, and lightning flies!
Amazed, confused, its fate unknown,
The world stands trembling at his throne.
While each pale sinner hangs his head,
10  Jove, nodding, shook the heav'ns, and said,
"Offending race of humankind,
By nature, reason, learning, blind;

---

1  The snuff is the wick end; tallow candles, made of animal fat, produced a particularly unpleasant smell as they went out.

You who through frailty stepped aside,
And you who never fell — through pride;
15    You who in different sects have shammed,
And come to see each other damned;
(So some folks told you, but they knew
No more of Jove's designs than you)
The world's mad business now is o'er,
20    And I resent these pranks no more.
I to such blockheads set my wit!
I damn such fools! — Go, go you're bit."°          *taken in, fooled*

*(1731)*                                    *(1774)*

---

## WILLIAM CONGREVE                    *English (1670-1729)*

# Song

Pious Selinda goes to prayers,
    If I but ask the favour;°                      *sexual favour*
And yet the tender fool's in tears,
    When she believes I'll leave her.

5    Would I were free from this restraint,
    Or else had hopes to win her;
Would she could make of me a saint,
    Or I of her a sinner.

*(1704)*

---

## ELIZABETH THOMAS                    *English (1675-1731)*

# The Forsaken Wife

    Methinks, 'tis strange you can't afford
One pitying look, one parting word;
Humanity claims this as due,
But what's humanity to you?

5        Cruel man! I am not blind,
Your infidelity I find;
Your want of love my ruin shows,
My broken heart, your broken vows.
Yet maugre° all your rigid hate,                      *in spite of*

I will be true in spite of fate;
And one preeminence I'll claim,
To be forever still the same.

Show me a man that dare be true,
That dares to suffer what I do;
That can for ever sigh unheard,
And ever love without regard:
I then will own your prior claim
To love, to honour, and to fame;
But till that time, my dear, adieu,
I yet superior am to you.

*(1722)*

---

# JOHN GAY

*English (1685-1732)*

# My Own Epitaph

Life is a jest, and all things show it;
I thought so once, but now I know it.

*(1720)*

## Songs from *The Beggar's Opera*

### I

Through all the employments of life,
    Each neighbour abuses his brother;
Whore and rogue they call husband and wife:
    All professions be-rogue one another.
5 The priest calls the lawyer a cheat,
    The lawyer be-knaves the divine;
And the statesman, because he's so great,
    Thinks his trade as honest as mine.[1]

### XI

A fox may steal your hens, sir,
A whore your health and pence, sir,
Your daughter rob your chest, sir,
Your wife may steal your rest, sir,
5     A thief your goods and plate.

---

1 Sung by Peachum, a fence or receiver of stolen goods.

But this is all but picking,
With rest, pence, chest, and chicken;
It ever was decreed, sir,
If lawyer's hand is fee'd, sir,
10     He steals your whole estate.

## XX

Let us take the road.[1]
     Hark! I hear the sound of coaches!
     The hour of attack approaches,
To your arms, brave boys, and load.

5     See the ball I hold!
Let the chymists toil like asses,
Our fire their fire surpasses,
     And turns all our lead to gold.

## XXII[2]

Youth's the season made for joys,
     Love is then our duty;
She alone who that employs,
     Well deserves her beauty.
5          Let's be gay,
          While we may,
Beauty's a flower despised in decay.

Let us drink and sport today,
     Ours is not to-morrow.
10   Love with youth flies swift away,
     Age is nought but sorrow.
          Dance and sing,
          Time's on the wing,
Life never knows the return of spring.

*(1728)*

---

1  Sung by the "hero," Macheath, a leader of highwaymen. In lines 6-8, he puns on the similarity of his profession and that of alchemists who attempt to heat base metal ("lead") into "gold" [coin].

2  Sung by a bevy of prostitutes. Cf. other "carpe diem" poems such as Ben Jonson's "Song [To Celia]" (p. 29), John Herrick's "To the Virgins, To Make Much of Time" (p. 32), and Andrew Marvell's "To His Coy Mistress" (p. 44).

# Epitaph on John Hewet and Sarah Drew in the Churchyard at Stanton Harcourt[1]

*Near this place lie the bodies of*
*John Hewet and Sarah Drew*
*an industrious young man, and*
*virtuous maiden of this parish;*
*contracted in marriage*
*who being with many others at harvest work,*
*were both in an instant killed*
*by lightning on the last day of July*
*1718*

Think not by rigorous judgement seized,
    A pair so faithful could expire;
Victims so pure Heav'n saw well pleased
    And snatched them in celestial fire.

5   Live well and fear no sudden fate;
        When God calls virtue to the grave,
    Alike tis justice, soon or late
        Mercy alike to kill or save.

Virtue unmoved can hear the call,
10  And face the flash that melts the ball.
*(1718)*                              *(1718)*

# Epitaph Intended for Sir Isaac Newton in Westminster-Abbey

Nature and Nature's laws lay hid in night.
God said, *Let Newton be!* and all was light.
*(ca. 1730)*                              *(1730)*

---

1   See a second epitaph on the same couple by Pope (p. 66) and one by his friend Lady Mary
Wortley Montagu (p. 67).

# Epigram from the French

Sir, I admit your gen'ral Rule
That every Poet is a Fool:
But you yourself may serve to show it,
That every Fool is not a Poet.

*(1732)*


# On a Certain Lady at Court[1]

I know the thing that's most uncommon
    (Envy be silent and attend!);
I know a reasonable woman,
    Handsome and witty, yet a friend.

5    Not warped by passion, awed by rumour,
        Not grave through pride, or gay through folly;
An equal mixture of good humour
    And sensible soft melancholy.

"Has she no faults, then (Envy says), sir?"
10    Yes, she has one, I must aver:
When all the world conspires to praise her,
    The woman's deaf, and does not hear.

*(ca. 1725)*                                *(1732)*


# Epigram. Engraved on the Collar of a Dog which I gave to his Royal Highness[2]

I am his Highness' dog at Kew;
Pray tell me, sir, whose dog are you?

*(1736-37)*                                *(1738)*

---

1  The lady is Henrietta, Countess of Suffolk, sometime mistress to George II. Pope alludes to her increasing deafness.

2  In 1736 Pope presented a puppy of his Great Dane Bounce to Frederick, Prince of Wales, whose anti-Whig politics he favoured.

# Epigram. On One who made long Epitaphs

Friend! for your Epitaphs I'm grieved,
    Where still so much is said,
One half will never be believed,
    The other never read.

*(1736)*                        *(1738)*


# Epitaph on the Stanton-Harcourt Lovers

Here lie two poor lovers, who had the mishap
Tho very chaste people, to die of a clap.

*(1718)*                        *(1950)*

---

## LADY MARY WORTLEY MONTAGU     *English (1689-1762)*


# Addressed to —

    With toilsome steps I pass through life's dull road,
No packhorse half so weary of his load;
And when this dirty journey will conclude,
To what new realms is then my way pursued?
5    Say, then, does the unbodied spirit fly
To happier climes and to a better sky;
Or sinking, mixes with its kindred clay,
And sleeps a whole eternity away?
Or shall this form be once again renewed,
10   With all its frailties and its hopes endued,
Acting once more on this detested stage
Passions of youth, infirmities of age?
    I see in Tully° what the ancients thought;            *Cicero*
And read unprejudiced what moderns taught;
15   But no conviction from my reading springs,
Most dubious on the most important things.
    Yet one short moment would at once explain
What all philosophy has sought in vain,
Would clear all doubt, and terminate all pain.
20   Why then not hasten that decisive hour,
Still in my view, and ever in my power?
Why should I drag along this life I hate,
Without one thought to mitigate the weight?
Whence this mysterious bearing to exist,

25  When every joy is lost, and every hope dismissed?
    In chains and darkness wherefore should I stay,
    And mourn in prison, while I keep the key?

*(1736)*                          *(1749)*


# Epitaph[1]

    Here lie John Hughes and Sarah Drew.
    Perhaps you'll say, what's that to you?
    Believe me, friend, much may be said
    On this poor couple that are dead.
5   On Sunday next they should have married:
    But see how oddly things are carried.
    On Thursday last it rained and lightened:
    These tender lovers, sadly frightened,
    Sheltered beneath the cocking hay,
10  In hopes to pass the storm away.
    But the bold thunder found them out
    (Commissioned for that end, no doubt)
    And, seizing on their trembling breath,
    Consigned them to the shades of death.
15  Who knows if 'twas not kindly done?
    For had they seen the next year's sun,
    A beaten wife and cuckold swain
    Had jointly cursed the marriage chain.
    Now they are happy in their doom,
20  For P[ope] has wrote upon their tomb.

*(1718)*                          *(1763)*


SAMUEL WESLEY                          *English (1691-1739)*


# On the Setting up Mr. Butler's Monument in Westminster Abbey

    While Butler, needy wretch! was yet alive,
    No gen'rous patron would a dinner give:
    See him, when starved to death and turned to dust,
    Presented with a monumental bust!

---

1   See Pope's two epitaphs on the same couple (pp. 64 and 66).

67

The poet's fate is here in emblem shown:
He asked for bread, and he received a stone.

*(1726)*

---

## SAMUEL JOHNSON    *English (1709-1784)*

# On the Death of Dr. Robert Levet[1]

Condemned to hope's delusive mine,
    As on we toil from day to day,
By sudden blasts, or slow decline,
    Our social comforts drop away.

5  Well tried through many a varying year,
    See Levet to the grave descend;
Officious,° innocent, sincere,                    *dutiful, kind*
    Of ev'ry friendless name the friend.

Yet still he fills affection's eye,
10    Obscurely wise, and coarsely° kind;        *roughly, rudely*
Nor, lettered arrogance, deny
    Thy praise to merit unrefined.

When fainting nature called for aid,
    And hov'ring death prepared the blow,
15  His vig'rous remedy displayed
    The power of art without the show.

In misery's darkest caverns known,
    His useful care was ever nigh,
Where hopeless anguish poured his groan,
20    And lonely want retired to die.

No summons mocked by chill delay,
    No petty gain disdained by pride,
The modest wants of ev'ry day
    The toil of ev'ry day supplied.

25  His virtues walked their narrow round,
    Nor made a pause, nor left a void;

---

1  A physician without medical degree (1705-82) who lived as a member of Johnson's household for many years and practiced among the extremely poor in London.

And sure th' Eternal Master found
　　The single talent well employed.[1]

The busy day, the peaceful night,
30　　Unfelt, uncounted, glided by;
His frame was firm, his powers were bright,
　　Though now his eightieth year was nigh.

Then with no throbbing fiery pain,
　　No cold gradations of decay,
35　Death broke at once the vital chain,
　　And freed his soul the nearest way.

*(1782)*　　　　　　　　　　　*(1783)*


# A Short Song of Congratulation: To Sir John Lade, on his Coming of Age

Long-expected one and twenty
　　Ling'ring year at last is flown,
Pomp and pleasure, pride and plenty,
　　Great Sir John, are all your own.

5　Loosened from the minor's tether,
　　Free to mortgage or to sell,
Wild as wind, and light as feather
　　Bid the slaves of thrift farewell.

Call the Bettys, Kates, and Jennys
10　　Ev'ry name that laughs at care,
Lavish of your grandsire's guineas,
　　Show the spirit of an heir.

All that prey on vice and folly
　　Joy to see their quarry fly,
15　Here the gamester light and jolly
　　There the lender grave and sly.

Wealth, Sir John, was made to wander,
　　Let it wander as it will;
See the jockey, see the pander,
20　　Bid them come, and take their fill.

---

1　See the biblical parable of the talents (Matthew 25:14-30).

When the bonny blade carouses,
    Pockets full, and spirits high,
What are acres? What are houses?
    Only dirt, or wet or dry.

25 If the guardian or the mother
    Tell the woes of willful waste,
Scorn their counsel and their pother,
    You can hang or drown at last.

*(1780)*                  *(1794)*

---

# Thomas Gray           *English (1716-1771)*

## Ode on the Death of a Favourite Cat, Drowned in a Tub of Gold Fishes[1]

'Twas on a lofty vase's side,
Where China's gayest art had dyed
    The azure flowers, that blow;°               *blossom*
Demurest of the tabby kind,
5 The pensive Selima reclined,
    Gazed on the lake below.

Her conscious tail her joy declared;
The fair round face, the snowy beard,
    The velvet of her paws,
10 Her coat that with the tortoise vies,
Her ears of jet and emerald eyes,
    She saw; and purred applause.

Still had she gazed; but 'midst the tide
Two angel forms were seen to glide,
15     The genii° of the stream:          *guardian spirits*
Their scaly armour's Tyrian hue°          *purple*
Through richest purple to the view
    Betrayed a golden gleam.

The hapless nymph with wonder saw:
20 A whisker first and then a claw,
    With many an ardent wish,

---

1 The "Cat Poem," as Samuel Johnson called it. This mock-heroic fable (complete with proverbial moral) was written at the request of his friend, Horace Walpole, as an epitaph for one of his cats.

She stretched in vain to reach the prize.
What female heart can gold despise?
    What cat's averse to fish?

25  Presumptuous maid! with looks intent
Again she stretched, again she bent,
    Nor knew the gulf between.
(Malignant Fate sat by, and smiled)
The slipp'ry verge° her feet beguiled,          *bank, rim*
30      She tumbled headlong in.

Eight times emerging from the flood
She mewed to ev'ry watry god,
    Some speedy aid to send.
No dolphin came,[1] no Nereid° stirred:          *sea nymph*
35  Nor cruel Tom, nor Susan° heard.               *servants*
    A fav'rite has no friend!

From hence, ye beauties, undeceived,
Know, one false step is ne'er retrieved,
    And be with caution bold.
40  Not all that tempts your wand'ring eyes
And heedless hearts, is lawful prize;
    Nor all that glisters, gold.

*(1747)*                                    *(1748)*


# On L[or]d H[ollan]d's Seat near M[argat]e, K[en]t[2]

Old and abandoned by each venal friend,
    Here H[olland] took the pious resolution
To smuggle some few years and strive to mend
    A broken character and constitution.
5   On this congenial spot he fixed his choice,
    Earl Godwin trembled for his neighbouring sand;[3]
Here seagulls scream and cormorants rejoice,
    And mariners, though shipwrecked, dread to land.
Here reign the blust'ring North and blighting East,

---

1   Such as occurred in the legend of the bard Arion, rescued from drowning by dolphins charmed by his song.

2   Henry Fox, first Baron Holland, accumulated a fortune as Paymaster-General after 1757, and was an astute leader of the House of Commons in Lord Bute's ministry after 1760, but was hated by many, especially in London, as an unscrupulous and corrupt self-seeker. He later quarrelled with the Prime Minister and other colleagues (see lines 17-18) and retired because of ill health to his villa in Kent in whose grounds were some fashionable imitation "Gothick" ruins which, Gray imagines, serve as the models for Holland's true intentions.

3   Goodwin Sands at the entrance to the Straits of Dover are supposedly part of an island owned in the eleventh century by Earl Godwin.

10      No tree is heard to whisper, bird to sing,
      Yet nature cannot furnish out the feast,
         Art he invokes new horrors still to bring.
      Now mould'ring fanes and battlements arise,
         Arches and turrets nodding to their fall,
15     Unpeopled palaces delude his eyes,
         And mimic desolation covers all.
      "Ah," said the sighing peer, "had Bute been true
         Nor Shelburne's, Rigby's, Calcraft's friendship vain,
      Far other scenes than these had blessed our view
20        And realised the ruins that we feign.°          *invent falsely*
      Purged by the sword and beautified by fire,
         Then had we seen proud London's hated walls,
      Owls might have hooted in St. Peter's° choir,     *Westminster Abbey*
         And foxes stunk and littered in St. Paul's."

*(1768)*                    *(1769)*

---

# WILLIAM COLLINS          *English (1721-1759)*

# Ode Written in the Beginning of the Year 1746

How sleep the brave,[1] who sink to rest,
By all their country's wishes blest!
When Spring, with dewy fingers cold,
Returns to deck their hallowed mould,
5   She there shall dress a sweeter sod
Than Fancy's feet have ever trod.

By fairy hands their knell is rung,
By forms unseen their dirge is sung;
There Honour comes, a pilgrim grey,
10  To bless the turf that wraps their clay;
And Freedom shall a while repair,
To dwell a weeping hermit there!

*(1746)*                    *(1746)*

---

1  The English troops who died at the battles of Preston Pans (September) and Falkirk (January) during the invasion by Bonnie Prince Charlie and his Scottish forces in 1745-46.

From *Jubilate Agno*[1]

# [My Cat Jeoffry]

For I will consider my Cat Jeoffry.
For he is the servant of the Living God
    duly and daily serving him.
For at the first glance of the glory of God in the
    East° he worships in his way.               *at sunrise*
For is this done by wreathing his body seven times round
    with elegant quickness.
5  For then he leaps up to catch the musk, w<sup>cho</sup> is the blessing    *which*
    of God upon his prayer.
For he rolls upon prank° to work it in.               *prankishly*
For having done duty and received blessing he begins
    to consider himself.
For this he performs in ten degrees.
For first he looks upon his fore-paws to see if they are clean.
10  For secondly he kicks up behind to clear away there.
For thirdly he works it upon stretch with the fore-paws extended.
For fourthly he sharpens his paws by wood.
For fifthly he washes himself
For Sixthly he rolls upon wash.
15  For Seventhly he fleas himself, that he may
    not be interrupted upon the beat.°         *on his daily round*
For Eighthly he rubs himself against a post.
For Ninthly he looks up for his instructions.
For Tenthly he goes in quest of food.
For having considered God and himself
    he will consider his neighbor.
20  For if he meets another cat he will kiss her in kindness.
For when he takes his prey he plays with it
    to give it a chance.
For one mouse in seven escapes by his dallying.
For when his day's work is done his business
    more properly begins.
For he keeps the Lord's watch in the night
    against the adversary.
25  For he counteracts the powers of darkness
    by his electrical skin & glaring eyes.

---

1  "Rejoice in the Lamb" (i.e. Christ, the Lamb of God), a complex and erudite poem written while Smart was confined for insanity. Much of the work has been lost, including the set of lines starting with *Let* which form an antiphonal parallel to these surviving lines (a *Let* line is followed by a corresponding *For* line).

For he counteracts the Devil, who is death,
    by brisking about the life.
For in his morning orisons° he loves the sun and         *prayers*
    the sun loves him.
For he is of the tribe of Tiger.
For the Cherub Cat is a term of the Angel Tiger.[1]
30  For he has the subtlety and hissing of a serpent,
    which in goodness he suppresses.
For he will not do destruction if he is well-fed,
    neither will he spit without provocation.
For he purrs in thankfulness, when God tells him
    he's a good Cat.
For he is an instrument for the children
    to learn benevolence upon.
For every house is incomplete without him & a blessing
    is lacking in the spirit.
35  For the Lord commanded Moses concerning the cats
    at the departure of the Children of Israel from Egypt.
For every family had one cat at least in the bag.
For the English Cats are the best in Europe.
For he is the cleanest in the use of his fore-paws
    of any quadruped.
For the dexterity of his defence is an instance of the love of God
    to him exceedingly.
40  For he is the quickest to his mark of any creature.
For he is tenacious of his point.
For he is a mixture of gravity and waggery.
For he knows that God is his Saviour.
For there is nothing sweeter than his peace when at rest.
45  For there is nothing brisker than his life when in motion.
For he is of the Lord's poor and so indeed is he called by
    benevolence perpetually — Poor Jeoffry! poor Jeoffry!
    the rat has bit thy throat.
For I bless the name of the Lord Jesus that Jeoffry is better.
For the divine spirit comes about his body
    to sustain it in complete cat.
For his tongue is exceeding pure so that it has
    in purity what it wants in music.
50  For he is docile and can learn certain things.
For he can set up with gravity which is patience
    upon approbation.
For he can fetch and carry, which is patience in employment.
For he can jump over a stick which is patience
    upon proof positive.
For he can spraggle° upon waggle at the word of command.     *sprawl*
55  For he can jump from an eminence into his master's bosom.

---

1  As a cherub is a small angel, so a cat is a miniature tiger.

For he can catch the cork and toss it again.
For he is hated by the hypocrite and miser.
For the former is afraid of detection.
For the latter refuses the charge.
60 For he camels his back to bear the first notion of business.
For he is good to think on, if a man would express himself neatly.
For he made a great figure in Egypt for his signal services.
For he killed the Icneumon-rat° very pernicious by land.          *mongoose*
For his ears are so acute that they sting again.
65 For from this proceeds the passing quickness of his attention.
For by stroking of him I have found out electricity.
For I perceived God's light about him both wax and fire.
For the Electrical fire is the spiritual substance, which God sends from
          heaven to sustain the bodies both of man and beast.
For God has blessed him in the variety of his movements.
70 For, though he cannot fly, he is an excellent clamberer.
For his motions upon the face of the earth are more than any other
          quadruped.
For he can tread to all the measures upon the music.
For he can swim for life.
For he can creep.

*(1759-63)*                              *(1939)*

---

## OLIVER GOLDSMITH                              *Irish (1730?-1774)*

# An Elegy on the Death of a Mad Dog

Good people all, of every sort,
     Give ear unto my song;
And if you find it wond'rous short,
     It cannot hold you long.

5   In Islington there was a man,
     Of whom the world might say
That still a godly race he ran,
     Whene'er he went to pray.

A kind and gentle heart he had,
10     To comfort friends and foes;
The naked every day he clad,
     When he put on his clothes.

And in that town a dog was found,
     As many dogs there be,

Both mongrel, puppy, whelp and hound,
    And curs of low degree.

This dog and man at first were friends;
    But when a pique began,
The dog, to gain some private ends,
    Went mad and bit the man.

Around from all the neighbouring streets
    The wondering neighbours ran,
And swore the dog had lost his wits,
    To bite so good a man.

The wound it seemed both sore and sad
    To every Christian eye;
And while they swore the dog was mad,
    They swore the man would die.

But soon a wonder came to light,
    That showed the rogues they lied:
The man recovered of the bite,
    The dog it was that died.

*(1766)*

---

**WILLIAM COWPER**　　　　　　　　　　*English (1731-1800)*

## Epitaph on a Hare

Here lies, whom hound did ne'er pursue,
    Nor swifter greyhound follow,
Whose foot ne'er tainted morning dew,
    Nor ear heard huntsman's "hallo,"

Old Tiney, surliest of his kind,
    Who, nursed with tender care,
And to domestic bounds confined,
    Was still a wild jack-hare.

Though duly from my hand he took
    His pittance ev'ry night,
He did it with a jealous look,
    And, when he could, would bite.

His diet was of wheaten bread,
    And milk, and oats, and straw,

15    Thistles, or lettuces instead,
          With sand to scour his maw.°                                    *stomach*

      On twigs of hawthorn he regaled,
          On pippins'° russet peel;                                    *[a kind of apple]*
      And, when his juicy salads failed,
20        Sliced carrot pleased him well.

      A Turkey carpet was his lawn,
          Whereon he loved to bound,
      To skip and gambol like a fawn,
          And swing his rump around.

25    His frisking was at evening hours,
          For then he lost his fear;
      But most before approaching show'rs,
          Or when a storm drew near.

      Eight years and five round-rolling moons
30        He thus saw steal away,
      Dozing out all his idle noons,
          And ev'ry night at play.

      I kept him for his humour's sake,
          For he would oft beguile
35    My heart of thoughts that made it ache,
          And force me to a smile.

      But now, beneath this walnut-shade
          He finds his long, last home,
      And waits in snug concealment laid,
40        Till gentler Puss shall come.

      He, still more agèd, feels the shocks
          From which no care can save,
      And, partner once of Tiney's box,
          Must soon partake his grave.

*(1783)*                                         *(1784)*


# On a Spaniel Called Beau
# Killing a Young Bird

A spaniel, Beau, that fares like you,
    Well-fed, and at his ease,
Should wiser be, than to pursue
    Each trifle that he sees.

5    But you have killed a tiny bird,
        Which flew not till to-day,
    Against my orders, whom you heard
        Forbidding you the prey.

    Nor did you kill, that you might eat,
10       And ease a doggish pain,
    For him, though chased with furious heat
        You left where he was slain.

    Nor was he of the thievish sort,
        Or one whom blood allures,
15    But innocent was all his sport,
        Whom you have torn for yours.

    My dog! what remedy remains,
        Since, teach you all I can,
    I see you after all my pains,
20       So much resemble man!

*(1793)*                          *(1803)*

# The Castaway[1]

    Obscurest night involved the sky,
        Th' Atlantic billows roared,
    When such a destined wretch as I,
        Washed headlong from on board,
5    Of friends, of hope, of all bereft,
    His floating home for ever left.

    No braver chief could Albion° boast           *Britain*
        Than he with whom he went,
    Nor ever ship left Albion's coast,
10       With warmer wishes sent.
    He loved them both, but both in vain,
    Nor him beheld, nor her again.

    Not long beneath the whelming brine,
        Expert° to swim, he lay;                *able*
15    Nor soon he felt his strength decline,
        Or courage die away;

---

1  Cowper's last poem — an allegory of his own religious despair — was based on a passage in Richard Walter's *A Voyage Round the World by George Anson* (1748), describing the fate of a sailor thrown overboard in a storm and lost. Anson is the "chief" of line 7.

But waged with death a lasting strife,
Supported by despair of life.

He shouted: nor his friends had failed
20      To check the vessel's course,
But so the furious blast prevailed,
        That, pitiless perforce.
They left their outcast mate behind,
And scudded still before the wind.

25   Some succor yet they could afford;
        And, such as storms allow,
The cask, the coop,° the floated cord,          *fish basket*
        Delayed not to bestow.
But he (they knew) nor ship, nor shore,
30   Whate'er they gave, should visit more.

Nor, cruel as it seemed, could he
        Their haste himself condemn,
Aware that flight, in such a sea,
        Alone could rescue them;
35   Yet bitter felt it still to die
Deserted, and his friends so nigh.

He long survives, who lives an hour
        In ocean, self-upheld:
And so long he, with unspent pow'r,
40      His destiny repelled;
And ever as the minutes flew,
Entreated help, or cried — "Adieu!"

At length, his transient respite past,
        His comrades, who before
45   Had heard his voice in ev'ry blast,
        Could catch the sound no more.
For then, by toil subdued, he drank
The stifling wave, and then he sank.

No poet wept him: but the page
50      Of narrative sincere,
That tells his name, his worth, his age,
        Is wet with Anson's tear.
And tears by bards or heroes shed
Alike immortalize the dead.

55   I therefore purpose not, or dream,
        Descanting° on his fate,          *commenting*
To give the melancholy theme
        A more enduring date:

But misery still delights to trace
60  Its 'semblance in another's case.

No voice divine the storm allayed
    No light propitious shone;
When, snatched from all effectual aid,
    We perished, each alone:
65  But I beneath a rougher sea,
And whelmed in deeper gulfs than he.

*(1799)*                        *(1803)*

---

## WILLIAM BLAKE                      *English (1757-1827)*

From *Songs of Innocence, 1789*

# The Chimney Sweeper

When my mother died I was very young,
And my father sold me while yet my tongue,
Could scarcely cry weep weep weep weep.[1]
So your chimneys I sweep & in soot I sleep.

5  Theres little Tom Dacre, who cried when his head
That curl'd like a lambs back, was shav'd, so I said.
Hush Tom never mind it, for when your head's bare,
You know that the soot cannot spoil your white hair.

And so he was quiet, & that very night,
10  As Tom was a sleeping he had such a sight,
That thousands of sweepers Dick, Joe Ned & Jack
Were all of them lock'd up in coffins of black

And by came an Angel who had a bright key,
And he open'd the coffins & set them all free.
15  Then down a green plain leaping laughing they run
And wash in a river and shine in the Sun.

Then naked & white, all their bags left behind,
They rise upon clouds, and sport in the wind.
And the Angel told Tom if he'd be a good boy,
20  He'd have God for his father & never want joy.

---

1  The child's lisping attempt to pronounce the street cry, "Sweep! Sweep!"

And so Tom awoke and we rose in the dark
And got with our bags & our brushes to work.
Tho' the morning was cold, Tom was happy & warm,
So if all do their duty, they need not fear harm.

*(1789)*

# The Lamb

Little Lamb who made thee
Dost thou know who made thee
Gave thee life & bid thee feed.
By the stream & o'er the mead;
5   Gave thee clothing of delight,
Softest clothing wooly bright;
Gave thee such a tender voice,
Making all the vales rejoice!
Little Lamb who made thee
10   Dost thou know who made thee

Little Lamb I'll tell thee,
Little Lamb I'll tell thee!
He is called by thy name,
For he calls himself a Lamb:
15   He is meek & he is mild,
He became a little child:
I a child & thou a lamb,
We are called by his name.
Little Lamb God bless thee.
20   Little Lamb God bless thee.

*(1789)*

From *Songs of Experience, 1794*

# A Poison Tree

I was angry with my friend;
I told my wrath, my wrath did end.
I was angry with my foe:
I told it not, my wrath did grow.

5   And I waterd it in fears,
Night & morning with my tears:
And I sunned it with smiles,
And with soft deceitful wiles.

And it grew both day and night.
10  Till it bore an apple bright.
And my foe beheld it shine.
And he knew that it was mine.

And into my garden stole,
When the night had veild the pole;
15  In the morning glad I see;
My foe outstretchd beneath the tree.

*(ca. 1793)*                    *(1794)*


# London

I wander thro' each charter'd[1] street,
Near where the charter'd Thames does flow.
And mark in every face I meet
Marks of weakness, marks of woe.

5  In every cry of every Man,
In every Infants cry of fear,
In every voice: in every ban,[2]
The mind-forg'd manacles I hear

How the Chimney-sweepers cry
10  Every blackning Church appalls,
And the hapless Soldiers sigh,
Runs in blood down Palace walls

But most thro' midnight streets I hear
How the youthful Harlots curse
15  Blasts the new-born Infants tear
And blights with plagues the Marriage hearse

*(ca. 1793)*                    *(1794)*

---

1  A multiple bitter pun: the rights and liberties of Englishmen established by Magna Carta (and now threatened by Prime Minister Pitt's repressive government); the chartering of commercial enterprises with exclusive rights and property; bounding and "charting" natural features such as the river and streets.

2  Another multiple pun: political and legal prohibition, curse, public proscription, proclamation (now normally of marriage and spelt *bann*).

# The Chimney Sweeper

A little black thing among the snow:
Crying weep, weep, in notes of woe!
Where are thy father & mother? say?
They are both gone up to the church to pray.

5    Because I was happy upon the heath,
And smil'd among the winters snow:
They clothed me in the clothes of death,
And taught me to sing the notes of woe.

And because I am happy, & dance & sing,
10   They think they have done me no injury:
And are gone to praise God & his Priest & King
Who make up a heaven of our misery.

*(1790-93)*                            *(1794)*

# The Garden of Love

I went to the Garden of Love,
And saw what I never had seen:
A Chapel was built in the midst,
Where I used to play on the green.

5    And the gates of this Chapel were shut,
And Thou shalt not writ over the door;
So I turn'd to the Garden of Love,
that so many sweet flowers bore,

And I saw it was filled with graves,
10   And tomb-stones where flowers should be:
And Priests in black gowns, were walking their rounds,
And binding with briars, my joys & desires.

*(ca. 1793)*                            *(1794)*

# The Sick Rose

O Rose thou art sick.
The invisible worm,
That flies in the night
In the howling storm:

5    Has found out thy bed
     Of crimson joy:
     And his dark secret love
     Does thy life destroy.

*(ca. 1793)*                              *(1794)*


# The Tyger

     Tyger Tyger, burning bright,
     In the forests of the night;
     What immortal hand or eye,
     Could frame thy fearful symmetry?

5    In what distant deeps or skies
     Burnt the fire of thine eyes!
     On what wings dare he aspire?
     What the hand, dare sieze the fire?[1]

     And what shoulder, & what art,
10   Could twist the sinews of thy heart?
     And when thy heart began to beat,
     What dread hand? & what dread feet?

     What the hammer? what the chain,
     In what furnace was thy brain?
15   What the anvil? what dread grasp,
     Dare its deadly terrors clasp?

     When the stars threw down their spears[2]
     And water'd heaven with their tears:
     Did he smile his work to see?
20   Did he who made the Lamb make thee?

     Tyger, Tyger burning bright,
     In the forests of the night:
     What immortal hand or eye,
     Dare frame thy fearful symmetry?

*(1790-93)*                              *(1794)*

---

1   The previous line and this probably allude to the myths of Icarus and Prometheus.

2   The stars=rebel angels of the war in heaven in Milton's *Paradise Lost* (who never surrender, in fact).

## Robert Burns
*Scottish (1759-1796)*

# A Red, Red Rose

O my Luve's like a red, red rose,
    That's newly sprung in June;
O My Luve's like the melodie
    That's sweetly play'd in tune.

5   As fair art thou, my bonie lass,
    So deep in luve am I;
And I will luve thee still, my dear,
    Till a' the seas gang° dry.                *go*

Till a' the seas gang dry, my Dear,
10    And the rocks melt wi' the sun:
O I will love thee still my dear,
    While the sands o' life shall run.

And fare thee weel, my only Luve!
    And fare thee weel, a while!
15 And I will come again, my Luve,
    Tho' it ware ten thousand mile!

                     *(1794)*

# For A' That and A' That

Is there, for honest Poverty
    That° hings his head, and a' that;       *one who*
The coward-slave, we pass him by,
    We dare be poor for a' that!
5    For a' that, and a' that,
      Our toils obscure, and a' that,
    The rank is but the guinea's stamp,
      The Man's the gowd° for a' that. —      *gold*

What though on hamely fare we dine,
10    Wear hoddin-grey,° and a' that.    *undyed wool*
Gie fools their silks, and knaves their wine,
    A Man's a Man for a' that.
    For a' that, and a' that,
      Their tinsel show, and a' that;
15    The honest man, tho e'er sae poor,
      Is king o' men for a' that. —

Ye see yon birkie,° ca'd a lord,          *young fellow*
    Wha struts, and stares, and a' that,
Tho' hundreds worship at his word,
20      He's but a coof° for a' that.        *idiot*
    For a' that, and a' that,
      His ribband, star and a' that,
    The man of independent mind,
      He looks and laughs at a' that. —

25 A prince can mak a belted° knight,      *decorated*
    A marquis, duke, and a' that;
But an honest man's aboon° his might,      *above*
    Gude faith he mauna fa'° that!   *must not claim*
    For a' that, and a' that,
30      Their dignities, and a' that,
    The pith o' Sense, and pride o' Worth,
    Are higher rank than a' that. —

Then let us pray that come it may,
    As come it will for a' that,
35 That sense and worth, o'er a' the earth
    Shall bear the gree,° and a' that.      *prize*
    For a' that, and a' that,
      It's comin yet for a' that,
    That man to man the warld o'er,
40      Shall brothers be for a' that. —
*(1794-95)*              *(1795)*

---

# WILLIAM WORDSWORTH       *English (1770-1850)*

## [A slumber did my spirit seal]

A slumber did my spirit seal;
    I had no human fears:
She seemed a thing that could not feel
    The touch of earthly years.

5  No motion has she now, no force;
    She neither hears nor sees;
Rolled round in earth's diurnal° course,    *daily*
    With rocks, and stones, and trees.

*(1798-99)*              *(1800)*

# Composed Upon Westminster Bridge, September 3, 1802

Earth has not anything to show more fair:
Dull would he be of soul who could pass by
A sight so touching in its majesty:
This City now doth, like a garment, wear
5   The beauty of the morning; silent, bare,
Ships, towers, domes, theatres, and temples lie
Open unto the fields, and to the sky;
All bright and glittering in the smokeless air.
Never did sun more beautifully steep
10  In his first splendour, valley, rock, or hill;
Ne'er saw I, never felt, a calm so deep!
The river glideth at his own sweet will:
Dear God! the very houses seem asleep;
And all that mighty heart is lying still!

*(1802)*                                  *(1807)*

# [I wandered lonely as a cloud]

I wandered lonely as a cloud
That floats on high o'er vales and hills,
When all at once I saw a crowd,
A host, of golden daffodils;
5   Beside the lake, beneath the trees,
Fluttering and dancing in the breeze.

Continuous as the stars that shine
And twinkle on the milky way,
They stretched in never-ending line
10  Along the margin of a bay:
Ten thousand saw I at a glance,
Tossing their heads in sprightly dance.

The waves beside them danced; but they
Outdid the sparkling waves in glee;
15  A poet could not but be gay,
In such a jocund company;
I gazed — and gazed — but little thought
What wealth the show to me had brought:

For oft, when on my couch I lie
20  In vacant or in pensive mood,
They flash upon that inward eye

Which is the bliss of solitude;
And then my heart with pleasure fills,
And dances with the daffodils.

*(1804)*                    *(1807)*

# [It is a beauteous evening, calm and free]

It is a beauteous evening, calm and free,
The holy time is quiet as a Nun
Breathless with adoration; the broad sun
Is sinking down in its tranquillity;
5   The gentleness of heaven broods o'er the Sea:
Listen! the mighty Being is awake,
And doth with his eternal motion make
A sound like thunder — everlastingly.
Dear Child! dear Girl!¹ that walkest with me here,
10  If thou appear untouched by solemn thought,
Thy nature is not therefore less divine:
Thou liest in Abraham's bosom° all the year;       *heaven*
And worshipp'st at the Temple's inner shrine,²
God being with thee when we know it not.

*(1802)*                    *(1807)*

# London, 1802

Milton! thou shouldst be living at this hour:
England hath need of thee: she is a fen
Of stagnant waters: altar, sword, and pen,
Fireside, the heroic wealth of hall and bower,
5   Have forfeited their ancient English dower
Of inward happiness. We are selfish men;
Oh! raise us up, return to us again;
And give us manners, virtue, freedom, power.
Thy soul was like a Star, and dwelt apart;
10  Thou hadst a voice whose sound was like the sea:
Pure as the naked heavens, majestic, free,
So didst thou travel on life's common way,
In cheerful godliness; and yet thy heart
The lowliest duties on herself did lay.

*(1802)*                    *(1807)*

---

1  The child is probably Caroline, Wordsworth's daughter by the French woman Annette Vallon.
2  The Holy of Holies of the Jewish Temple, entered only once a year by the High Priest, at Yom Kippur.

# [The world is too much with us]

The world is too much with us; late and soon,
Getting and spending, we lay waste our powers:
Little we see in Nature that is ours;
We have given our hearts away, a sordid boon!°        *gift*
5    This Sea that bares her bosom to the moon;
The winds that will be howling at all hours,
And are up-gathered now like sleeping flowers;
For this, for every thing, we are out of tune;
It moves us not. — Great God! I'd rather be
10   A Pagan suckled in a creed outworn;
So might I, standing on this pleasant lea,°      *meadow*
Have glimpses that would make me less forlorn;
Have sight of Proteus rising from the sea;
Or hear old Triton blow his wreathèd horn.°   *[Classical sea deities]*

*(1802-04)*                  *(1807)*

---

## SAMUEL TAYLOR COLERIDGE       *English (1772-1834)*

# Kubla Khan

*Or, a Vision in a Dream. A Fragment.*[1]

In Xanadu did Kubla Khan
A stately pleasure-dome decree:
Where Alph, the sacred river, ran
Through caverns measureless to man
5      Down to a sunless sea.
So twice five miles of fertile ground
With walls and towers were girdled round:
And there were gardens bright with sinuous rills,
Where blossomed many an incense-bearing tree;
10   And here were forests ancient as the hills,
Enfolding sunny spots of greenery.

---

1   In a preface and note to this poem, Coleridge admitted to have fallen into an opium-induced "reverie" during his reading of the section describing Xanadu in Samuel Purchas's *Purchas His Pilgrimage* (1613): "In Xanadu did Cublai Can build a stately Palace, encompassing sixteen miles of plaine ground with a wall, wherein are fertile meddows, pleasant springs, delightful streams ... and in the middest thereof a sumptuous house of pleasure ...." Upon awakening, he began to write down the "two to three hundred lines" he had composed in his head during his "sleep," but was disturbed by a visitor, and after an hour away from the poem, he could add no more to this fragment.

But oh! that deep romantic chasm which slanted
Down the green hill athwart a cedarn cover!
A savage place! as holy and enchanted
15 As e'er beneath a waning moon was haunted
By woman wailing for her demon-lover!
And from this chasm, with ceaseless turmoil seething,
As if this earth in fast thick pants were breathing,
A mighty fountain momently was forced:
20 Amid whose swift half-intermitted burst
Huge fragments vaulted like rebounding hail,
Or chaffy grain beneath the thresher's flail:
And 'mid these dancing rocks at once and ever
It flung up momently the sacred river.
25 Five miles meandering with a mazy motion
Through wood and dale the sacred river ran,
Then reached the caverns measureless to man,
And sank in tumult to a lifeless ocean:
And 'mid this tumult Kubla heard from far
30 Ancestral voices prophesying war!
     The shadow of the dome of pleasure
     Floated midway on the waves;
     Where was heard the mingled measure
     From the fountain and the caves.
35 It was a miracle of rare device,
A sunny pleasure-dome with caves of ice!

     A damsel with a dulcimer
     In a vision once I saw:
     It was an Abyssinian maid,
40      And on her dulcimer she played,
     Singing of Mount Abora.
     Could I revive within me
     Her symphony and song,
     To such a deep delight 'twould win me,
45 That with music loud and long,
I would build that dome in air,
That sunny dome! those caves of ice!
And all who heard should see them there,
And all should cry, Beware! Beware!
50 His flashing eyes, his floating hair!
Weave a circle round him thrice,
And close your eyes with holy dread,
For he on honey-dew hath fed,
And drunk the milk of Paradise.

*(1797)*                          *(1816)*

# GEORGE GORDON, LORD BYRON     *English (1788-1824)*

## She Walks in Beauty[1]

### 1

She walks in Beauty, like the night
    Of cloudless climes and starry skies;
And all that's best of dark and bright
    Meet in her aspect and her eyes:
5   Thus mellowed to that tender light
    Which Heaven to gaudy day denies.

### 2

One shade the more, one ray the less,
    Had half impaired the nameless grace
Which waves in every raven tress,
10    Or softly lightens o'er her face;
Where thoughts serenely sweet express,
    How pure, how dear their dwelling-place.

### 3

And on that cheek, and o'er that brow,
    So soft, so calm, yet eloquent,
15   The smiles that win, the tints that glow,
    But tell of days in goodness spent,
A mind at peace with all below,
    A heart whose love is innocent!

*(1814)*                             *(1815)*

## Sonnet on Chillon[2]

Eternal Spirit of the chainless Mind!
    Brightest in dungeons, Liberty! thou art:
    For there thy habitation is the heart —
The heart which love of thee alone can bind;

---

1  Written the morning after attending a ball at which the poet met his beautiful young cousin, Lady Wilmot Horton, dressed in a be-spangled black mourning gown.

2  François Bonivard, a sixteenth-century Swiss political and religious martyr, was imprisoned for seven years in the Castle of Chillon on Lake Geneva by the Duke of Savoy.

5   And when thy sons to fetters are consigned —
      To fetters, and the damp vault's dayless gloom,
      Their country conquers with their martyrdom,
  And Freedom's fame finds wings on every wind.
  Chillon! thy prison is a holy place,
10      And thy sad floor an altar — for 'twas trod,
  Until his very steps have left a trace
     Worn, is if thy cold pavement were a sod,
  By Bonnivard! — May none those marks efface!
     For they appeal from tyranny to God.

*(1816)*                     *(1816)*

# Fragment on the back of the poet's ms. of canto the first [of Don Juan]

I would to Heaven that I were so much clay,
    As I am blood, bone, marrow, passion, feeling —
Because at least the past were passed away,
    And for the future — (but I write this reeling,
5 Having got drunk exceedingly to-day,
    So that I seem to stand upon the ceiling)
I say — the future is a serious matter —
And so — for God's sake — hock° and soda-water!       *Rhine wine*

*(1818)*                     *(1819)*

# On This Day I Complete My Thirty-sixth Year

*Missolonghi, 22nd January, 1824*[1]

1

'Tis time this heart should be unmoved,
    Since others it hath ceased to move:
Yet, though I cannot be beloved,
    Still let me love!

---

1  Byron was to die three months later, a martyr to the cause of Greek independence from the Turks.

5    My days are in the yellow leaf;
        The flowers and fruits of Love are gone;
    The worm, the canker, and the grief
        Are mine alone!

3

    The fire that on my bosom preys
10       Is lone as some Volcanic isle;
    No torch is kindled at its blaze —
        A funeral pile!

4

    The hope, the fear, the jealous care,
        The exalted portion of the pain
15    And power of love, I cannot share,
        But wear the chain.

5

    But 'tis not *thus* — and 'tis not *here* —
        Such thoughts should shake my soul, nor *now*,
    Where Glory decks the hero's bier,
20       Or binds his brow.

6

    The Sword, the Banner, and the Field,
        Glory and Greece, around me see!
    The Spartan, borne upon his shield,
        Was not more free.

7

25    Awake! (not Greece — she *is* awake!)
        Awake, my spirit! Think through *whom*
    Thy life-blood tracks its parent lake,
        And then strike home!

8

    Tread those reviving passions down,
30       Unworthy manhood! — unto thee
    Indifferent should the smile or frown
        Of Beauty be.

If thou regret'st thy youth, *why live?*
   The land of honourable death
35 Is here: — up to the Field, and give
    Away thy breath!

Seek out — less often sought than found —
   A soldier's grave, for thee the best;
Then look around, and choose thy ground,
40     And take thy Rest.

*(1824)*                         *(1824)*

---

## PERCY BYSSHE SHELLEY           *English (1792-1822)*

# Ozymandias[1]

I met a traveller from an antique land
Who said: Two vast and trunkless legs of stone
Stand in the desert ... Near them, on the sand,
Half sunk, a shattered visage lies, whose frown,
5 And wrinkled lip, and sneer of cold command,
Tell that its sculptor well those passions read
Which yet survive, stamped on these lifeless things,
The hand that mocked° them, and the heart that fed;       *imitated, derided*
And on the pedestal these words appear:
10 "My name is Ozymandias, king of kings:
Look on my works, ye Mighty, and despair!"
Nothing beside remains. Round the decay
Of that colossal wreck, boundless and bare
The lone and level sands stretch far away.

*(1817)*                         *(1818)*

---

1 The Greek name of the Pharaoh Rameses II (13th Century B.C.), reknowned for building enormous monuments and temples.

# England in 1819¹

An old, mad, blind, despised, and dying king, —
Princes, the dregs of their dull race, who flow
Through public scorn, — mud from a muddy spring, —
Rulers who neither see, nor feel, nor know,
5   But leech-like to their fainting country cling,
Till they drop, blind in blood, without a blow, —
A people starved and stabbed in the untilled field, —
An army, which liberticide and prey
Makes as a two-edged sword to all who wield, —
10  Golden and sanguine laws which tempt and slay;
Religion Christless, Godless — a book sealed;
A Senate, — Time's worst statute unrepealed, —
Are graves, from which a glorious Phantom may
Burst, to illumine our tempestuous day.

*(1819)*                               *(1839)*

---

JOHN KEATS                           *English (1795-1821)*

# On First Looking into Chapman's Homer²

Much have I travelled in the realms of gold,
   And many goodly states and kingdoms seen;
   Round many western islands have I been
Which bards in fealty to Apollo hold.
5  Oft of one wide expanse had I been told
   That deep-browed Homer ruled as his demesne;°        *realm*
   Yet did I never breathe its pure serene°          *clear air*
Till I heard Chapman speak out loud and bold:
Then felt I like some watcher of the skies
10   When a new planet swims into his ken;
Or like stout Cortez³ when with eagle eyes
   He stared at the Pacific — and all his men

---

1  The blind and insane George III was in the last year of his reign; his sons, especially George, the Prince Regent, were unpopular and Shelley blames a repressive government both for the "Peterloo Massacre" (August 16, 1819) at which troops charged a crowd attending a peaceful rally near Manchester (line 7) and for maintaining repressive religious laws (line 12).

2  Keats had spent the night before writing this poem reading George Chapman's Elizabethan translation of Homer with his former schoolmaster Charles Cowden Clarke. Clarke received the sonnet in the ten o'clock post that morning.

3  A famous error: it was Balboa who first saw the Pacific Ocean in 1513.

Looked at each other with a wild surmise —
    Silent, upon a peak in Darien.

*(1816)*                          *(1816)*

# La Belle Dame Sans Merci[1]

## A Ballad

O, what can ail thee, knight-at-arms,
    Alone and palely loitering?
The sedge has withered from the lake,
    And no birds sing.

5    O, what can ail thee, knight-at-arms,
    So haggard and so woe-begone?
The squirrel's granary is full,
    And the harvest's done.

I see a lily on thy brow,
10    With anguish moist and fever dew;
And on thy cheeks a fading rose
    Fast withereth too.

I met a lady in the meads,
    Full beautiful — a faery's child,
15    Her hair was long, her foot was light,
    And her eyes were wild.

I made a garland for her head,
    And bracelets too, and fragrant zone;°             *girdle*
She looked at me as she did love,
20    And made sweet moan.

I set her on my pacing steed,
    And nothing else saw all day long;
For sidelong would she bend, and sing
    A faery's song.

25    She found me roots of relish sweet,
    And honey wild, and manna dew,
And sure in language strange she said —
    "I love thee true."

---

1  Keats took his title, meaning "The Beautiful Lady without Pity" — but not his subject matter —
from a medieval poem by Alain Chartier.

She took me to her elfin grot,
30      And there she wept and sighed full sore,
And there I shut her wild wild eyes
         With kisses four.

And there she lullèd me asleep
         And there I dreamed — Ah! woe betide!
35  The latest° dream I ever dreamed                    *last*
         On the cold hill side.

I saw pale kings and princes too,
         Pale warriors, death-pale were they all;
They cried — "La Belle Dame sans Merci
40      Hath thee in thrall!"

I saw their starved lips in the gloam,
         With horrid warning gapèd wide,
And I awoke and found me here,
         On the cold hill's side.

45  And this is why I sojourn here
         Alone and palely loitering,
Though the sedge has withered from the lake,
         And no birds sing.

*(1819)*                                *(1820)*


# To Autumn

### I

Season of mists and mellow fruitfulness,
         Close bosom-friend of the maturing sun;
Conspiring with him how to load and bless
         With fruit the vines that round the thatch-eves run;
5  To bend with apples the mossed cottage-trees,
         And fill all fruit with ripeness to the core;
                  To swell the gourd, and plump the hazel shells
With a sweet kernel; to set budding more,
         And still more, later flowers for the bees,
10      Until they think warm days will never cease,
                  For Summer has o'er-brimmed their clammy cells.

### II

Who hath not seen thee oft amid thy store?
         Sometimes whoever seeks abroad may find
Thee sitting careless on a granary floor,

15      Thy hair soft-lifted by the winnowing wind;
Or on a half-reaped furrow sound asleep,
    Drowsed with the fume of poppies, while thy hook°           *scythe*
        Spares the next swath and all its twinèd flowers:
And sometimes like a gleaner thou dost keep
20     Steady thy laden head across a brook;
      Or by a cider-press, with patient look,
        Thou watchest the last oozings hours by hours.

### III

Where are the songs of Spring? Aye, where are they?
     Think not of them, thou hast thy music too, —
25  While barred clouds bloom the soft-dying day,
     And touch the stubble-plains with rosy hue;
Then in a wailful choir the small gnats mourn
     Among the river sallows,° borne aloft           *willows*
       Or sinking as the light wind lives or dies;
30  And full-grown lambs loud bleat from hilly bourn;°      *region*
     Hedge-crickets sing; and now with treble soft
     The red-breast whistles from a garden-croft;°    *enclosed field*
       And gathering swallows twitter in the skies.

*(1819)*                      *(1820)*

# [When I have fears that I may cease to be]

When I have fears that I may cease to be
     Before my pen has gleaned my teeming brain,
Before high-piled books, in charactry,°          *printed characters*
     Hold like rich garners the full ripened grain;
5  When I behold, upon the night's starred face,
     Huge cloudy symbols of a high romance,
And think that I may never live to trace
     Their shadows, with the magic hand of chance;
And when I feel, fair creature of an hour,
10    That I shall never look upon thee more,
Never have relish in the faery power
     Of unreflecting love; — then on the shore
Of the wide world I stand alone, and think
Till love and fame to nothingness do sink.

*(1818)*                      *(1848)*

# [The tide rises, the tide falls]

The tide rises, the tide falls,
The twilight darkens, the curlew calls;
Along the sea-sands damp and brown
The traveller hastens toward the town,
5      And the tide rises, the tide falls.

Darkness settles on roofs and walls,
But the sea, the sea in the darkness calls;
The little waves, with their soft, white hands,
Efface the footprints in the sands,
10     And the tide rises, the tide falls.

The morning breaks; the steeds in their stalls
Stamp and neigh, as the hostler calls;
The day returns, but nevermore
Returns the traveller to the shore,
15     And the tide rises, the tide falls.

*(1879)*                         *(1880)*

---

# Sonnet — To Science

Science! true daughter of Old Time thou art!
    Who alterest all things with thy peering eyes.
Why preyest thou thus upon the poet's heart,
    Vulture, whose wings are dull realities?
5  How should he love thee? or how deem thee wise,
    Who wouldst not leave him in his wandering
To seek for treasure in the jewelled skies,
    Albeit he soared with an undaunted wing?
Hast thou not dragged Diana[1] from her car?
10    And driven the Hamadryad° from the wood         *tree nymph*
To seek a shelter in some happier star?
    Hast thou not torn the Naiad° from her flood,      *river nymph*

---

1  Virgin goddess of the hunt and the moon ("her car").

99

The Elfin from the green grass, and from me
The summer dream beneath the tamarind° tree?          *[oriental fruit]*

*(1829)*                              *(1829, 1845)*


# T̶ɦe Haunte∂ Palace

In the greenest of our valleys
    By good angels tenanted,
Once a fair and stately palace —
    Radiant palace — reared its head.
5  In the monarch Thought's dominion —
    It stood there!
Never seraph spread a pinion
    Over fabric half so fair!

Banners yellow, glorious, golden,
10    On its roof did float and flow —
(This — all this — was in the olden
    Time long ago)
And every gentle air that dallied,
    In that sweet day,
15 Along the ramparts plumed and pallid,
    A wingèd odor went away.

Wanderers in that happy valley,
    Through two luminous windows, saw
Spirits moving musically,
20    To a lute's well-tunèd law,
Round about a throne where, sitting,
    Porphyrogene°,          *in royal purple*
In state his glory well befitting
    The ruler of the realm was seen.

25 And all with pearl and ruby glowing
    Was the fair palace door,
Through which came flowing, flowing, flowing,
    And sparkling evermore,
A troop of Echoes whose sweet duty
30    Was but to sing,
In voices of surpassing beauty,
    The wit and wisdom of their king.

But evil things, in robes of sorrow,
    Assailed the monarch's high estate.
35 (Ah, let us mourn! — for never morrow
    Shall dawn upon him, desolate!)

And round about his home the glory
  That blushed and bloomed,
Is but a dim-remembered story
40  Of the old-time entombed.

And travellers, now, within that valley,
  Through the encrimsoned windows see
Vast forms that move fantastically
  To a discordant melody,
45 While, like a ghastly rapid river,
  Through the pale door
A hideous throng rush out forever
  And laugh — but smile no more.

      *(1845)*

---

## ALFRED, LORD TENNYSON     *English (1809-1892)*

# [Break, break, break]

Break, break, break,
  On thy cold gray stones, O Sea!
And I would that my tongue could utter
  The thoughts that arise in me.

5 O, well for the fisherman's boy,
  That he shouts with his sister at play!
O, well for the sailor lad,
  That he sings in his boat on the bay!

And the stately ships go on
10  To their haven under the hill;
But O for the touch of a vanish'd hand,
  And the sound of a voice that is still!

Break, break, break,
  At the foot of thy crags, O Sea!
15 But the tender grace of a day that is dead
  Will never come back to me.

*(1834)*        *(1842)*

# Ulysses

It little profits that an idle king,[1]
By this still hearth, among these barren crags,
Match'd with an aged wife, I mete and dole
Unequal laws[2] unto a savage race,
5   That hoard, and sleep, and feed, and know not me.
I cannot rest from travel; I will drink
Life to the lees. All times I have enjoyed
Greatly, have suffered greatly, both with those
That loved me, and alone; on shore, and when
10   Thro' scudding drifts the rainy Hyades°            *springtime stars*
Vext the dim sea. I am become a name;
For always roaming with a hungry heart
Much have I seen and known, — cities of men
And manners, climates, councils, governments,
15   Myself not least, but honoured of them all, —
And drunk delight of battle with my peers,
Far on the ringing plains of windy Troy.
I am a part of all that I have met;
Yet all experience is an arch wherethro'
20   Gleams that untravelled world whose margin fades
For ever and for ever when I move.
How dull it is to pause, to make an end,
To rust unburnished, not to shine in use!
As tho' to breathe were life! Life piled on life
25   Were all too little, and of one to me
Little remains; but every hour is saved
From that eternal silence, something more,
A bringer of new things; and vile it were
For some three suns° to store and hoard myself,          *years*
30   And this grey spirit yearning in desire
To follow knowledge like a sinking star,
Beyond the utmost bound of human thought.
      This is my son, mine own Telemachus,
To whom I leave the sceptre and the isle, —
35   Well-loved of me, discerning to fulfil
This labour, by slow prudence to make mild
A rugged people, and thro' soft degrees
Subdue them to the useful and the good.
Most blameless is he, centred in the sphere
40   Of common duties, decent not to fail

---

1  By suggesting Ulysses' boredom upon resuming his kingship, Tennyson combines Homer's account of the Greek hero's return to his home on Ithaca after the Trojan War with Dante's notion that he never did so, but set out on a daring westward quest with his men.

2  Measure and deal out rewards and punishments.

In offices of tenderness, and pay
Meet adoration to my household gods,
When I am gone. He works his work, I mine.
    There lies the port; the vessel puffs her sail;
45    There gloom the dark, broad seas. My mariners,
Souls that have toiled, and wrought, and thought with me, —
That ever with a frolic welcome took
The thunder and the sunshine, and opposed
Free hearts, free foreheads, — you and I are old;
50    Old age hath yet his honour and his toil.
Death closes all; but something ere the end,
Some work of noble note, may yet be done,
Not unbecoming men that strove with Gods.
The lights begin to twinkle from the rocks;
55    The long day wanes; the slow moon climbs; the deep
Moans round with many voices. Come, my friends.
'Tis not too late to seek a newer world.
Push off, and sitting well in order smite
The sounding furrows; for my purpose holds
60    To sail beyond the sunset, and the baths
Of all the western stars, until I die.
It may be that the gulfs will wash us down;
It may be we shall touch the Happy Isles,[1]
And see the great Achilles, whom we knew.
65    Tho' much is taken, much abides; and tho'
We are not now that strength which in old days
Moved earth and heaven, that which we are, we are, —
One equal temper of heroic hearts,
Made weak by time and fate, but strong in will
70    To strive, to seek, to find, and not to yield.
*(1833)*                              *(1842)*

## Two Songs from *The Princess*

# [Now sleeps the crimson petal]

    Now sleeps the crimson petal, now the white;
Nor waves the cypress in the palace walk;
Nor winks the gold fin in the porphyry font.
The fire-fly wakens; waken thou with me.

5    Now droops the milk-white peacock like a ghost,
And like a ghost she glimmers on to me.

---

[1]  Islands of the Blessed: the abode of heroes after death in the far-western ocean beyond Gibraltar.

Now lies the Earth all Danaë[1] to the stars,
And all thy heart lies open unto me.

Now slides the silent meteor on, and leaves
10  A shining furrow, as thy thoughts in me.

Now folds the lily all her sweetness up,
And slips into the bosom of the lake.
So fold thyself, my dearest, thou, and slip
Into my bosom and be lost in me.

*(1847)*

# [Tears, idle tears]

Tears, idle tears, I know not what they mean,
Tears from the depth of some divine despair
Rise in the heart, and gather to the eyes,
In looking on the happy autumn-fields,
5  And thinking of the days that are no more.

Fresh as the first beam glittering on a sail,
That brings our friends up from the underworld,
Sad as the last which reddens over one
That sinks with all we love below the verge;
10  So sad, so fresh, the days that are no more.

Ah, sad and strange as in dark summer dawns
The earliest pipe of half-awakened birds
To dying ears, when unto dying eyes
The casement slowly grows a glimmering square;
15  So sad, so strange, the days that are no more.

Dear as remembered kisses after death,
And sweet as those by hopeless fancy feigned
On lips that are for others; deep as love,
Deep as first love, and wild with all regret;
20  O Death in Life, the days that are no more!

*(1847)*

---

1  Zeus visited the imprisoned Greek princess in a shower of gold; their offspring was the hero Perseus.

# ROBERT BROWNING

*English (1812-1889)*

## Porphyria's Lover

The rain set early in tonight,
　　The sullen wind was soon awake,
It tore the elm-tops down for spite,
　　And did its worst to vex the lake:
5　　　I listened with heart fit to break.
When glided in Porphyria; straight
　　She shut the cold out and the storm,
And kneeled and made the cheerless grate
　　Blaze up, and all the cottage warm;
10　　　Which done, she rose, and from her form
Withdrew the dripping cloak and shawl,
　　And laid her soiled gloves by, untied
Her hat and let the damp hair fall,
　　And, last, she sat down by my side
15　　　And called me. When no voice replied,
She put my arm about her waist,
　　And made her smooth white shoulder bare,
And all her yellow hair displaced,
　　And, stooping, made my cheek lie there,
20　　　And spread, o'er all, her yellow hair,
Murmuring how she loved me — she
　　Too weak, for all her heart's endeavour,
To set its struggling passion free
　　From pride, and vainer ties dissever,
25　　　And give herself to me forever.
But passion sometimes would prevail,
　　Nor could tonight's gay feast restrain
A sudden thought of one so pale
　　For love of her, and all in vain:
30　　　So, she was come through wind and rain.
Be sure I looked up at her eyes
　　Happy and proud; at last I knew
Porphyria worshiped me; surprise
　　Made my heart swell, and still it grew
35　　　While I debated what to do.
That moment she was mine, mine, fair,
　　Perfectly pure and good: I found
A thing to do, and all her hair
　　In one long yellow string I wound
40　　　Three times her little throat around,
And strangled her. No pain felt she;
　　I am quite sure she felt no pain.
As a shut bud that holds a bee,

I warily oped her lids: again
45      Laughed the blue eyes without a stain.
And I untightened next the tress
        About her neck; her cheek once more
Blushed bright beneath my burning kiss:
        I propped her head up as before,
50      Only, this time my shoulder bore
Her head, which droops upon it still:
        The smiling rosy little head,
So glad it has its utmost will,
        That all it scorned at once is fled,
55      And I, its love, am gained instead!
Porphyria's love: she guessed not how
        Her darling one wish would be heard.
And thus we sit together now,
        And all night long we have not stirred,
60      And yet God has not said a word!

*(1834)*                                        *(1836, 1842)*


# My Last Duchess

## *FERRARA*

That's my last Duchess painted on the wall,
Looking as if she were alive. I call
That piece a wonder, now: Frà Pandolf's¹ hands
Worked busily a day, and there she stands.
5    Will't please you sit and look at her? I said
"Fra Pandolf" by design, for never read
Strangers like you that pictured countenance,
The depth and passion of its earnest glance,
But to myself they turned (since none puts by
10   The curtain I have drawn for you, but I)
And seemed as they would ask me, if they durst,°                    *dared*
How such a glance came there; so, not the first
Are you to turn and ask thus. Sir, 'twas not
Her husband's presence only called that spot
15   Of joy into the Duchess' cheek: perhaps
Frà Pandolf chanced to say "Her mantle laps
Over my lady's wrist too much," or "Paint
Must never hope to reproduce the faint
Half-flush that dies along her throat:" such stuff
20   Was courtesy, she thought, and cause enough
For calling up that spot of joy. She had

---

1   An imaginary painter (also a monk); Claus of Innsbruck (line 56) is similarly invented.

A heart — how shall I say? — too soon made glad,
Too easily impressed; she liked whate'er
She looked on, and her looks went everywhere.
25 Sir, 'twas all one! My favour° at her breast,                    *gift, jewel*
The dropping of the daylight in the West,
The bough of cherries some officious° fool                        *meddling*
Broke in the orchard for her, the white mule
She rode with round the terrace — all and each
30 Would draw from her alike the approving speech,
Or blush, at least. She thanked men, — good! but thanked
Somehow — I know not how — as if she ranked
My gift of a nine-hundred-years-old name
With anybody's gift. Who'd stoop to blame
35 This sort of trifling? Even had you skill
In speech — (which I have not) — to make your will
Quite clear to such an one, and say, "Just this
Or that in you disgusts me; here you miss,
Or there exceed the mark" — and if she let
40 Herself be lessoned so, nor plainly set
Her wits to yours, forsooth, and made excuse,
— E'en then would be some stooping; and I choose
Never to stoop. Oh sir, she smiled, no doubt,
Whene'er I passed her; but who passed without
45 Much the same smile? This grew; I gave commands;
Then all smiles stopped together. There she stands
As if alive. Will't please you rise? We'll meet
The company below, then. I repeat,
The Count your master's known munificence°                        *great generosity*
50 Is ample warrant that no just pretence
Of mine for dowry will be disallowed;
Though his fair daughter's self, as I avowed
At starting, is my object. Nay, we'll go
Together down, sir. Notice Neptune, though,
55 Taming a sea-horse, thought a rarity,
Which Claus of Innsbruck cast in bronze for me!

*(1842)*                                    *(1842)*

# Soliloquy of the Spanish Cloister

## I

GR-R-R— there go, my heart's abhorrence!
    Water your damned flower-pots, do!
If hate killed men, Brother Lawrence,
    God's blood, would not mine kill you!
5 What? your myrtle-bush wants trimming?
    Oh, that rose has prior claims —
Needs its leaden vase filled brimming?
    Hell dry you up with its flames!

## II

At the meal we sit together:
10     *Salve tibi!*[1] I must hear
Wise talk of the kind of weather,
    Sort of season, time of year:
*Not a plenteous cork-crop: scarcely*
    *Dare we hope oak-galls,*[2] *I doubt:*
15 *What's the Latin name for "parsley"?*
    What's the Greek name for Swine's Snout?°       *dandelion*

## III

Whew! We'll have our platter burnished,
    Laid with care on our own shelf!
With a fire-new spoon we're furnished,
20     And a goblet for ourself,
Rinsed like something sacrificial
    Ere 'tis fit to touch our chaps° —      *lips*
Marked with L. for our initial!
    (He-he! There his lily snaps!)

## IV

25 *Saint*, forsooth! While brown Dolores
    Squats outside the Convent bank
With Sanchicha, telling stories,
    Steeping tresses in the tank,
Blue-black, lustrous, thick like horsehairs,
30     — Can't I see his dead eye glow,
Bright as 'twere a Barbary corsair's°?      *African pirate's*
    (That is, if he'd let it show!)

---

1 "Hail to thee." Here and in lines 13-15, the speaker mockingly quotes Brother Lawrence's conversation.

2 A growth or tumour on oak trees useful for tanning, medicine and ink-making.

## V

When he finishes refection,°                           *dinner*
    Knife and fork he never lays
35 Cross-wise, to my recollection,
    As do I, in Jesu's praise.
I the Trinity illustrate,
    Drinking watered orange-pulp —
In three sips the Arian[1] frustrate;
40     While he drains his at one gulp.

## VI

Oh, those melons? If he's able
    We're to have a feast! so nice!
One goes to the Abbot's table,
    All of us get each a slice.
45 How go on your flowers? None double?
    Not one fruit-sort can you spy?
Strange!—And I, too, at such trouble,
    Keep them close-nipped on the sly!

## VII

There's a great text in Galatians,[2]
50     Once you trip on it, entails
Twenty-nine distinct damnations,
    One sure, if another fails:
If I trip him just a-dying,
    Sure of heaven as sure can be,
55 Spin him round and send him flying
    Off to hell, a Manichee?[3]

## VIII

Or, my scrofulous° French novel                    *pornographic*
    On grey paper with blunt type!
Simply glance at it, you grovel
60     Hand and foot in Belial's gripe°:           *Satan's grip*
If I double down its pages
    At the woeful° sixteenth print,             *scandalous*
When he gathers his greengages,
    Ope a sieve and slip it in't?

---

1  Follower of the fourth-century heresy that denied the Trinity.

2  In Galatians 5:19-21, St. Paul specifies the various "works of the flesh" that lead to damnation (but not "twenty-nine," nor "distinct").

3  Follower of another early heresy which believed in the eternal conflict of God and Satan. The speaker would appear to believe in this dualism himself.

## IX

65 Or, there's Satan! — one might venture
    Pledge one's soul to him, yet leave
Such a flaw in the indenture°            *contract*
    As he'd miss till, past retrieve,
Blasted lay that rose-acacia
70     We're so proud of! *Hy, Zy, Hine*[1]...
'St, there's Vespers°! *Plena gratiâ*      *evening prayers*
    *Ave, Virgo°!* Gr-r-r — you swine!    *Hail, Virgin, full of grace*

*(ca. 1839)*                        *(1842)*

---

**EMILY BRONTË**                     *English (1818-1848)*

## *Stanzas*

Often rebuked, yet always back returning
    To those first feelings that were born with me,
And leaving busy chase of wealth and learning
    For idle dreams of things which cannot be:

5 Today, I will seek not the shadowy region;
    Its unsustaining vastness waxes drear;
And visions rising, legion after legion,
    Bring the unreal world too strangely near.

I'll walk, but not in old heroic traces,
10     And not in paths of high morality,
And not among the half-distinguished faces
    The clouded forms of long-past history.

I'll walk where my own nature would be leading —
    It vexes me to choose another guide —
15 Where the grey flocks in ferny glens are feeding,
    Where the wild wind blows on the mountainside.

What have those lonely mountains worth revealing?
    More glory and more grief than I can tell:
The earth that wakes one human heart to feeling
20     Can centre both the worlds of Heaven and Hell.

              *(1850)*

---

1  The start of a curse against Brother Lawrence, or incantation to summon Satan.

## The Latest Decalogue

Thou shalt have one God only; who
Would be at the expense of two?
No graven images may be
Worshipped, except the currency:
5   Swear not at all; for for thy curse
Thine enemy is none the worse:
At church on Sunday to attend
Will serve to keep the world thy friend:
Honour thy parents; that is, all
10  From whom advancement may befall:
Thou shalt not kill; but needst not strive
Officiously to keep alive:
Do not adultery commit;
Advantage rarely comes of it:
15  Thou shalt not steal; an empty feat,
When it's so lucrative to cheat:
Bear not false witness; let the lie
Have time on its own wings to fly:
Thou shalt not covet; but tradition
20  Approves all forms of competition.

The sum of all is, thou shalt love,
If any body, God above:
At any rate shall never labour
*More* than thyself to love thy neighbour.

*(1849)*                              *(1862)*

---

## When I Heard the Learn'd Astronomer

When I heard the learn'd astronomer,
When the proofs, the figures, were ranged in columns before me,
When I was shown the charts and diagrams, to add, divide, and measure
    them,
When I sitting heard the astronomer where he lectured with much applause
    in the lecture-room,
5   How soon unaccountable I became tired and sick,
Till rising and gliding out I wandered off by myself,

In the mystical moist night-air, and from time to time,
Looked up in perfect silence at the stars.

*(1865)*                                    *(1865)*


# A Noiseless Patient Spider

A noiseless patient spider,
I marked where on a little promontory it stood isolated,
Marked how to explore the vacant vast surrounding,
It launched forth filament, filament, filament, out of itself,
5    Ever unreeling them, ever tirelessly speeding them.

And you O my soul where you stand,
Surrounded, detached, in measureless oceans of space,
Ceaselessly musing, venturing, throwing, seeking the spheres
        to connect them,
Till the bridge you will need be formed, till the ductile° anchor hold,        *pliable*
10    Till the gossamer thread you fling catch somewhere, O my soul.

*(1868)*                                    *(1881)*

**MATTHEW ARNOLD**                          *English (1822-1888)*

# Dover Beach

The sea is calm tonight.
The tide is full, the moon lies fair
Upon the straits; — on the French coast the light
Gleams and is gone; the cliffs of England stand,
5    Glimmering and vast, out in the tranquil bay.
Come to the window, sweet is the night-air!

Only, from the long line of spray
Where the sea meets the moon-blanched land,
Listen! you hear the grating roar
10    Of pebbles which the waves draw back, and fling,
At their return, up the high strand,
Begin, and cease, and then again begin,
With tremulous cadence slow, and bring
The eternal note of sadness in.

15    Sophocles long ago
Heard it on the Ægæan, and it brought
Into his mind the turbid ebb and flow

Of human misery; we
Find also in the sound a thought,
20  Hearing it by this distant northern sea.

The Sea of Faith
Was once, too, at the full, and round earth's shore
Lay like the folds of a bright girdle furled.
But now I only hear
25  Its melancholy, long, withdrawing roar,
Retreating, to the breath
Of the night-wind, down the vast edges drear
And naked shingles° of the world.                    *pebble beaches*

Ah, love, let us be true
30  To one another! for the world, which seems
To lie before us like a land of dreams,
So various, so beautiful, so new,
Hath really neither joy, nor love, nor light,
Nor certitude, nor peace, nor help for pain;
35  And we are here as on a darkling plain
Swept with confused alarms of struggle and flight,
Where ignorant armies clash by night.

*(1848-51)*                              *(1867)*


# Growing Old

What is it to grow old?
Is it to lose the glory of the form,
The lustre of the eye?
Is it for beauty to forego her wreath?
5  — Yes, but not this alone.

Is it to feel our strength —
Not our bloom only, but our strength — decay?
Is it to feel each limb
Grow stiffer, every function less exact,
10  Each nerve more loosely strung?

Yes, this, and more; but not
Ah, 'tis not what in youth we dreamed 'twould be!
'Tis not to have our life
Mellowed and softened as with sunset-glow,
15  A golden day's decline.

'Tis not to see the world
As from a height, with rapt prophetic eyes,
And heart profoundly stirred;

113

And weep, and feel the fulness of the past,
20   The years that are no more.

It is to spend long days
And not once feel that we were ever young;
It is to add, immured°                                                              *confined*
In the hot prison of the present, month
25   To month with weary pain.

It is to suffer this,
And feel but half, and feebly, what we feel.
Deep in our hidden heart
Festers the dull remembrance of a change,
30   But no emotion — none.

It is — last stage of all —
When we are frozen up within, and quite
The phantom of ourselves,
To hear the world applaud the hollow ghost
35   Which blamed the living man.

                              *(1867)*

---

# GEORGE MEREDITH                              *English (1828-1909)*

## from *Modern Love*

### 17

At dinner, she is hostess, I am host.
Went the feast ever cheerfuller? She keeps
The Topic over intellectual deeps
In buoyancy afloat. They see no ghost.
5   With sparkling surface-eyes we ply the ball:
It is in truth a most contagious game:
HIDING THE SKELETON, shall be its name.
Such play as this, the devils might appal!
But here's the greater wonder; in that we
10   Enamoured of an acting nought can tire,
Each other, like true hypocrites, admire;
Warm-lighted looks, Love's ephemerioe,°                      *short-lived insects*
Shoot gaily o'er the dishes and the wine.
We waken envy of our happy lot.
15   Fast, sweet, and golden, shows the marriage-knot.
Dear guests, you now have seen Love's corpse-light[1] shine.

                              *(1862)*

---

1   Phosphorescent light in marshes; in a cemetery it portended a funeral.

## DANTE GABRIEL ROSSETTI  *English (1828-1882)*

from *The House of Life: A Sonnet Sequence*

## [A Sonnet is a moment's monument]

A Sonnet is a moment's monument, —
    Memorial from the Soul's eternity
    To one dead deathless hour. Look that it be
Whether for lustral° rite or dire° portent         *purification / tragic*
5  Of its own arduous fulness reverent:
    Carve it in ivory or in ebony,
    As Day or Night may rule; and let Time see
Its flowering crest impearled and orient.°        *intricately Eastern*

A Sonnet is a coin: its face reveals
10    The soul, — its converse, to what Power 'tis due: —
Whether for tribute to the august appeals
    Of Life, or dower in Love's high retinue,
It serve; or, 'mid the dark wharf's° cavernous breath,    *underworld's*
In Charon's[1] palm it pay the toll to Death.

*(1880)*                          *(1881)*

---

## EMILY DICKINSON  *American (1830-1866)*

### 435

Much Madness is divinest Sense —
To a discerning Eye —
Much Sense — the starkest Madness —
'Tis the Majority
5  In this, as All, prevail —
Assent — and you are sane —
Demur — you're straightway dangerous —
And handled with a Chain —

*(1862)*                          *(1890)*

---

1  For a fee, the ferryman rowed the souls of the dead across the River Styx.

### 465

I heard a Fly buzz — when I died —
The Stillness in the Room
Was like the Stillness in the Air —
Between the Heaves of Storm —

5    The Eyes around — had wrung them dry —
And Breaths were gathering firm
For that last Onset — when the King
Be witnessed — in the Room —

I willed my Keepsakes — Signed away
10  What portion of me be
Assignable — and then it was
There interposed a Fly —

With Blue — uncertain stumbling Buzz —
Between the light — and me —
15  And then the Windows failed — and then
I could not see to see —

*(1862)*                               *(1896)*

### 712

Because I could not stop for Death —
He kindly stopped for me —
The Carriage held but just Ourselves —
And Immortality.

5    We slowly drove — He knew no haste
And I had put away
My labor and my leisure too,
For His Civility —

We passed the School, where Children strove
10  At Recess — in the Ring —
We passed the Fields of Gazing Grain —
We passed the Setting Sun —

Or rather — He passed Us —
The Dews drew quivering and chill —
15  For only Gossamer, my Gown —
My Tippet° — only Tulle° —                *shoulder cape / fine (silk) net*

We paused before a House that seemed
A Swelling of the Ground —

The Roof was scarcely visible —
20 The Cornice — in the Ground —

Since then — 'tis Centuries — and yet
Feels shorter than the Day
I first surmised the Horses Heads
Were toward Eternity —

*(1863)* *(1890)*


### 986

A narrow Fellow in the Grass
Occasionally rides —
You may have met Him — did you not
His notice sudden is —

5 The Grass divides as with a Comb —
A spotted shaft is seen —
And then it closes at your feet
And opens further on —

He likes a Boggy Acre
10 A Floor too cool for Corn —
Yet when a Boy, and Barefoot —
I more than once at Noon
Have passed, I thought, a Whip lash
Unbraiding in the Sun
15 When stooping to secure it
It wrinkled, and was gone —

Several of Nature's People
I know, and they know me —
I feel for them a transport
20 Of cordiality —

But never met this Fellow
Attended, or alone
Without a tighter breathing
And Zero at the Bone —

*(1866)*


### 1129

Tell all the Truth but tell it slant —
Success in Circuit lies
Too bright for our infirm Delight
The Truth's superb surprise

<sup>5</sup> As Lightning to the Children eased
With explanation kind
The Truth must dazzle gradually
Or every man be blind —

*(1945)*

---

## CHRISTINA ROSSETTI *English (1830-1894)*

# In An Artist's Studio<sup>1</sup>

One face looks out from all his canvases,
    One selfsame figure sits or walks or leans;
    We found her hidden just behind those screens,
That mirror gave back all her loveliness.
<sup>5</sup> A queen in opal or in ruby dress,
    A nameless girl in freshest summer-greens,
    A saint, an angel; — every canvas means
The same one meaning, neither more nor less.
He feeds upon her face by day and night,
<sup>10</sup>     And she with true kind eyes looks back on him
Fair as the moon and joyful as the light:
    Not wan with waiting, not with sorrow dim;
Not as she is, but was when hope shone bright;
    Not as she is, but as she fills his dream.

*(1856)*                         *(1896)*

---

## LEWIS CARROLL<sup>2</sup> *English (1832-1898)*

# Jabberwocky<sup>3</sup>

'Twas brillig, and the slithy toves
    Did gyre and gimble in the wabe;

---

1 The artist is Dante Gabriel Rossetti, Christina's brother, who later married Miss Siddal, his favourite model.

2 Charles Lutwidge Dodgson.

3 The poem appears in *Through the Looking Glass*, Chapter 6. Humpty Dumpty rather unconvincingly explains to Alice that " 'brillig' means four o'clock in the afternoon — the time when you begin *broiling* things for dinner," and that " 'slithy' means 'lithe' and 'slimy.' 'Lithe' is the same as 'active.' You see it's like a portmanteau — there are two meanings packed into one word."

All mimsy were the borogoves,
    And the mome raths outgrabe.

5    "Beware the Jabberwock, my son!
       The jaws that bite, the claws that catch!
    Beware the Jubjub bird, and shun
       The frumious Bandersnatch!"

He took his vorpal sword in hand;
10      Long time the manxome foe he sought —
So rested he by the Tumtum tree,
    And stood awhile in thought.

And, as in uffish thought he stood,
    The Jabberwock, with eyes of flame,
15   Came whiffling through the tulgey wood,
    And burbled as it came!

One, two! One, two! And through and through
    The vorpal blade went snicker-snack!
He left it dead, and with its head
20     He went galumphing back.

"And hast thou slain the Jabberwock?
    Come to my arms, my beamish boy
O frabjous day! Callooh! Callay!"
    He chortled in his joy.

25   'Twas brillig, and the slithy toves
    Did gyre and gimble in the wabe;
All mimsy were the borogoves,
    And the mome raths outgrabe.

*(1855)*                      *(1871)*

---

# Sir William Schwenk Gilbert    *English (1836-1911)*

# [Anglicized Utopia][1]

Society has quite forsaken all her wicked courses,
Which empties our police courts, and abolishes divorces.
            (Divorce is nearly obsolete in England.)
No tolerance we show to undeserving rank and splendour;
5   For the higher his position is, the greater the offender.
            (That's a maxim that is prevalent in England.)

---

1  Originally a song by Paramount the First, King of Utopia, and the chorus (lines in parentheses) in Gilbert and Sullivan's *Utopia Limited* (1893), a satire on visionary social ideas common in the 1880s and 1890s. Line 18 mentions an elegant London square and streets.

No Peeress at our Drawing-Room° before the Presence passes    *court reception*
Who wouldn't be accepted by the lower-middle classes;
Each shady dame, whatever be her rank, is bowed out neatly.
10 (In short, this happy country has been Anglicized completely!
     It really is surprising
     What a thorough Anglicizing
  We've brought about — Utopia's quite another land;
     In her enterprising movements,
15      She is England — with improvements,
  Which we dutifully offer to our mother-land!)

Our city we have beautified — we've done it willy-nilly —
And all that isn't Belgrave Square is Strand and Piccadilly.
              (They haven't any slummeries in England.)
20 We have solved the labour question with discrimination polished
So poverty is obsolete and hunger is abolished —
              (They are going to abolish it in England.)
The Chamberlain our native stage has purged, beyond a question
Of "risky" situation and indelicate suggestion;
25 No piece is tolerated if it's costumed indiscreetly —
(In short, this happy country has been Anglicized completely!
     It really is surprising
     What a thorough Anglicizing
  We've brought about — Utopia's quite another land;
30      In her enterprising movements,
     She is England — with improvements,
  Which we dutifully offer to our motherland!)

Our Peerage we've remodelled on an intellectual basis,
Which certainly is rough on our hereditary races —
35               (They are going to remodel it in England.)
The Brewers and the Cotton Lords no longer seek admission,
And Literary Merit meets with proper recognition —
              (As Literary Merit does in England!)
Who knows but we may count among our intellectual chickens
40 Like them an Earl of Thackeray and p'raps a Duke of Dickens —
Lord Fildes[1] and Viscount Millais (when they come) we'll welcome
   sweetly —
(And then, this happy country will be Anglicized completely!
     It really is surprising
     What a thorough Anglicizing
45   We've brought about — Utopia's quite another land;
     In her enterprising movements,
     She is England — with improvements,
  Which we dutifully offer to our mother-land!)

*(1892-93)*                                    *(1893)*

---

1   Sir Luke Fildes (1844-1927), a facile but popular painter and portraitist.

# The Ruined Maid

"O 'Melia, my dear, this does everything crown!
Who could have supposed I should meet you in Town?
And whence such fair garments, such prosperi-ty?" —
"O didn't you know I'd been ruined?" said she.

5    — "You left us in tatters, without shoes or socks,
Tired of digging potatoes, and spudding° up docks;°          *rooting / weeds*
And now you've gay bracelets and bright feathers three!" —
"Yes: that's how we dress when we're ruined," said she.

— "At home in the barton° you said 'thee' and 'thou,'          *farmyard*
10   And 'thik oon,' and 'theäs oon,' and 't'other'; but now
Your talking quite fits 'ee for high compa-ny!" —
"Some polish is gained with one's ruin," said she.

— "Your hands were like paws then, your face blue and bleak
But now I'm bewitched by your delicate cheek,
15   And your little gloves fit as on any la-dy!" —
"We never do work when we're ruined," said she.

— "You used to call home-life a hag-ridden dream,
And you'd sigh, and you'd sock°; but at present you seem          *sigh*
To know not of megrims° or melancho-ly!" —          *(morbid) depression*
20   "True. One's pretty lively when ruined," said she.

— "I wish I had feathers, a fine sweeping gown,
And a delicate face, and could strut about Town!" —
"My dear — a raw country girl, such as you be,
Cannot quite expect that. You ain't ruined," said she.

*(1866)*                              *(1901)*


# Channel Firing[1]

That night your great guns, unawares,
Shook all our coffins as we lay,
And broke the chancel° window-squares,          *area around a church alter*
We thought it was the Judgment-day

---

1   Written four months before the start of World War I, the title refers to German and British gunnery
practice by warships in the English Channel.

5    And sat upright. While drearisome
       Arose the howl of wakened hounds:
       The mouse let fall the altar-crumb,
       The worms drew back into the mounds,

       The glebe° cow drooled. Till God called, "No;      *grazing field beside a church*
10   It's gunnery practice out at sea
       Just as before you went below;
       The world is as it used to be:

       "All nations striving strong to make
       Red war yet redder. Mad as hatters
15   They do no more for Christés sake
       Than you who are helpless in such matters.

       "That this is not the judgment-hour
       For some of them's a blessed thing,
       For if it were they'd have to scour
20   Hell's floor for so much threatening ....

       "Ha, ha. It will be warmer when
       I blow the trumpet (if indeed
       I ever do; for you are men,
       And rest eternal sorely need)."

25   So down we lay again. "I wonder,
       Will the world ever saner be,"
       Said one, "than when He sent us under
       In our indifferent century!"

       And many a skeleton shook his head.
30   "Instead of preaching forty year,"
       My neighbour Parson Thirdly said,
       "I wish I had stuck to pipes and beer."

       Again the guns disturbed the hour,
       Roaring their readiness to avenge,
35   As far inland as Stourton Tower,
       And Camelot, and starlit Stonehenge.[1]

*(1914)*                  *(1914)*

---

1  Stonehenge is a famous prehistoric stone circle on Salisbury Plain; Stourton Tower in Dorset commemorates Alfred the Great's defeat of a Danish invasion in 879. Camelot (supposedly near Glastonbury) is the legendary location of King Arthur's court.

# The Convergence of the Twain

*(Lines on the loss of the "Titanic")*[1]

## I

In a solitude of the sea
Deep from human vanity,
And the Pride of Life that planned her, stilly couches she.

## II

      Steel chambers, late the pyres
5        Of her salamandrine[2] fires,
Cold currents thrid,° and turn to rhythmic tidal lyres.        *threaded among*

## III

Over the mirrors meant
To glass the opulent
The sea-worm crawls — grotesque, slimed, dumb, indifferent.

## IV

10        Jewels in joy designed
To ravish the sensuous mind
Lie lightless, all their sparkles bleared and black and blind.

## V

Dim moon-eyed fishes near
Gaze at the gilded gear
15 And query: "What does this vaingloriousness down here?" . . .

## VI

Well: while was fashioning
This creature of cleaving wing,
The Immanent Will that stirs and urges everything[3]

---

1  This "unsinkable" ocean liner collided with an iceberg on her maiden voyage to New York and sank with loss of over 800 lives on April 15, 1912.

2  In legend, salamanders were thought to be able to live in fire. Here, the word "salamandrine" seems to stress the extreme heat of the ship's furnaces.

3  According to Hardy's philosophy, the blind force that drives the world.

## VII

Prepared a sinister mate
    For her — so gaily great —
A Shape of Ice, for the time far and dissociate.

## VIII

And as the smart ship grew
    In stature, grace, and hue,
In shadowy silent distance grew the Iceberg too.

## IX

Alien they seemed to be:
    No mortal eye could see
The intimate welding of their later history,

## X

Or sign that they were bent
    By paths coincident
On being anon twin halves of one august event,

## XI

Till the Spinner of the Years
    Said "Now!" And each one hears,
And consummation comes, and jars two hemispheres.

*(1912)*                                    *(1914)*


# The Workbox

"See, here's the workbox, little wife,
    That I made of polished oak."
He was a joiner,° of village life;                          *cabinetmaker*
    She came of borough° folk.                         *town, municipality*

He holds the present up to her
    As with a smile she nears
And answers to the profferer,
    "'Twill last all my sewing years!"

"I warrant it will. And longer too.
10     'Tis a scantling° that I got                    *leftover piece*
Off poor John Wayward's coffin, who
        Died of they knew not what.

"The shingled pattern that seems to cease
        Against your box's rim
15 Continues right on in the piece
        That's underground with him.

"And while I worked it made me think
        Of timber's varied doom:
One inch where people eat and drink,
20      The next inch in a tomb.

"But why do you look so white, my dear,
        And turn aside your face?
You knew not that good lad, I fear,
        Though he came from your native place?"

25 "How could I know that good young man,
        Though he came from my native town,
When he must have left far earlier than
        I was a woman grown?"

"Ah, no. I should have understood!
30      It shocked you that I gave
To you one end of a piece of wood
        Whose other is in a grave?"

"Don't, dear, despise my intellect,
        Mere accidental things
35 Of that sort never have effect
        On my imaginings."

Yet still her lips were limp and wan,
        Her face still held aside,
As if she had known not only John,
40      But known of what he died.

                    *(1914)*

## God's Grandeur

The world is charged with the grandeur of God.
    It will flame out, like shining from shook foil;[1]
    It gathers to a greatness, like the ooze of oil°         *[from olives]*
Crushed. Why do men then now not reck his rod?°        *disobey his laws*
5  Generations have trod, have trod, have trod;
    And all is seared with trade; bleared, smeared with toil;
    And wears man's smudge and shares man's smell: the soil
Is bare now, nor can foot feel, being shod.

And for° all this, nature is never spent;             *despite*
10    There lives the dearest freshness deep down things;
And though the last lights off the black West went
    Oh, morning, at the brown brink eastward, springs —
Because the Holy Ghost over the bent
    World broods with warm breast and with ah! bright wings.

*(1877)*                    *(1918)*

## Pied[2] Beauty

Glory be to God for dappled things —
    For skies of couple-colour as a brinded° cow;        *streaked*
        For rose-moles all in stipple° upon trout that swim;    *dots*
Fresh-firecoal chestnut-falls;[3] finches' wings;
5    Landscape plotted and pieced — fold, fallow, and plough;
        And áll trádes, their gear and tackle and trim.°    *equipment*
All things counter, original, spare°, strange;         *rare*
    Whatever is fickle, freckled (who knows how?)
        With swift, slow; sweet, sour; adazzle, dim;
10  He fathers forth whose beauty is past change:
                      Praise him.

*(1877)*                    *(1918)*

---

1  In a letter, Hopkins explained this image: "I mean foil in its sense of leaf or tinsel .... Shaken gold foil gives off broad glares like sheet lightning...."

2  Spotted, many-coloured, variegated.

3  i.e. newly-fallen chestnuts, brightly glowing like coals.

# Spring and Fall

### To a young child

Márgarét, áre you gríeving
Over Goldengrove unleaving?°                              *losing leaves*
Leáves, líke the things of man, you
With your fresh thoughts care for, can you?
5   Áh! ás the heart grows older
It will come to such sights colder
By and by, nor spare a sigh
Though worlds of wanwood leafmeal[1] lie;
And yet you *will* weep and know why.
10  Now no matter, child, the name:
Sórrow's spríngs áre the same.
Nor mouth had, no nor mind, expressed
What heart heard of, ghost° guessed:                      *spirit, soul*
It ís the blight man was born for,
15  It is Margaret you mourn for.

*(1880)*                          *(1918)*


# The Windhover[2]

### To Christ our Lord

I caught this morning morning's minion,° king-          *beloved*
    dom of daylight's dauphin,[3] dapple-dawn-drawn Falcon, in his riding
    Of the rolling level underneath him steady air, and striding
High there, how he rung upon the rein[4] of a wimpling° wing     *rippling*
5   In his ecstasy! then off, off forth on swing,
    As a skate's heel sweeps smooth on a bow-bend: the hurl and gliding
    Rebuffed the big wind. My heart in hiding
Stirred for a bird, — the achieve of, the mastery of the thing!

Brute beauty and valour and act, oh, air, pride, plume, here
10      Buckle![5] AND the fire that breaks from thee then, a billion
Times told lovelier, more dangerous, O my chevalier!°          *knight*

---

1   Pale woods with mouldering leaves.
2   The sparrow-hawk or kestrel noted for hovering in the wind, even head-on.
3   Heir to the throne.
4   Circled or checked at end of a rein, as in "ringing a horse."
5   A multiple pun: prepare for action, fasten (together), collapse or give way.

No wonder of it: shéer plód makes plough down sillion°       *furrow-ridge*
Shine, and blue-bleak embers, ah my dear,
    Fall, gall° themselves, and gash gold-vermilion.       *break open*

*(1877)*                              *(1918)*

---

# A.E. HOUSMAN                   *English (1859-1936)*

## from *A Shropshire Lad*

### XIII

When I was one-and-twenty
    I heard a wise man say,
"Give crowns and pounds and guineas
    But not your heart away;
5  Give pearls away and rubies
    But keep your fancy free."
But I was one-and-twenty,
    No use to talk to me.

When I was one-and-twenty
10    I heard him say again,
"The heart out of the bosom
    Was never given in vain;
'Tis paid with sighs a plenty
    And sold for endless rue."
15  And I am two-and-twenty,
    And oh, 'tis true, 'tis true.

                    *(1896)*

### XIX

# To An Athlete Dying Young

The time you won your town the race
We chaired you through the market-place;
Man and boy stood cheering by,
And home we brought you shoulder-high.

5  To-day, the road all runners come,
Shoulder-high we bring you home,
And set you at your threshold down,
Townsman of a stiller town.

Smart lad, to slip betimes away
10  From fields where glory does not stay

And early though the laurel grows
It withers quicker than the rose.

Eyes the shady night has shut
Cannot see the record cut,°                                    *broken*
15  And silence sounds no worse than cheers
After earth has stopped the ears:

Now you will not swell the rout
Of lads that wore their honours out,
Runners whom renown outran
20  And the name died before the man.

So set, before its echoes fade,
The fleet foot on the sill of shade,
And hold to the low lintel up
The still-defended challenge-cup.

25  And round that early-laurelled head
Will flock to gaze the strengthless dead,
And find unwithered on its curls
The garland briefer than a girl's.

                                           *(1896)*

---

WILFRED CAMPBELL                 *Canadian (1861-1918)*

# The Winter Lakes

Out in a world of death far to the northward lying,
    Under the sun and the moon, under the dusk and the day;
Under the glimmer of stars and the purple of sunsets dying,
    Wan and waste and white, stretch the great lakes away.

5  Never a bud of spring, never a laugh of summer,
    Never a dream of love, never a song of bird;
But only the silence and white, the shores that grow chiller and dumber,
    Wherever the ice winds sob, and the griefs of winter are heard.

Crags that are black and wet out of the grey lake looming,
10    Under the sunset's flush and the pallid, faint glimmer of dawn;
Shadowy, ghost-like shores, where midnight surfs are booming
    Thunders of wintry woe over the spaces wan.

Lands that loom like spectres, whited regions of winter,
    Wastes of desolate woods, deserts of water and shore:

15 A world of winter and death, within these regions who enter,
     Lost to summer and life, go to return no more.

Moons that glimmer above, waters that lie white under,
     Miles and miles of lake far out under the night;
Foaming crests of waves, surfs that shoreward thunder,
20     Shadowy shapes that flee, haunting the spaces white.

Lonely hidden bays, moon-lit, ice-rimmed, winding,
     Fringed by forests and crags, haunted by shadowy shores;
Hushed from the outward strife, where the mighty surf is grinding
     Death and hate on the rocks, as sandward and landward it roars.

*(1889)*

---

ARCHIBALD LAMPMAN                    *Canadian (1861-1899)*

# Heat

From plains that reel to southward, dim,
     The road runs by me white and bare;
Up the steep hill it seems to swim
     Beyond, and melt into the glare.
5 Upward half-way, or it may be
     Nearer the summit, slowly steals
A hay-cart, moving dustily
     With idly clacking wheels.

By his cart's side the wagoner
10     Is slouching slowly at his ease,
Half-hidden in the windless blur
     Of white dust puffing to his knees.
This wagon on the height above,
     From sky to sky on either hand,
15 Is the sole thing that seems to move
     In all the heat-held land.

Beyond me in the fields the sun
     Soaks in the grass and hath his will;
I count the marguerites one by one;
20     Even the buttercups are still.
On the brook yonder not a breath
     Disturbs the spider or the midge.
The water-bugs draw close beneath
     The cool gloom of the bridge.

25 Where the far elm-tree shadows flood
         Dark patches in the burning grass,
  The cows, each with her peaceful cud,
         Lie waiting for the heat to pass.
  From somewhere on the slope near by
30       Into the pale depth of the noon
  A wandering thrush slides leisurely
         His thin revolving tune.

  In intervals of dreams I hear
         The cricket from the droughty ground;
35 The grasshoppers spin into mine ear
         A small innumerable sound.
  I lift mine eyes sometimes to gaze:
         The burning sky-line blinds my sight:
  The woods far off are blue with haze:
40       The hills are drenched in light.

  And yet to me not this or that
         Is always sharp or always sweet;
  In the sloped shadow of my hat
         I lean at rest, and drain the heat;
45 Nay more, I think some blessèd power
         Hath brought me wandering idly here:
  In the full furnace of this hour
         My thoughts grow keen and clear.

                    *(1888)*

---

# DUNCAN CAMPBELL SCOTT             *Canadian (1862-1947)*

# The Onondaga[1] Madonna [and Child]

  She stands full-throated and with careless pose,
  This woman of a weird and waning race,
  The tragic savage lurking in her face,
  Where all her pagan passion burns and glows;
5 Her blood is mingled with her ancient foes,
  And thrills with war and wildness in her veins;
  Her rebel lips are dabbled with the stains
  Of feuds and forays and her father's woes.

---

1  One of the Six Nations of the Iroquois Confederacy.

And closer in the shawl about her breast,
10  The latest promise of her nation's doom,
Paler than she her baby clings and lies,
The primal warrior gleaming from his eyes;
He sulks, and burdened with his infant gloom,
He draws his heavy brows and will not rest.

*(ca. 1894)*                          *(1894, 1898)*

---

## WILLIAM BUTLER YEATS                          *Irish (1865-1939)*

# The Second Coming[1]

Turning and turning in the widening gyre
The falcon cannot hear the falconer;
Things fall apart; the center cannot hold;
Mere anarchy is loosed upon the world,
5   The blood-dimmed tide is loosed, and everywhere
The ceremony of innocence is drowned;
The best lack all conviction, while the worst
Are full of passionate intensity.

Surely some revelation is at hand;
10  Surely the Second Coming is at hand.
The Second Coming! Hardly are those words out
When a vast image out of *Spiritus Mundi*[2]
Troubles my sight: somewhere in sands of the desert
A shape with lion body and the head of a man,
15  A gaze blank and pitiless as the sun,
Is moving its slow thighs, while all about it
Reel shadows of the indignant desert birds.
The darkness drops again; but now I know
That twenty centuries of stony sleep
20  Were vexed to nightmare by a rocking cradle,
And what rough beast, its hour come round at last,
Slouches towards Bethlehem to be born?

*(1919)*                          *(1921)*

---

1  Though this title refers to Christian belief in the return of Christ (see Matthew 24), it is ironic, for this new Nativity produces a Sphinx-like beast, which (unlike that of the Book of Revelation) is unconquerable. Yeats believed in 2000-year cycles of history (he called them "gyres" — conical-spiral turnings of time); the Irish "troubles," World War I, and the Russian Revolution convinced him that the era starting with Christ's birth was coming to an end, to be replaced by an era antithetical to it. See also "Leda and the Swan" (p. 133) which deals with the beginning of the Greco-Roman gyre which preceded the Christian one.

2  The Soul of the Universe, the "Great Memory," a universal subconscious repository of human memories and images.

# Leda and the Swan[1]

A sudden blow: the great wings beating still
Above the staggering girl, her thighs caressed
By the dark webs, her nape caught in his bill,
He holds her helpless breast upon his breast.

5   How can those terrified vague fingers push
The feathered glory from her loosening thighs?
And how can body, laid in that white rush,
But feel the strange heart beating where it lies?

A shudder in the loins engenders there
10  The broken wall, the burning roof and tower
And Agamemnon dead.
                    Being so caught up,
So mastered by the brute blood of the air,
Did she put on his knowledge with his power
15  Before the indifferent beak could let her drop?

*(1923)*                            *(1928)*


# Crazy Jane Talks with the Bishop[2]

I met the Bishop on the road
And much said he and I.
"Those breasts are flat and fallen now,
Those veins must soon be dry;
5   Live in a heavenly mansion,
Not in some foul sty."

"Fair and foul are near of kin,
And fair needs foul," I cried.
"My friends are gone, but that's a truth
10  Nor grave nor bed denied,
Learned in bodily lowliness
And in the heart's pride.

---

1  In Greek mythology, Zeus, in the form of a swan, raped Leda, who gave birth to Helen and Clytemnestra. Each married a King, Menelaus and Agammemnon respectively. Helen eloped with the Trojan prince Paris and Agammemnon led the Greek armies in the ten-year Trojan War. Following the destruction of Troy, Agammemnon returned home and was murdered by his unfaithful wife.

2  This is the sixth in a series of poems inspired by an old woman (originally called "Cracked Mary") renowned for her out-spokenness. Here this "wise fool" defends sexuality and the sensuality of her youth against the "respectable" orthodoxy of the Bishop.

"A woman can be proud and stiff
When on love intent;
15 But Love has pitched his mansion in
The place of excrement;
For nothing can be sole or whole
That has not been rent."

*(1929-31)*                    *(1932)*


# Long-Legged Fly

That civilisation may not sink,
Its great battle lost,
Quiet the dog, tether the pony
To a distant post;
5 Our master Caesar is in the tent
Where the maps are spread,
His eyes fixed upon nothing,
A hand under his head.
*Like a long-legged fly upon the stream*
10 *His mind moves upon silence.*

That the topless towers° be burnt                    *[of Troy]*
And men recall that face,
Move most gently if move you must
In this lonely place.
15 She° thinks, part woman, three parts a child,    *[Helen of Troy]*
That nobody looks; her feet
Practise a tinker shuffle
Picked up on a street.
*Like a long-legged fly upon the stream*
20 *Her mind moves upon silence.*

That girls at puberty may find
The first Adam in their thought,
Shut the door of the Pope's chapel,°              *[the Sistine Chapel]*
Keep those children out.
25 There on that scaffolding reclines
Michael Angelo.
With no more sound than the mice make
His hand moves to and fro.
*Like a long-legged fly upon the stream*
30 *His mind moves upon silence.*

*(1937)*                    *(1939)*

EDWIN ARLINGTON ROBINSON        *American (1869-1935)*

# Richard Cory

Whenever Richard Cory went down town,
We people on the pavement looked at him:
He was a gentleman from sole to crown,
Clean favored, and imperially slim.

5   And he was always quietly arrayed,
And he was always human when he talked;
But still he fluttered pulses when he said,
"Good-morning," and he glittered when he walked.

And he was rich, — yes, richer than a king, —
10  And admirably schooled in every grace:
In fine,° we thought that he was everything                    *briefly*
To make us wish that we were in his place.

So on we worked, and waited for the light,
And went without the meat, and cursed the bread;
15  And Richard Cory, one calm summer night,
Went home and put a bullet through his head.

*(1896)*

# Miniver Cheevy

Miniver Cheevy, child of scorn,
    Grew lean while he assailed the seasons;
He wept that he was ever born,
    And he had reasons.

5   Miniver loved the days of old
    When swords were bright and steeds were prancing;
The vision of a warrior bold
    Would set him dancing.

Miniver sighed for what was not,
10      And dreamed, and rested from his labors;
He dreamed of Thebes and Camelot,
    And Priam's neighbors.[1]

---

1  Thebes was the setting of Sophocles' tragedy *Oedipus Rex*; Camelot the legendary seat of King Arthur; Priam's neighbours were his subjects during the ten-year Trojan War.

Miniver mourned the ripe renown
    That made so many a name so fragrant;
15  He mourned Romance, now on the town,
    And Art, a vagrant.

Miniver loved the Medici,[1]
    Albeit he had never seen one;
He would have sinned incessantly
20    Could he have been one.

Miniver cursed the commonplace
    And eyed a khaki suit with loathing;
He missed the mediaeval grace
    Of iron clothing.

25  Miniver scorned the gold he sought,
    But sore annoyed was he without it;
Miniver thought, and thought, and thought,
    And thought about it.

Miniver Cheevy, born too late,
30    Scratched his head and kept on thinking;
Miniver coughed, and called it fate,
    And kept on drinking.

              *(1910)*

# Mr. Flood's Party

Old Eben Flood, climbing alone one night
Over the hill between the town below
And the forsaken upland hermitage
That held as much as he should ever know
5  On earth again of home, paused warily.
The road was his with not a native near;
And Eben, having leisure, said aloud,
For no man else in Tilbury Town to hear:

"Well, Mr. Flood, we have the harvest moon
10  Again, and we may not have many more;
The bird is on the wing, the poet says,
And you and I have said it here before.
Drink to the bird." He raised up to the light
The jug that he had gone so far to fill,

---

1  Family of wealthy merchants, later Dukes, of Florence and famed art patrons.

15    And answered huskily: "Well, Mr. Flood,
       Since you propose it, I believe I will."

       Alone, as if enduring to the end
       A valiant armor of scarred hopes outworn,
       He stood there in the middle of the road
20    Like Roland's ghost winding a silent horn.[1]
       Below him, in the town among the trees,
       Where friends of other days had honored him,
       A phantom salutation of the dead
       Rang thinly till old Eben's eyes were dim.

25    Then, as a mother lays her sleeping child
       Down tenderly, fearing it may awake,
       He set the jug down slowly at his feet
       With trembling care, knowing that most things break;
       And only when assured that on firm earth
30    It stood, as the uncertain lives of men
       Assuredly did not, he paced away,
       And with his hand extended paused again:

       "Well, Mr. Flood, we have not met like this
       In a long time; and many a change has come
35    To both of us, I fear, since last it was
       We had a drop together. Welcome home!"
       Convivially returning with himself,
       Again he raised the jug up to the light;
       And with an acquiescent quaver said:
40    "Well, Mr. Flood, if you insist, I might.

       "Only a very little, Mr. Flood —
       For auld lang syne.[2] No more, sir; that will do."
       So, for the time, apparently it did,
       And Eben evidently thought so too;
45    For soon amid the silver loneliness
       Of night he lifted up his voice and sang,
       Secure, with only two moons listening,
       Until the whole harmonious landscape rang —

       "For auld lang syne." The weary throat gave out,
50    The last word wavered, and the song was done.
       He raised again the jug regretfully
       And shook his head, and was again alone.
       There was not much that was ahead of him,

---

[1] Charlemagne's nephew, hero of the medieval epic *The Song of Roland* (ca. 1000), blew his horn for aid just before dying at the futile battle of Roncevalles (A.D. 778).

[2] "For the days of long ago," the Scots dialectical refrain of Burn's famous song of comradeship and parting.

And there was nothing in the town below —
55 Where strangers would have shut the many doors
That many friends had opened long ago.

*(1921)*

---

## Stephen Crane

*American (1871-1900)*

# A Man Said to the Universe

A man said to the universe:
"Sir, I exist!"
"However," replied the universe,
"The fact has not created in me
5 A sense of obligation."

*(1899)*

---

## Paul Laurence Dunbar

*American (1872-1906)*

# We Wear the Mask

We wear the mask that grins and lies,
It hides our cheeks and shades our eyes, —
This debt we pay to human guile;
With torn and bleeding hearts we smile,
5 And mouth with myriad subtleties.

Why should the world be over-wise,
In counting all our tears and sighs?
Nay, let them only see us, while
We wear the mask.

10 We smile, but, O great Christ, our cries
To thee from tortured souls arise.
We sing, but oh the clay is vile
Beneath our feet, and long the mile;
But let the world dream otherwise,
15 We wear the mask!

*(1896)*

# After Apple-Picking

My long two-pointed ladder's sticking through a tree
Toward heaven still,
And there's a barrel that I didn't fill
Beside it, and there may be two or three
5   Apples I didn't pick upon some bough.
But I am done with apple-picking now.
Essence of winter sleep is on the night,
The scent of apples: I am drowsing off.
I cannot rub the strangeness from my sight
10   I got from looking through a pane of glass
I skimmed this morning from the drinking trough
And held against the world of hoary grass.
It melted, and I let it fall and break.
But I was well
15   Upon my way to sleep before it fell,
And I could tell
What form my dreaming was about to take.
Magnified apples appear and disappear,
Stem end and blossom end,
20   And every fleck of russet showing clear.
My instep arch not only keeps the ache,
It keeps the pressure of a ladder-round.
I feel the ladder sway as the boughs bend.
And I keep hearing from the cellar bin
25   The rumbling sound
Of load on load of apples coming in.
For I have had too much
Of apple-picking: I am overtired
Of the great harvest I myself desired.
30   There were ten thousand thousand fruit to touch,
Cherish in hand, lift down, and not let fall.
For all
That struck the earth,
No matter if not bruised or spiked with stubble,
35   Went surely to the cider-apple heap
As of no worth.
One can see what will trouble
This sleep of mine, whatever sleep it is.
Were he not gone,
40   The woodchuck could say whether it's like his
Long sleep, as I describe its coming on,
Or just some human sleep.

*(1914)*

# Mending Wall

Something there is that doesn't love a wall,
That sends the frozen-ground-swell under it,
And spills the upper boulders in the sun,
And makes gaps even two can pass abreast.
5  The work of hunters is another thing:
I have come after them and made repair
Where they have left not one stone on a stone,
But they would have the rabbit out of hiding,
To please the yelping dogs. The gaps I mean,
10  No one has seen them made or heard them made,
But at spring mending-time we find them there.
I let my neighbor know beyond the hill;
And on a day we meet to walk the line
And set the wall between us once again.
15  We keep the wall between us as we go.
To each the boulders that have fallen to each.
And some are loaves and some so nearly balls
We have to use a spell to make them balance:
"Stay where you are until our backs are turned!"
20  We wear our fingers rough with handling them.
Oh, just another kind of outdoor game,
One on a side. It comes to little more:
There where it is we do not need the wall:
He is all pine and I am apple orchard.
25  My apple trees will never get across
And eat the cones under his pines, I tell him.
He only says, "Good fences make good neighbors."
Spring is the mischief in me, and I wonder
If I could put a notion in his head:
30  "*Why* do they make good neighbors? Isn't it
Where there are cows? But here there are no cows.
Before I built a wall I'd ask to know
What I was walling in or walling out,
And to whom I was like to give offense.
35  Something there is that doesn't love a wall,
That wants it down." I could say "Elves" to him,
But it's not elves exactly, and I'd rather
He said it for himself. I see him there,
Bringing a stone grasped firmly by the top
40  In each hand, like an old-stone savage armed.
He moves in darkness as it seems to me,
Not of woods only and the shade of trees.
He will not go behind his father's saying,
And he likes having thought of it so well
45  He says again, "Good fences make good neighbors."

*(1914)*

# Fire and Ice

Some say the world will end in fire,
Some say in ice.
From what I've tasted of desire
I hold with those who favor fire.
5    But if it had to perish twice,
I think I know enough of hate
To say that for destruction ice
Is also great
And would suffice.

*(1923)*

# Nothing Gold Can Stay

Nature's first green is gold,
Her hardest hue to hold.
Her early leaf's a flower;
But only so an hour.
5    Then leaf subsides to leaf.
So Eden sank to grief,
So dawn goes down to day.
Nothing gold can stay.

*(1923)*

# The Silken Tent

She is as in a field a silken tent
At midday when a sunny summer breeze
Has dried the dew and all its ropes relent,
So that in guys° it gently sways at ease,            *ropes*
5    And its supporting central cedar pole,
That is its pinnacle to heavenward
And signifies the sureness of the soul,
Seems to owe naught to any single cord,
But strictly held by none, is loosely bound
10   By countless silken ties of love and thought
To everything on earth the compass round,
And only by one's going slightly taut
In the capriciousness of summer air
Is of the slightest bondage made aware.

*(1942)*

# Patterns

I walk down the garden-paths,
And all the daffodils
Are blowing, and the bright blue squills.
I walk down the patterned garden-paths
5  In my stiff, brocaded gown.
With my powdered hair and jeweled fan,
I too am a rare
Pattern. As I wander down
The garden-paths.
10  My dress is richly figured,
And the train
Makes a pink and silver stain
On the gravel, and the thrift°                    *flowering perennial*
Of the borders.
15  Just a plate of current fashion,
Tripping by in high-heeled, ribboned shoes.
Not a softness anywhere about me,
Only whalebone and brocade.
And I sink on a seat in the shade
20  Of a lime tree.° For a passion                  *linden*
Wars against the stiff brocade.
The daffodils and squills
Flutter in the breeze
As they please.
25  And I weep;
For the lime-tree is in blossom
And one small flower has dropped upon my bosom.

And the plashing of waterdrops
In the marble fountain
30  Comes down the garden-paths.
The dripping never stops.
Underneath my stiffened gown
Is the softness of a woman bathing in a marble basin,
A basin in the midst of hedges grown
35  So thick, she cannot see her lover hiding,
But she guesses he is near,
And the sliding of the water
Seems the stroking of a dear
Hand upon her.
40  What is Summer in a fine brocaded gown!
I should like to see it lying in a heap upon the ground.
All the pink and silver crumpled up on the ground.

I would be the pink and silver as I ran along the paths,
And he would stumble after,
45 Bewildered by my laughter.
I should see the sun flashing from his sword-hilt
and the buckles on his shoes.
I would choose
To lead him in a maze along the patterned paths,
A bright and laughing maze for my heavy-booted lover.
50 Till he caught me in the shade,
And the buttons of his waistcoat bruised my body as he clasped me,
Aching, melting, unafraid.
With the shadows of the leaves and the sundrops,
And the plopping of the waterdrops,
55 All about us in the open afternoon —
I am very like to swoon
With the weight of this brocade,
For the sun sifts through the shade.

Underneath the fallen blossom
60 In my bosom
Is a letter I have hid.
It was brought to me this morning by a rider from the Duke.[1]
"Madam, we regret to inform you that Lord Hartwell
Died in action Thursday se'nnight."°                                  *week*
65 As I read it in the white, morning sunlight,
The letters squirmed like snakes.
"Any answer, Madam," said my footman.
"No," I told him.
"See that the messenger takes some refreshment.
70 No, no answer."
And I walked into the garden,
Up and down the patterned paths,
In my stiff, correct brocade.
The blue and yellow flowers stood up proudly in the sun,
75 Each one.
I stood upright too,
Held rigid to the pattern
By the stiffness of my gown;
Up and down I walked,
80 Up and down.

In a month he would have been my husband.
In a month, here, underneath this lime,
We would have broke the pattern;
He for me, and I for him,

---

1  John Churchill, Duke of Marlborough, General of British and Allied Forces, fighting the French
on the continent during the war of the Spanish Succession (1702-1713).

He as Colonel, I as Lady,
On this shady seat.
He had a whim
That sunlight carried blessing.
And I answered, "It shall be as you have said."
90 Now he is dead.

In Summer and in Winter I shall walk
Up and down
The patterned garden-paths
In my stiff, brocaded gown.
95 The squills and daffodils
Will give place to pillared roses, and to asters, and to snow.
I shall go
Up and down
In my gown.
100 Gorgeously arrayed,
Boned and stayed.
And the softness of my body will be guarded from embrace
By each button, hook, and lace.
For the man who should loose me is dead,
105 Fighting with the Duke in Flanders,
In a pattern called a war.
Christ! What are patterns for?

*(1916)*


# The Dinner-Party

### FISH

"So ..." they said,
With their wineglasses delicately poised,
Mocking at the thing they cannot understand.
"So ..." they said again,
5 Amused and insolent.
The silver on the table glittered,
And the red wine in the glasses
Seemed the blood I had wasted
In a foolish cause.

### GAME

10 The gentleman with the grey-and-black whiskers
Sneered languidly over his quail.
Then my heart flew up and labored,
Then I burst from my own holding
And hurled myself forward.
15 With straight blows I beat upon him,
Furiously, with red-hot anger, I thrust against him.

But my weapon slithered over his polished surface,
And I recoiled upon myself,
Panting.

### DRAWING-ROOM

20 In a dress all softness and half-tones,
Indolent and half-reclined,
She lay upon a couch,
With the firelight reflected in her jewels.
But her eyes had no reflection,
25 They swam in a grey smoke,
The smoke of smoldering ashes,
The smoke of her cindered heart.

### COFFEE

They sat in a circle with their coffee-cups.
One dropped in a lump of sugar,
30 One stirred with a spoon.
I saw them as a circle of ghosts
Sipping blackness out of beautiful china,
And mildly protesting against my coarseness
In being alive.

### TALK

35 They took dead men's souls
And pinned them on their breasts for ornament;
Their cuff-links and tiaras
Were gems dug from a grave;
They were ghouls battening on exhumed thoughts;
40 And I took a green liqueur from a servant
So that he might come near me
And give me the comfort of a living thing.

### ELEVEN O'CLOCK

The front door was hard and heavy,
It shut behind me on the house of ghosts.
45 I flattened my feet on the pavement
To feel it solid under me;
I ran my hand along the railings
And shook them,
And pressed their pointed bars
50 Into my palms.
The hurt of it reassured me,
And I did it again and again
Until they were bruised.
When I woke in the night
55 I laughed to find them aching,
For only living flesh can suffer.

*(1916)*

## WILLIAM CARLOS WILLIAMS     *American (1883-1963)*

# The Red Wheelbarrow

so much depends
upon

a red wheel
barrow

5   glazed with rain
water

beside the white
chickens

*(1923)*

# This Is Just to Say

I have eaten
the plums
that were in
the icebox

5   and which
you were probably
saving
for breakfast

Forgive me
10  they were delicious
so sweet
and so cold

*(1934)*

# The Dance

In Breughel's[1] great picture, The Kermess,°         *Flemish village fair*
the dancers go round, they go round and

---

1   Pieter Breughel (or Brueghel) the elder (1525/30-1569), painter of Flemish peasant life.

around, the squeal and the blare and the
tweedle of bagpipes, a bugle and fiddles
5    tipping their bellies (round as the thick-
sided glasses whose wash they impound)
their hips and their bellies off balance
to turn them. Kicking and rolling about
the Fair Grounds, swinging their butts, those
10    shanks must be sound to bear up under such
rollicking measures, prance as they dance
in Breughel's great picture, The Kermess.

*(1944)*

# D.H. Lawrence    *English (1885-1930)*

## Piano

Softly, in the dusk, a woman is singing to me;
Taking me back down the vista of years, till I see
A child sitting under the piano, in the boom of the tingling strings
And pressing the small, poised feet of a mother who smiles as she sings.

5    In spite of myself, the insidious mastery of song
Betrays me back, till the heart of me weeps to belong
To the old Sunday evenings at home, with winter outside
And hymns in the cozy parlour, the tinkling piano our guide.

So now it is vain for the singer to burst into clamour
10    With the great black piano appassionato.° The glamour    *passionately*
Of childish days is upon me, my manhood is cast
Down in the flood of remembrance, I weep like a child for the past.

*(1918)*

## Snake

A snake came to my water-trough
On a hot, hot day, and I in pyjamas for the heat,
To drink there.

In the deep, strange-scented shade of the great dark carob-tree
5    I came down the steps with my pitcher
And must wait, must stand and wait, for there he was at the trough
      before me.

He reached down from a fissure in the earth-wall in the gloom
And trailed his yellow-brown slackness soft-bellied down, over the
     edge of the stone trough
And rested his throat upon the stone bottom,
10  And where the water had dripped from the tap, in a small clearness,
He sipped with his straight mouth,
Softly drank through his straight gums, into his slack long body,
Silently.

Someone was before me at my water-trough,
15  And I, like a second comer, waiting.

He lifted his head from his drinking, as cattle do,
And looked at me vaguely, as drinking cattle do,
And flickered his two-forked tongue from his lips, and mused a
     moment,
And stooped and drank a little more,
20  Being earth-brown, earth-golden from the burning bowels of the earth
On the day of Sicilian July, with Etna° smoking.        *[Italian volcano]*

The voice of my education said to me
He must be killed,
For in Sicily the black, black snakes are innocent, the gold are
     venomous.

25  And voices in me said, if you were a man
You would take a stick and break him now, and finish him off.
But I must confess how I liked him,
How glad I was he had come like a guest in quiet, to drink at my
     water-trough
And depart peaceful, pacified, and thankless,
30  Into the burning bowels of this earth.

Was it cowardice, that I dared not kill him?
Was it perversity, that I longed to talk to him?
Was it humility, to feel so honoured?
I felt so honoured.

35  And yet those voices:
*If you were not afraid, you would kill him!*

And truly I was afraid, I was most afraid,
But even so, honoured still more
That he should seek my hospitality
40  From out the dark door of the secret earth.

He drank enough
And lifted his head, dreamily, as one who has drunken,
And flickered his tongue like a forked night on the air, so black;

Seeming to lick his lips,
45 And looking around like a god, unseeing, into the air,
And slowly turned his head,
And slowly, very slowly, as if thrice adream,
Proceeded to draw his slow length curving round
And climb again the broken bank of my wall-face.

50 And as he put his head into that dreadful hole,
And as he slowly drew up, snake-easing his shoulders, and entered farther,
A sort of horror, a sort of protest against his withdrawing into that horrid
    black hole,
Deliberately going into the blackness, and slowly drawing himself after,
Overcame me now his back was turned.

55 I looked round, I put down my pitcher,
I picked up a clumsy log
And threw it at the water-trough with a clatter.

I think it did not hit him,
But suddenly that part of him that was left behind convulsed in undignified
    haste,
60 Writhed like lightning, and was gone
Into the black hole, the earth-lipped fissure in the wall-front,
At which, in the intense still noon, I stared with fascination.

And immediately I regretted it.
I thought how paltry, how vulgar, what a mean act!
65 I despised myself and the voices of my accursed human education.

And I thought of the albatross,[1]
And I wished he would come back, my snake.

For he seemed to me again like a king,
Like a king in exile, uncrowned in the underworld,
70 Now due to be crowned again.

And so, I missed my chance with one of the lords
Of life.
And I have something to expiate;
A pettiness.

*(1920)*                                    *(1921, 1923)*

---

[1]  In Coleridge's *The Rime of the Ancient Mariner*, this huge seabird is shot by the seaman who, with his crew, suffers severe punishment for this sin against nature.

# How Beastly the Bourgeois Is

How beastly the bourgeois is
especially the male of the species —

Presentable eminently presentable —
shall I make you a present of him?

5    Isn't he handsome? isn't he healthy? isn't he a fine specimen?
doesn't he look the fresh clean englishman, outside?
Isn't it god's own image? tramping his thirty miles a day
after partridges, or a little rubber ball?
wouldn't you like to be like that, well off, and quite the thing?

10   Oh, but wait!
Let him meet a new emotion, let him be faced with another man's
    need,
let him come home to a bit of moral difficulty, let life face him with a
    new demand on his understanding
and then watch him go soggy, like a wet meringue.
Watch him turn into a mess, either a fool or a bully.
15   Just watch the display of him, confronted with a new demand on his
    intelligence,
a new life-demand.

How beastly the bourgeois is
especially the male of the species —

Nicely groomed, like a mushroom
20   standing there so sleek and erect and eyeable —
and like a fungus, living on the remains of bygone life
sucking his life out of the dead leaves of greater life than his own.

And even so, he's stale, he's been there too long.
Touch him, and you'll find he's all gone inside
25   just like an old mushroom, all wormy inside, and hollow
under a smooth skin and an upright appearance.

Full of seething, wormy, hollow feelings
rather nasty —
How beastly the bourgeois is!

30   Standing in their thousands, these appearances, in damp England
what a pity they can't all be kicked over
like sickening toadstools, and left to melt back, swiftly
into the soil of England.

*(1929)*

# In a Station of the Metro

The apparition of these faces in the crowd;
Petals on a wet, black bough.

*(1916)*

# Ancient Music[1]

Winter is icummen in,
Lhude sing Goddamm,
Raineth drop and staineth slop,
And how the wind doth ramm!
5          Sing: Goddamm.
Skiddeth bus and sloppeth us,
An ague hath my ham.
Freezeth river, turneth liver,
          Damn you, sing: Goddamm.
10   Goddamm, Goddamm, 'tis why I am, Goddamm,
          So 'gainst the winter's balm.
Sing goddamm, damm, sing Goddamm,
Sing goddamm, sing goddamm, DAMM.

*(1917)*

# Bells for John Whiteside's Daughter

There was such speed in her little body,
And such lightness in her footfall,
It is no wonder her brown study°                      *sombre reverie*
Astonishes us all.

5   Her wars were bruited° in our high window.         *heard, spread through*
We looked among orchard trees and beyond

---

1   Compare the medieval lyric "Sumer is icumen in" (p. 1).

Where she took arms against her shadow,
Or harried unto the pond

The lazy geese, like a snow cloud
10   Dripping their snow on the green grass,
Tricking and stopping, sleepy and proud,
Who cried in goose, Alas,

For the tireless heart within the little
Lady with rod that made them rise
15   From their noon apple-dreams and scuttle
Goose-fashion under the skies!

But now go the bells, and we are ready,
In one house we are sternly stopped
To say we are vexed at her brown study,
20   Lying so primly propped.

*(1924)*

---

ISAAC ROSENBERG                    *English (1890-1918)*

# Break of Day in the Trenches

The darkness crumbles away.
It is the same old druid° Time as ever,          *ancient Celtic priest*
Only a live thing leaps my hand,
A queer sardonic rat,
5   As I pull the parapet's° poppy                   *top of trench wall*
To stick behind my ear.
Droll rat, they would shoot you if they knew
Your cosmopolitan sympathies.
Now you have touched this English hand
10   You will do the same to a German
Soon, no doubt, if it be your pleasure
To cross the sleeping green between.
It seems you inwardly grin as you pass
Strong eyes, fine limbs, haughty athletes,
15   Less chanced than you for life,
Bonds to the whims of murder,
Sprawled in the bowels of the earth,
The torn fields of France.
What do you see in our eyes
20   At the shrieking iron and flame
Hurled through still heavens?
What quaver — what heart aghast?

Poppies whose roots are in man's veins
Drop, and are ever dropping;
25  But mine in my ear is safe —
Just a little white with the dust.

*(1916)*                              *(1922)*

---

## Edna St. Vincent Millay          *American (1892-1950)*

# Elegy before Death

There will be rose and rhododendron
    When you are dead and under ground;
Still will be heard from white syringas°                                    *lilacs*
    Heavy with bees, a sunny sound;

5  Still will the tamaracks be raining
    After the rain has ceased, and still
Will there be robins in the stubble,
    Grey sheep upon the warm green hill.

Spring will not ail nor autumn falter;
10      Nothing will know that you are gone, —
Saving alone some sullen plough-land
    None but yourself sets foot upon;

Saving the may-weed and the pig-weed
    Nothing will know that you are dead, —
15  These, and perhaps a useless wagon
    Standing beside some tumbled shed.

Oh, there will pass with your great passing
    Little of beauty not your own, —
Only the light from common water,
20      Only the grace from simple stone!

*(1920, 1921)*

# [What lips my lips have kissed, and where, and why]

What lips my lips have kissed, and where, and why,
I have forgotten, and what arms have lain
Under my head till morning; but the rain
Is full of ghosts tonight, that tap and sigh
5  Upon the glass and listen for reply,
And in my heart there stirs a quiet pain
For unremembered lads that not again

Will turn to me at midnight with a cry.
Thus in the winter stands the lonely tree,
10  Nor knows what birds have vanished one by one,
Yet knows its boughs more silent than before:
I cannot say what loves have come and gone,
I only know that summer sang in me
A little while, that in me sings no more.

*(1922, 1923)*

---

## WILFRED OWEN                                   *English (1893-1918)*

# Dulce et Decorum Est[1]

Bent double, like old beggars under sacks,
Knock-kneed, coughing like hags, we cursed through sludge,
Till on the haunting flares we turned our backs
And towards our distant rest began to trudge.
5   Men marched asleep. Many had lost their boots
But limped on, blood-shod. All went lame; all blind;
Drunk with fatigue; deaf even to the hoots
Of tired, outstripped Five-Nines° that                    *5.9 in.-calibre gas shells*
                dropped behind.

Gas! GAS! Quick, boys! — An ecstasy of fumbling,
10  Fitting the clumsy helmets just in time;
But someone still was yelling out and stumbling
And flound'ring like a man in fire or lime ...
Dim, through the misty panes° and thick green light,        *[of gas masks]*
As under a green sea, I saw him drowning.

15  In all my dreams, before my helpless sight,
He plunges at me, guttering, choking, drowning.

If in some smothering dreams you too could pace
Behind the wagon that we flung him in,
And watch the white eyes writhing in his face,
20  His hanging face, like a devil's sick of sin;
If you could hear, at every jolt, the blood
Come gargling from the froth-corrupted lungs,

---

1  British schoolboys well knew the whole line from Horace's *Odes* (III.2.13) quoted in the last two lines of the poem: *It is sweet and honourable to die for your country.* As with many of his countrymen, Owen radically changed his attitude to the war as it progressed; in 1914, ironically, he had written:

        O meet it is and passing sweet
        To live in peace with others,
        But sweeter still and far more meet,
        To die in war for brothers.

Obscene as cancer, bitter as the cud
Of vile, incurable sores on innocent tongues, —
25   My friend, you would not tell with such high zest
To children ardent for some desperate glory,
The old Lie: Dulce et decorum est
Pro patria mori.

*(1917-18)*                    *(1920)*

---

## E.E. CUMMINGS                    *American (1894-1963)*

---

# [in Just-]

in Just-
spring      when the world is mud-
luscious the little
lame balloonman

5    whistles      far      and wee

and eddieandbill come
running from marbles and
piracies and it's
spring

10   when the world is puddle-wonderful

the queer
old balloonman whistles
far      and      wee
and bettyandisbel come dancing

15   from hop-scotch and jump-rope and

it's
spring
and
      the

20            goat-footed

balloonMan      whistles
far
and
wee

*(1920, 1923)*

# ["next to of course god america i]

"next to of course god america i
love you land of the pilgrims' and so forth oh
say can you see by the dawn's early my
country 'tis of centuries come and go
5    and are no more what of it we should worry
in every language even deafanddumb
thy sons acclaim your glorious name by gorry
by jingo by gee by gosh by gum
why talk of beauty what could be more beaut-
10   iful than these heroic happy dead
who rushed like lions to the roaring slaughter
they did not stop to think they died instead
then shall the voice of liberty be mute?"

He spoke.  And drank rapidly a glass of water
*(1926)*

# [anyone lived in a pretty how town]

anyone lived in a pretty how town
(with up so floating many bells down)
spring summer autumn winter
he sang his didn't he danced his did.

5    Women and men(both little and small)
cared for anyone not at all
they sowed their isn't they reaped their same
sun moon stars rain

children guessed(but only a few
10   and down they forgot as up they grew
autumn winter spring summer)
that noone loved him more by more

when by now and tree by leaf
she laughed his joy she cried his grief
15   bird by snow and stir by still
anyone's any was all to her

someones married their everyones
laughed their cryings and did their dance
(sleep wake hope and then)they
20   said their nevers they slept their dream

stars rain sun moon
(and only the snow can begin to explain
how children are apt to forget to remember
with up so floating many bells down)

25 one day anyone died i guess
(and noone stooped to kiss his face)
busy folk buried them side by side
little by little and was by was

all by all and deep by deep
30 and more by more they dream their sleep
noone and anyone earth by april
wish by spirit and if by yes.

Women and men(both dong and ding)
summer autumn winter spring
35 reaped their sowing and went their came
sun moon stars rain

*(1940)*

---

# F.R. SCOTT                                    *Canadian (1899-1985)*

## The Canadian Authors Meet[1]

Expansive puppets percolate self-unction°                    *anointment*
Beneath a portrait of the Prince of Wales.
Miss Crotchet's muse has somehow failed to function,
Yet she's a poetess. Beaming, she sails

5 From group to chattering group, with such a dear
Victorian saintliness, as is her fashion,
Greeting the other unknowns with a cheer —
Virgins of sixty who still write of passion.

The air is heavy with Canadian topics,
10 And Carman, Lampman, Roberts, Campbell, Scott,
Are measured for their faith and philanthropics,
Their zeal for God and King, their earnest thought.

---

1 This poem was written after Scott attended a meeting of the Canadian Authors' Association (founded 1921) in the spring of 1925. One topic discussed was the appointment of a Poet Laureate.

The cakes are sweet, but sweeter is the feeling
That one is mixing with the *literati*;°                    *the learned class*
15   It warms the old, and melts the most congealing.
Really, it is a most delightful party.

Shall we go round the mulberry bush, or shall
We gather at the river, or shall we
Appoint a Poet Laureate this fall,
20   Or shall we have another cup of tea?

O Canada, O Canada, Oh can
A day go by without new authors springing
To paint the native maple, and to plan
More ways to set the selfsame welkin° ringing?         *sky (archaic)*

*(1925)*                               *(1927, 1945)*

# W.L.M.K.[1]

How shall we speak of Canada,
Mackenzie King dead?
The Mother's boy in the lonely room
With his dog, his medium and his ruins?

5   He blunted us.

We had no shape
Because he never took sides,
And no sides
Because he never allowed them to take shape.

10   He skilfully avoided what was wrong
Without saying what was right,
And never let his on the one hand
Know what his on the other hand was doing.

The height of his ambition
15   Was to pile a Parliamentary Committee on a Royal Commission,
To have "conscription if necessary
But not necessarily conscription,"
To let Parliament decide —
Later.

---

1   The initials of William Lyon Mackenzie King (1874-1950), Prime Minister of Canada 1921-30 and 1935-48. Though it was little known at the time, he consulted psychics for political advice and to contact the spirits of his mother and, later, his dog Pat. He also had artificial ruins constructed on his estate at Kingsmere, Quebec.

20  Postpone, postpone, abstain.

Only one thread was certain:
After World War I
Business as usual,

After World War II
25  Orderly decontrol.
Always he led us back to where we were before.

He seemed to be in the centre
Because we had no centre,
No vision
30  To pierce the smoke-screen of his politics.

Truly he will be remembered
Wherever men honour ingenuity,
Ambiguity, inactivity, and political longevity.

Let us raise up a temple
35  To the cult of mediocrity,
Do nothing by halves
Which can be done by quarters.

*(1954)*

---

## ROBERT FINCH                    *Canadian (1900-1995)*

# Egg-and-Dart[1]

This never-ended searching for the eyes
Wherein the unasked question's answer lies;
This beating, beating, beating of the heart
Because a contour seems to fit the part;
5   The long, drear moment of the look that spoils
The little bud of hope; the word that soils
The immaculate pact, so newly born;
The noisy silence of the old self-scorn;
These, and the sudden leaving in the lurch;
10  Then the droll recommencement of the search.

*(1946)*

---

1 A carved ornamental moulding consisting of an egg-shaped design alternating with one resembling an elongated javelin or arrowhead. See line drawing above.

# At the San Francisco Airport

## *To My Daughter, 1954*

This is the terminal: the light
Gives perfect vision, false and hard;
The metal glitters, deep and bright.
Great planes are waiting in the yard —
5   They are already in the night.

And you are here beside me, small,
Contained and fragile, and intent
On things that I but half recall —
Yet going whither you are bent.
10   I am the past, and that is all.

But you and I in part are one:
The frightened brain, the nervous will,
The knowledge of what must be done,
The passion to acquire the skill
15   To face that which you dare not shun.

The rain of matter upon sense
Destroys me momently. The score:
There comes what will come. The expense
Is what one thought, and something more —
20   One's being and intelligence.

This is the terminal, the break.
Beyond this point, on lines of air,
You take the way that you must take;
And I remain in light and stare —
25   In light, and nothing else, awake.

*(1954)*                                          *(1960)*

ROBERT FRANCIS                    *American (1901-1987)*

# Pitcher

His art is eccentricity, his aim
How not to hit the mark he seems to aim at,

His passion how to avoid the obvious,
His technique how to vary the avoidance.

5    The others throw to be comprehended. He
Throws to be a moment misunderstood

Yet not too much. Not errant, arrant, wild,
But every seeming aberration willed.

Not to, yet still, still to communicate
10   Making the batter understand too late.

*(1960)*

---

LANGSTON HUGHES                    *American (1902-1967)*

# The Negro Speaks of Rivers

I've known rivers:
I've known rivers ancient as the world and older than the flow of human
   blood in human veins.

My soul has grown deep like the rivers.

I bathed in the Euphrates[1] when dawns were young.
5    I built my hut near the Congo and it lulled me to sleep.
I looked upon the Nile and raised the pyramids above it.
I heard the singing of the Mississippi when Abe Lincoln went down to New
   Orleans, and I've seen its muddy bosom turn all golden in the sunset.

I've known rivers:
Ancient, dusky rivers.

10   My soul has grown deep like the rivers.

*(1920)*                              *(1921, 1926)*

---

1   Major river in the Near East, the cradle of Ancient Babylon.

# Harlem

What happens to a dream deferred?

Does it dry up
like a raisin in the sun?
Or fester like a sore —
5 and then run?

Does it stink like rotten meat?
Or crust and sugar over —
like a syrupy sweet?

Maybe it just sags
10 like a heavy load.

*Or does it explode?*

*(1951)*

---

**STEVIE SMITH**                    *English (1902-1971)*

# Not Waving but Drowning

Nobody heard him, the dead man,
But still he lay moaning:
I was much further out than you thought
And not waving but drowning.

5 Poor chap, he always loved larking
And now he's dead
It must have been too cold for him his heart gave way,
They said.

Oh, no no no, it was too cold always
10 (Still the dead one lay moaning)
I was much too far out all my life
And not waving but drowning.

*(1957)*

# Bushed[1]

He invented a rainbow but lightning struck it
shattered it into the lake-lap of a mountain
so big his mind slowed when he looked at it

Yet he built a shack on the shore
5   learned to roast porcupine belly and
wore the quills on his hatband

At first he was out with the dawn
whether it yellowed bright as wood-columbine
or was only a fuzzed moth in a flannel of storm
10   But he found the mountain was clearly alive
sent messages whizzing down every hot morning
boomed proclamations at noon and spread out
a white guard of goat
before falling asleep on its feet at sundown

15   When he tried his eyes on the lake      ospreys°                    *sea-hawks*
would fall like valkyries[2]
choosing the cut-throat°                                              *B.C. trout*
He took then to waiting
till the night smoke rose from the boil of the sunset

20   But the moon carved unknown totems
out of the lakeshore
owls in the beardusky woods derided him
moosehorned cedars circled his swamps and tossed
their antlers up to the stars
25   then he knew      though the mountain slept      the winds
were shaping its peak to an arrowhead
poised

And now he could only
bar himself in and wait
30   for the great flint to come singing into his heart
*(1951)*                          *(1952)*

---

1  Trapper's term for someone who has gone insane after long isolation in the wilderness.
2  In Norse mythology, handmaidens of Odin who conduct the souls of slain warriors to Valhalla, the great hall of the gods.

# In Westminster Abbey

Let me take this other glove off
    As the *vox humana*° swells,                 *voice-like organ stop*
And the beauteous fields of Eden
    Bask beneath the Abbey bells.
5  Here, where England's statesmen lie,
Listen to a lady's cry.

Gracious Lord, oh bomb the Germans.
    Spare their women for Thy Sake,
And if that is not too easy
10     We will pardon Thy Mistake.
But, gracious Lord, whate'er shall be,
Don't let anyone bomb me.

Keep our Empire undismembered
    Guide our Forces by Thy Hand,
15  Gallant blacks from far Jamaica,
    Honduras and Togoland;
Protect them Lord in all their fights,
And, even more, protect the whites.

Think of what our Nation stands for,
20     Books from Boots,[1] and country lanes,
Free speech, free passes, class distinction,
    Democracy and proper drains.
Lord, put beneath Thy special care
One-eighty-nine Cadogan Square.°       *[the speaker's fashionable address]*

25  Although dear Lord I am a sinner,
    I have done no major crime;
Now I'll come to Evening Service
    Whensoever I have the time.
So, Lord, reserve for me a crown,
30  And do not let my shares° go down.          *stocks*

I will labour for Thy Kingdom,
    Help our lads to win the war,
Send white feathers to the cowards
    Join the Women's Army Corps,

---

1  A chain of pharmacies with circulating libraries.

35 Then wash the Steps around Thy Throne
In the Eternal Safety Zone.

Now I feel a little better,
    What a treat to hear Thy Word,
Where the bones of leading statesmen,
40    Have so often been interr'd.
And now, dear Lord, I cannot wait
Because I have a luncheon date.

*(1939-40)*                    *(1940)*

---

# W.H. AUDEN            *British-American (1907-1973)*

# The Unknown Citizen

*(To JS/07/M/378
This Marble Monument
Is Erected by the State)*

He was found by the Bureau of Statistics to be
One against whom there was no official complaint,
And all the reports on his conduct agree
That, in the modern sense of an old-fashioned word, he was a saint,
5 For in everything he did he served the Greater Community.
Except for the War till the day he retired
He worked in a factory and never got fired,
But satisfied his employers, Fudge Motors Inc.
Yet he wasn't a scab or odd in his views,
10 For his Union reports that he paid his dues,
(Our report on his Union shows it was sound)
And our Social Psychology workers found
That he was popular with his mates and liked a drink.
The Press are convinced that he bought a paper every day
15 And that his reactions to advertisements were normal in every way.
Policies taken out in his name prove that he was fully insured,
And his Health-card shows he was once in hospital but left it cured.
Both Producers Research and High-Grade Living declare
He was fully sensible to the advantages of the Instalment Plan
20 And had everything necessary to the Modern Man,
A phonograph, radio, a car and a frigidaire.
Our researchers into Public Opinion are content
That he held the proper opinions for the time of year;
When there was peace, he was for peace; when there was war, he went.
25 He was married and added five children to the population,

165

Which our Eugenist[1] says was the right number for a parent of his
      generation,
And our teachers report that he never interfered with their education.
Was he free? Was he happy? The question is absurd:
Had anything been wrong, we should certainly have heard.

                              *(1940)*

---

## THEODORE ROETHKE                    *American (1908-1963)*

# My Papa's Waltz

The whiskey on your breath
Could make a small boy dizzy;
But I hung on like death:
Such waltzing was not easy.

5   We romped until the pans
Slid from the kitchen shelf;
My mother's countenance
Could not unfrown itself.

The hand that held my wrist
10  Was battered on one knuckle;
At every step you missed
My right ear scraped a buckle.

You beat time on my head
With a palm caked hard by dirt,
15  Then waltzed me off to bed
Still clinging to your shirt.

                              *(1948)*

---

1   A scientist who studies population and ways to improve the characteristics of children.

# The Sun in the Garden

Wallace Stevens is wrong: he says,
"A poem need not have a meaning
And like most things in nature
Often does not have." He is slipshod.
5   He was in the insurance business,
He ought to have known better.

I examine this slug that has crawled up
Into the saucer of my cup of tea.
It has two protrusions out of its head
10   And apparently absorbs food
Through its foot's peristalsis:°                 *contractions*
Repugnance after my sugar.

Also after the roses. The garden
Looks like it. The protuberances
15   Move out almost imperceptibly
But it doesn't fool what it senses
Or me. Beauty is taken in,
Blind repugnance or not. It squashes.

I snip it with my fingers off
20   The saucer, enough of it had. I walk
The rest of the day in the garden knowing
Something is futile. I have meaning.
I have to counteract it. I look up
*Evolution, religion, love.*

                     *(1981)*

# Grain Elevator

Up from the low-roofed dockyard warehouses
it rises blind and babylonian
like something out of legend. Something seen
in a children's coloured book. Leviathan
5   swamped on our shore? The cliffs of some other river?
The blind ark lost and petrified? A cave

built to look innocent, by pirates? Or
some eastern tomb a travelled patron here makes local?

But even when known, it's more than what it is:
10   for here, as in a Josephdream,° bow down                 *[see Genesis 41]*
the sheaves, the grains, the scruples of the sun
garnered for darkness; and Saskatchewan
is rolled like a rug of a thick and golden thread.
O prison of prairies, ship in whose galleys roll
15   sunshines like so many shaven heads,
waiting the bushel-burst out of the beached bastille!°            *prison*

Sometimes, it makes me think Arabian,
the grain picked up, like tic-tacs out of time:
first one; an other; singly; one by one; —
20   to save life. Sometimes, some other races claim
the twinship of my thought, — as the river stirs
restless in a white Caucasian sleep,
or, as in the steerage of the elevators,
the grains, Mongolian and crowded, dream.

25   A box: cement, hugeness, and rightangles —
merely the sight of it leaning in my eyes
mixes up continents and makes a montage
of inconsequent time and uncontiguous space.
It's because it's bread. It's because
30   bread is its theme, an absolute. Because
always this great box flowers over us
with all the coloured faces of mankind....

                 *(1948)*

---

# DOROTHY LIVESAY                        *Canadian (1909-   )*

# Green Rain

I remember long veils of green rain
Feathered like the shawl of my grandmother —
Green from the half-green of the spring trees
Waving in the valley.

5   I remember the road
Like the one which leads to my grandmother's house,
A warm house, with green carpets,
Geraniums, a trilling canary
And shining horse-hair chairs;

10 And the silence, full of the rain's falling
   Was like my grandmother's parlour
   Alive with herself and her voice, rising and falling —
   Rain and wind intermingled.

   I remember on that day
15 I was thinking only of my love
   And of my love's house.
   But now I remember the day
   As I remember my grandmother.
   I remember the rain as the feathery fringe of her shawl.

*(1929, 1932)*

## Bartok[1] and the Geranium

   She lifts her green umbrellas
   Towards the pane
   Seeking her fill of sunlight
   Or of rain;
5 Whatever falls
   She has no commentary
   Accepts, extends,
   Blows out her furbelows,°          *flounces, ruffles*
   Her bustling boughs;

10 And all the while he whirls
   Explodes in space,
   Never content with this small room:
   Not even can he be
   Confined to sky
15 But must speed high and higher still
   From galaxy to galaxy,
   Wrench from the stars their momentary notes
   Steal music from the moon.

   She's daylight
20 He is dark
   She's heaven-held breath
   He storms and crackles
   Spits with hell's own spark.

   Yet in this room, this moment now
25 These together breathe and be:
   She, essence of serenity,
   He in a mad intensity

---

1   Bela Bartok (1881-1945), important modernist composer, whose compositions are noted for their energy and intensity.

Soars beyond sight
Then hurls, lost Lucifer,
30  From heaven's height.

And when he's done, he's out:
She leans a lip against the glass
And preens herself in light.

*(1955, 1957)*

---

## Irving Layton                                    *Canadian (1912-    )*

# On Seeing the Statuettes of Ezekiel and Jeremiah in the Church of Notre Dame[1]

They have given you French names
        and made you captive, my rugged
troublesome compatriots;
        your splendid beards, here, are epicene,°                 *sexless*
5   plaster white
                and your angers
unclothed with Palestinians hills quite lost
in this immense and ugly edifice.

You are bored — I see it — sultry prophets
10          with priests and nuns
(What coarse jokes must pass between you!)
        and with those morbidly religious,
i.e. my prize brother-in-law
                ex-Lawrencian
15  pawing his rosary, and his wife
sick with many guilts.

Believe me I would gladly take you
        from this spidery church
its bad melodrama, its musty smell of candle
20          and set you both free again
in no make-believe world
                of sin and penitence
but the sunlit square opposite
alive at noon with arrogant men.

---

1  That is, the Church of Notre Dame in Montreal.

25 Yet cheer up Ezekiel and you Jeremiah
          who were once cast into a pit;
    I shall not leave you here incensed, uneasy
          among alien Catholic saints
    but shall bring you from time to time
30              my hot Hebrew heart
    as passionate as your own, and stand
    with you here awhile in aching confraternity.

                    *(1956)*

---

ROBERT HAYDEN                          *American (1913-1980)*

# Those Winter Sundays

Sundays too my father got up early
and put his clothes on in the blueblack cold,
then with cracked hands that ached
from labor in the weekday weather made
5   banked fires blaze. No one ever thanked him.

I'd wake and hear the cold splintering, breaking.
When the rooms were warm, he'd call,
and slowly I would rise and dress,
fearing the chronic angers of that house,

10  Speaking indifferently to him,
who had driven out the cold
and polished my good shoes as well.
What did I know, what did I know
of love's austere and lonely offices?°              *duties*

                    *(1962)*

---

KARL SHAPIRO                           *American (1913-    )*

# Auto Wreck

Its quick soft silver bell beating, beating,
And down the dark one ruby flare
Pulsing out red light like an artery,
The ambulance at top speed floating down
5   Past beacons and illuminated clocks
Wings in a heavy curve, dips down,

And brakes speed, entering the crowd.
The doors leap open, emptying light;
Stretchers are laid out, the mangled lifted
10   And stowed into the little hospital.
Then the bell, breaking the hush, tolls once,
And the ambulance with its terrible cargo
Rocking, slightly rocking, moves away,
As the doors, an afterthought, are closed.

15   We are deranged, walking among the cops
Who sweep glass and are large and composed.
One is still making notes under the light.
One with a bucket douches ponds of blood
Into the street and gutter.
20   One hangs lanterns on the wrecks that cling,
Empty husks of locusts, to iron poles.

Our throats were tight as tourniquets,
Our feet were bound with splints, but now,
Like convalescents intimate and gauche,°          *socially awkward*
25   We speak through sickly smiles and warn
With the stubborn saw° of common sense,          *wise saying, advice*
The grim joke and the banal resolution.
The traffic moves around with care,
But we remain, touching a wound
30   That opens to our richest horror.
Already old, the question Who shall die?
Becomes unspoken Who is innocent?

For death in war is done by hands;
Suicide has cause and stillbirth, logic;
35   And cancer, simple as a flower, blooms.
But this invites the occult mind,
Cancels our physics with a sneer,
And spatters all we knew of denouement°          *outcome, conclusion*
Across the expedient and wicked stones.

*(1941)*

---

# Henry Reed                           *English (1914-1986)*

from *Lessons of the War*

# Naming of Parts

Today we have naming of parts. Yesterday,
We had daily cleaning. And tomorrow morning,

We shall have what to do after firing. But today,
Today we have naming of parts. Japonica°          *a red-flowered shrub*
5   Glistens like coral in all of the neighbouring gardens,
        And today we have naming of parts.

This is the lower sling swivel. And this
Is the upper sling swivel, whose use you will see,
When you are given your slings. And this is the piling swivel,
10  Which in your case you have not got. The branches
Hold in the gardens their silent, eloquent gestures,
        Which in our case we have not got.

This is the safety-catch, which is always released
With an easy flick of the thumb. And please do not let me
15  See anyone using his finger. You can do it quite easy
If you have any strength in your thumb. The blossoms
Are fragile and motionless, never letting anyone see
        Any of them using their finger.

And this you can see is the bolt. The purpose of this
20  Is to open the breech, as you see. We can slide it
Rapidly backwards and forwards: we call this
Easing the spring. And rapidly backwards and forwards
The early bees are assaulting and fumbling the flowers:
        They call it easing the Spring.

25  They call it easing the Spring: it is perfectly easy
If you have any strength in your thumb; like the bolt,
And the breech, and the cocking-piece, and the point of balance,
Which in our case we have not got; and the almond-blossom
Silent in all of the gardens and the bees going backwards and forwards,
30      For today we have naming of parts.

                        *(1946)*

---

**WILLIAM STAFFORD**                    *American (1914-1993)*

# Traveling Through the Dark

Traveling through the dark I found a deer
dead on the edge of the Wilson River road.
It is usually best to roll them into the canyon:
that road is narrow; to swerve might make more dead.

By glow of the tail-light I stumbled back of the car
and stood by the heap, a doe, a recent killing;
she had stiffened already, almost cold.
I dragged her off; she was large in the belly.

My fingers touching her side brought me the reason —
10   her side was warm; her fawn lay there waiting,
alive, still, never to be born.
Beside that mountain road I hesitated.

The car aimed ahead its lowered parking lights;
under the hood purred the steady engine.
15   I stood in the glare of the warm exhaust turning red;
around our group I could hear the wilderness listen.

I thought hard for us all — my only swerving —,
then pushed her over the edge into the river.

*(1960)*

---

## DYLAN THOMAS — *Welsh (1914-1953)*

# Fern Hill[1]

Now as I was young and easy under the apple boughs
About the lilting house and happy as the grass was green,
    The night above the dingle° starry,       *small wooded valley*
      Time let me hail and climb
5       Golden in the heydays of his eyes,
And honoured among wagons I was prince of the apple towns
And once below a time I lordly had the trees and leaves
      Trail with daisies and barley
    Down the rivers of the windfall light.

10   And as I was green and carefree, famous among the barns
About the happy yard and singing as the farm was home,
      In the sun that is young once only,
      Time let me play and be
    Golden in the mercy of his means,
15   And green and golden I was huntsman and herdsman, the calves
Sang to my horn, the foxes on the hills barked clear and cold,
      And the sabbath rang slowly
    In the pebbles of the holy streams.

---

1  Name of the farm of the poet's aunt, where he spent summer holidays.

All the sun long it was running, it was lovely, the hay
20 Fields high as the house, the tunes from the chimneys, it was air
    And playing, lovely and watery
        And fire green as grass.
    And nightly under the simple stars
As I rode to sleep the owls were bearing the farm away,
25 All the moon long I heard, blessed among stables, the nightjars[1]
    Flying with the ricks,° and the horses           *haystacks*
        Flashing into the dark.

And then to awake, and the farm, like a wanderer white
With the dew, come back, the cock on his shoulder: it was all
30     Shining, it was Adam and maiden,
        The sky gathered again
    And the sun grew round that very day.
So it must have been after the birth of the simple light
In the first, spinning place, the spellbound horses walking warm
35     Out of the whinnying green stable
        On to the fields of praise.

And honoured among foxes and pheasants by the gay house
Under the new made clouds and happy as the heart was long,
    In the sun born over and over,
40         I ran my heedless ways,
    My wishes raced through the house high hay
And nothing I cared, at my sky blue trades, that time allows
    In all his tuneful turning so few and such morning songs
    Before the children green and golden
45         Follow him out of grace.

Nothing I cared, in the lamb white days, that time would take me
Up to the swallow thronged loft by the shadow of my hand,
    In the moon that is always rising,
        Nor that riding to sleep
50     I should hear him fly with the high fields
And wake to the farm forever fled from the childless land.
Oh as I was young and easy in the mercy of his means,
    Time held me green and dying
    Though I sang in my chains like the sea.

           *(1946)*

---

1  Nocturnal birds with raucous cries.

# Do Not Go Gentle into That Good Night

Do not go gentle into that good night,
Old age should burn and rave at close of day;
Rage, rage against the dying of the light.

Though wise men at their end know dark is right,
5    Because their words had forked no lightning they
Do not go gentle into that good night.

Good men, the last wave by, crying how bright
Their frail deeds might have danced in a green bay,
Rage, rage against the dying of the light.

10   Wild men who caught and sang the sun in flight,
And learn, too late, they grieved it on its way,
Do not go gentle into that good night.

Grave men, near death, who see with blinding sight
Blind eyes could blaze like meteors and be gay,
15   Rage, rage against the dying of the light.

And you, my father, there on the sad height,
Curse, bless, me now with your fierce tears, I pray.
Do not go gentle into that good night.
Rage, rage against the dying of the light.

*(1951)*                              *(1957)*

---

MIRIAM WADDINGTON            *Canadian (1917-   )*

# Advice to the Young

1

Keep bees and
grow asparagus,
watch the tides
and listen to the
5    wind instead of
the politicians
make up your own
stories and believe
them if you want to
10   live the good life.

2

All rituals
are instincts
never fully
trust them but
15  study to im-
prove biology
with reason.

3

Digging trenches
for asparagus
20  is good for the
muscles and
waiting for the
plants to settle
teaches patience
25  to those who are
usually in too
much of a hurry.

4

There is morality
in bee-keeping
30  it teaches how
not to be afraid
of the bee swarm
it teaches how
not to be afraid of
35  finding new places
and building in them
all over again.

*(1972)*

AL PURDY                                    *Canadian (1918-    )*

# Lament for the Dorsets

*(Eskimos extinct in the 14th century A.D.)*

Animal bones and some mossy tent rings
scrapers and spearheads    carved ivory swans
all that remains of the Dorset giants
who drove the Vikings back to their long ships
5   talked to spirits of earth and water

— a picture of terrifying old men
so large they broke the backs of bears
so small they lurk behind bone rafters
in the brain of modern hunters
10   among good thoughts and warm things
and come out at night
to spit on the stars

The big men with clever fingers
who had no dogs and hauled their sleds
15   over the frozen northern oceans
awkward giants
                    killers of seal
they couldn't compete with little men
who came from the west with dogs
Or else in a warm climatic cycle
20   the seals went back to cold waters
and the puzzled Dorsets scratched their heads
with hairy thumbs around 1350 A.D.
— couldn't figure it out
went around saying to each other
25   plaintively
              "What's wrong? What happened?
              Where are the seals gone?"
And died

Twentieth century people
30   apartment dwellers
executives of neon death
warmakers with things that explode
— they have never imagined us in their future
how could we imagine them in the past
35   squatting among the moving glaciers
six hundred years ago
with glowing lamps?
As remote or nearly
as the trilobites and swamps
40   when coal became
or the last great reptile hissed
at a mammal the size of a mouse
that squeaked and fled

Did they ever realize at all
45   what was happening to them?
Some old hunter with one lame leg
a bear had chewed
sitting in a caribou skin tent
— the last Dorset?
50   Let's say his name was Kudluk

carving 2-inch ivory swans
for a dead grand-daughter
taking them out of his mind
the places in his mind
55   where pictures are
He selects a sharp stone tool
to gouge a parallel pattern of lines
on both sides of the swan
holding it with his left hand
60   bearing down and transmitting
his body's weight
from brain to arm and right hand
and one of his thoughts
turns to ivory
65   The carving is laid aside
in beginning darkness
at the end of hunger
after a while wind
blows down the tent and snow
70   begins to cover him
After 600 years
the ivory thought
is still warm

*(1968)*

---

LAWRENCE FERLINGHETTI          *American (1919-    )*

## [Constantly risking absurdity and death]

Constantly risking absurdity
              and death
    whenever he performs
             above the heads
5                of his audience
   the poet like an acrobat
      climbs on rime
         to a high wire of his own making
and balancing on eyebeams
10            above a sea of faces
    paces his way
        to the other side of day
   performing entrechats
         and sleight-of-foot tricks
15  and other high theatrics
     and all without mistaking

any thing
              for what it may not be

     For he's the super realist
20                    who must perforce perceive
          taut truth
                    before the taking of each stance or step

     in his supposed advance
                    toward that still higher perch
25   where Beauty stands and waits
                    with gravity
                              to start her death-defying leap
     And he
          a little charleychaplin man
30                        who may or may not catch
          her fair eternal form
                    spreadeagled in the empty air
          of existence

                    *(1958)*

---

R<small>AYMOND</small> S<small>OUSTER</small>                              *Canadian (1921-    )*

# The Lilac Poem

Before lilac-time is over and each fragrant branch
becomes a shrunken stalk hanging down very limp and dead,
I want to write a poem about lilacs and their beauty
brief and star-shining as a young girl's beauty.

5   Because there's so much made of strength and wealth and power,
because the little things are often lost in this world,
I write this poem about lilacs knowing well that both
are this day's only: tomorrow they will lie forgotten.

                    *(1952, 1980)*

# Richard Wilbur

*American (1921-    )*

## A Simile for Her Smile

Your smiling, or the hope, the thought of it,
Makes in my mind such pause and abrupt ease
As when the highway bridgegates fall,
Balking the hasty traffic, which must sit
5    On each side massed and staring, while
Deliberately the drawbridge starts to rise:

Then horns are hushed, the oilsmoke rarefies,
Above the idling motors one can tell
The packet's° smooth approach, the slip,          *boat's*
10   Slip of the silken river past the sides,
The ringing of clear bells, the dip
And slow cascading of the paddle wheel.

*(1950)*

---

# Elizabeth Brewster

*Canadian (1922-    )*

## The Night Grandma Died

"Here's Grandmother in here," Cousin Joy said,
Standing beside me at the bedroom door,
One hand on my shoulder. "You see, she's only sleeping."
But I, nine years old and frightened,
5    Knew it was a lie. Grandmother's shell
Lay on the bed, hands folded, head on one side,
The spirit that had groaned so loud an hour ago
Gone out of her. I looked, and turned and ran,
First to the kitchen. There were the aunts
10   Who had laid her out, still weeping
Over a good hot cup of tea: Aunt Stella,
Large, dominant; Aunt Alice, a plump, ruffled hen of a woman;
My small, quick mother; Aunt Grace, youngest and shyest,
Awkward on the edge of the group: "Shush," she was saying
15   To Cousin Pauline, who was lying on the floor
Pretending to be Grandma.

And they all got up and came into the parlour,
Where suddenly everyone was jovial,
And Aunt April sat in the best chair

20   Nursing her newest baby,
     And the uncles sat talking of crops and weather,
     And Uncle Harry, who had come from Maine,
     Pumped the hands of people he hadn't seen in twenty years,
     And Grandma's nephew Eb from up the road
25   Played everybody's favourite tune on the piano.
     Now and then, remembering the corpse, he burst into a Baptist hymn,
     His rich bass voice, dark and deep as molasses,
     Flowing protectively over the women,
     While his eyes, also dark,
30   Wrapped them warm with sympathy.

     And I, sitting on a footstool in a corner,
     Was sometimes warmed by the voice,
     And sometimes chilled remembering
     In the room next door
35   Grandmother, dead, whom I had never liked.

*(1969)*

---

## PHILIP LARKIN                    *English (1922-1985)*

# Church Going

     Once I am sure there's nothing going on
     I step inside, letting the door thud shut.
     Another church: matting, seats, and stone,
     And little books; sprawlings of flowers, cut
5   For Sunday, brownish now; some brass and stuff
     Up at the holy end; the small neat organ;
     And a tense, musty, unignorable silence,
     Brewed God knows how long. Hatless, I take off
     My cycle-clips in awkward reverence,

10  Move forward, run my hand around the font.
     From where I stand, the roof looks almost new —
     Cleaned, or restored? Someone would know: I don't.
     Mounting the lectern, I peruse a few
     Hectoring large-scale verses, and pronounce
15  "Here endeth" much more loudly than I'd meant.
     The echoes snigger briefly. Back at the door
     I sign the book, donate an Irish sixpence,[1]
     Reflect the place was not worth stopping for.

---

[1]  Larkin worked as a librarian at Queen's University, Belfast, from 1950-1955.

Yet stop I did: in fact I often do,
20  And always end much at a loss like this,
Wondering what to look for; wondering, too,
When churches fall completely out of use
What we shall turn them into, if we shall keep
A few cathedrals chronically on show,
25  Their parchment, plate and pyx¹ in locked cases,
And let the rest rent-free to rain and sheep.
Shall we avoid them as unlucky places?

Or, after dark, will dubious women come
To make their children touch a particular stone;
30  Pick simples° for a cancer; or on some                    *herbs*
Advised night see walking a dead one?
Power of some sort or other will go on
In games, in riddles, seemingly at random;
But superstition, like belief, must die,
35  And what remains when disbelief has gone?
Grass, weedy pavement, brambles, buttress, sky,

A shape less recognisable each week,
A purpose more obscure. I wonder who
Will be the last, the very last, to seek
40  This place for what it was; one of the crew
That tap and jot and know what rood-lofts² were?
Some ruin-bibber,° randy° for antique,          *"drunkard" / lustful*
Or Christmas-addict, counting on a whiff
Of gown-and-bands° and organ-pipes and myrrh?    *clerical collar strips*
45  Or will he be my representative,

Bored, uninformed, knowing the ghostly silt
Dispersed, yet tending to this cross of ground
Through suburb scrub because it held unspilt
So long and equably what since is found
50  Only in separation — marriage, and birth,
And death, and thoughts of these — for which was built
This special shell? For, though I've no idea
What this accoutred° frowsty° barn is worth,          *outfitted / musty*
It pleases me to stand in silence here;

55  A serious house on serious earth it is,
In whose blent° air all our compulsions meet,               *mixed*
Are recognised, and robed as destinies.

---

1  Gold or silver container for Eucharist wafers.
2  Galleries bearing a cross ("rood") atop carved screens, separating the nave from the choir area
of a church.

And that much never can be obsolete,
Since someone will forever be surprising
60  A hunger in himself to be more serious,
And gravitating with it to this ground,
Which, he once heard, was proper to grow wise in,
If only that so many dead lie round.

*(1954)*                                    *(1955)*

---

## Eli Mandel

*Canadian (1922-    )*

# City Park Merry-Go-Round

Freedom is seldom what you now believe.
Mostly you circle round and round the park:
Night follows day, these horses never leave.

Like children, love whatever you conceive,
5   See then your world as lights whirled in the dark.
Freedom is seldom what you now believe.

Your world moves up and down or seems to weave
And still you pass you pass the same ringed mark.
Night follows day, these horses never leave.

10  You thought your past was here, you might retrieve
That wild illusion whirling in the dark.
Freedom is seldom what you now believe.

Sick on that circle you begin to grieve.
You wish the ride would end you could escape the park.
15  Night follows day, these horses never leave.

Mostly you circle round and round the park.
You'd give your life now to be free to leave.
Freedom is seldom what you now believe.
Night follows day, these horses never leave.

*(1960)*

# A Poet's Progress

Like snooker balls thrown on the table's faded green,
Rare ivory and weighted with his best ambitions,
At first his words are launched: not certain what they mean,
He loves to see them roll, rebound, assume positions
5     Which — since not he — some power beyond him has assigned.
But now the game begins: dead players, living critics
Are watching him — and suddenly one eye goes blind,
The hand that holds the cue shakes like a paralytic's,
Till every thudding, every clinking sound portends
10    New failure, new defeat. Amazed, he finds that still
It is not he who guides his missiles to their ends
But an unkind geometry that mocks his will.

If he persists, for years he'll practise patiently,
Lock all the doors, learn all the tricks, keep noises out,
15    Though he may pick a ghost or two for company
Or pierce the room's inhuman silence with a shout.
More often silence wins; then soon the green felt seems
An evil playground, lawless, lost to time, forsaken,
And he a fool caught in the water weeds of dreams
20    Whom only death or frantic effort can awaken.

At last, a master player, he can face applause,
Looks for a fit opponent, former friends, emerges;
But no one knows him now. He questions his own cause,
And has forgotten why he yielded to those urges,
25    Took up a wooden cue to strike a coloured ball.
Wise now, he goes on playing; both his house and heart
Unguarded solitudes, hospitable to all
Who can endure the cold intensity of art.

*(1949)*                    *(1950)*

---

# It Wasn't a Major Operation

the surgeon joined us
with a long wire he threaded
through your left earhole
and into my right one

when we woke up from the anesthetic
we had to begin practicing at once
every time you nodded your head
I inclined mine
we bobbed together this way and that

10 when the wire was too taut
there was a knotted feeling in my head
when it was too slack
it looped and caught in my necklace

but now we have got used to
15 the continual lolling motion
and are able to go
for a short walk every day

this morning while we were
admiring the lilies
20 a row of birds sat down on our wire

night has fallen now
and they are still here
nine sparrows and a kingbird

*(1987)*

---

## ROBERT KROETSCH                    *Canadian (1927-    )*

# Elegy for Wong Toy

Charlie    you are dead now
but I dare to speak because
in China the living speak
to their kindred    dead.
5 And you are one of my fathers.

Your iron bachelorhood perplexed
our horny youth:    we were born
to the snow of a prairie town
to the empty streets of our
10 longing.    You built a railway
                    to get there.

You were your own enduring    winter.
You were your abacus,° your Chinaman's        *Chinese calculator*
eyes.    You were the long reach up
15    to the top of that bright showcase
where    for a few pennies
we bought a whole childhood.

Only a Christmas calendar
told us your name:
20    Wong Toy, prop., Canada Cafe:
above the thin pad of months,
under the almost naked girl
in the white leather boots
who was never allowed to undress
25    in the rows of God-filled houses

which you were never
invited to enter.

Charlie, I knew my first touch
of Ellen Kiefer's young breasts
30    in the second booth from the back
                in your cafe.
It was the night of a hockey game.
You were out in the kitchen
making sandwiches and coffee.

35    You were your own enduring
winter.    You were our spring
and we    like meadowlarks
hearing the sun    boom
under the flat horizon
40    cracked the still dawn alive
with one ferocious    song.

So Charlie    this is a thank you
poem.    You are twenty years
dead.    I hope they buried you
45    sitting upright in your grave
the way you sat    pot-bellied
behind your jawbreakers
and your licorice plugs,
behind your tins of Ogden's fine cut,
50    your treasury of cigars,

and the heart-shaped box of chocolates
that no one ever took home.

*(1975)*

# Africa

Thus she had lain
sugarcane sweet
deserts her hair
golden her feet
5   mountains her breasts
two Niles her tears
Thus she has lain
Black through the years.

Over the white seas
10  rime white and cold
brigands ungentled
icicle bold
took her young daughters
sold her strong sons
15  churched her with Jesus
bled her with guns.
Thus she has lain.

Now she is rising
remember her pain
20  remember the losses
her screams loud and vain
remember her riches
her history slain
now she is striding
25  although she had lain.

*(1975)*

---

# Wild Strawberry

*For Helene*

And I rode the Greyhound down to Brooklyn
where I sit now eating woody strawberries
grown on the backs of Mexican farmers

imported from the fields of their hands,
5  juices without color or sweetness

     my wild blood berries of spring meadows
     sucked by June bees and protected by hawks
     have stained my face and honeyed
     my tongue ... healed the sorrow in my flesh

10   vines crawl across the grassy floor
     of the north, scatter to the world
     seeking the light of the sun and innocent
     tap of the rain to feed the roots
     and bud small white flowers that in June
15   will burst fruit and announce spring
     when wolf will drop winter fur
     and wrens will break the egg

     my blood, blood berries that brought laughter
     and the ache in the stooped back that vied
20   with dandelions for the plucking,
     and the wines nourished our youth and heralded
     iris, corn and summer melon

     we fought bluebirds for the seeds
     armed against garter snakes, field mice;
25   won the battle with the burning sun
     which blinded our eyes and froze our hands
     to the vines and the earth where knees knelt
     and we laughed in the morning dew like worms
     and grubs; we scented age and wisdom

30   my mother wrapped the wounds of the world
     with a sassafras poultice and we ate
     wild berries with their juices running
     down the roots of our mouths and our joy

I sit here in Brooklyn eating Mexican
35  berries which I did not pick, nor do
I know the hands which did, nor their stories ...
January snow falls, listen ...

                    *(1981)*

# ADRIENNE RICH

*American (1929-    )*

## Aunt Jennifer's Tigers

Aunt Jennifer's tigers prance across a screen,
Bright topaz denizens of a world of green.
They do not fear the men beneath the tree;
They pace in sleek chivalric certainty.

5    Aunt Jennifer's fingers fluttering through her wool
Find even the ivory needle hard to pull.
The massive weight of Uncle's wedding band
Sits heavily upon Aunt Jennifer's hand.

When Aunt is dead, her terrified hands will lie
10   Still ringed with ordeals she was mastered by.
The tigers in the panel that she made
Will go on prancing, proud and unafraid.

*(1951)*

---

# ELIZABETH COOK-LYNN

*Crow Creek Sioux/American (1930-    )*

## Grandfather at the Indian Health Clinic

It's cold at last and cautious winds creep
softly into coves along the riverbank. At my insistence
he wears his denim cowboy coat high on his neck; averse to
an unceremonious world, he follows me through
5    hallways pushing down the easy rage he always has
with me, a youngest child, and smiles.
This morning the lodge is closed to the dance
and he reminds me these are not the men who
raise the bag above the painted marks; for the young
10   intern from New Jersey he bares his chest
but keeps a scarf tied on his steel-gray braids
and thinks of days that have no turning: he wore
yellow chaps and went as far as Canada to ride
Mad Dog and then came home to drive the Greenwood Woman's
15   cattle to his brother's place,
two hundred miles
along the timber line
the trees were bright
he turned his hat brim down in summer rain.

Now winter's here, he says, in this white lighted place
where lives are sometimes saved by
throwing blankets over spaces where the leaves are brushed away
and giving brilliant gourd-shell rattles
to everyone who comes.

*(1988)*

---

# IAN ADAM                                    *Canadian (1932-    )*

## Hallowe'en

we've hurled an orange up    the moon    it
hurtles through the wisps of clouds
flicks shadows on the streets we roam
in groups of five or six to talk or howl

5    too old for topless outhouse towers toppled
dogs    or wolves    on scent of marauders
and flashlights down alleys and pell-mell scurry
ancient as treats or tricks or apples bobbing

no costumes now but cigarettes and swearing
10    and ritual contraceptive-ring-marked-wallets
and richer devilry on the heroic scale
our plotting tonight to latch onto legends

of dances in cornfields and stolen cob roasting
of beet wine procured from Hutterite neighbours
15    or girls had in golf courses under bridges in gymnasiums
or rackety battles by the river    blood noses

we'll blockade the main street with wagons
saw horses    old cars    junk and debris
dawn will spread light    news of achievement
20    talk in the pool hall and photographs    scandal

we'll bask    downtown sun    advertise brazen secrets
conceived in rye whiskey drunk in the Commerce°        *a Canadian bank*
(where Mike the bank clerk lets us in quiet
and we happy lush in the velvety darkness

25    while Barry and Jimmy's girl back in the corner
mumble and mash and scramble together
take shares of the bottle with hands stretching out
like meshed tag team wrestlers    reach for relief)

then outside scour alleys and lots    haul sweat and
30    heave sprain fingers grunt curse shove and pile
the dark line of clutter gathers on high street
and skeleton shadows crisscross the bright gravel

we scatter and wander    a fog white is rising
Pete's Indian drunk    drags a scarecrow from somewhere
35    limbs over barbed wire to the high water tower
scrambles to the girder some forty feet up

works a noose round the neck of his placid companion
and dangles him limp from the beam to the night
and the fog getting thicker and wetter    a cloud
40    jack-o-lanterns from windows are sparks on a moor

noises of struggle    shouts    Jimmy's found Barry
scuffle and thudding    all hell is broke loose
"bastard don't touch I'll"    Jane crying stop
and trousers removed and thrown to a roof

45    and hooting and shouting    bare-assed Barry's grim curses
and slip through the mist    walk now for home
and the outline of hanged man as we pass by the tower
the winter sometime nearer in the cool air.

*(1981)*

---

PETER MEINKE                          *American (1932-    )*

---

# Advice to My Son

*— for Tim*

The trick is, to live your days
as if each one may be your last
(for they go fast, and young men lose their lives
in strange and unimaginable ways)
5    but at the same time, plan long range
(for they go slow: if you survive
the shattered windshield and the bursting shell
you will arrive
at our approximation here below
10    of heaven or hell).

192

To be specific, between the peony and the rose
plant squash and spinach, turnips and tomatoes;
beauty is nectar
and nectar, in a desert, saves —
15  but the stomach craves stronger sustenance
than the honied vine.
Therefore, marry a pretty girl
after seeing her mother;
speak truth to one man,
20  work with another;
and always serve bread with your wine.

But, son,
always serve wine.

*(1965)*


---

## LINDA PASTAN                              *American (1932-    )*


# Marks

My husband gives me an A
for last night's supper,
an incomplete for my ironing
a B plus in bed.
5  My son says I am average,
an average mother, but if
I put my mind to it
I could improve.
My daughter believes
10  in Pass/Fail and tells me
I pass. Wait 'til they learn
I'm dropping out.

*(1978)*


---

## SYLVIA PLATH                              *American (1932-1963)*


# Metaphors

I'm a riddle in nine syllables,
An elephant, a ponderous house,
A melon strolling on two tendrils.

O red fruit, ivory, fine timbers!
5   This loaf's big with its yeasty rising.
Money's new-minted in this fat purse.
I'm a means, a stage, a cow in calf.
I've eaten a bag of green apples,
Boarded the train there's no getting off.

*(1960)*


# Tulips

The tulips are too excitable, it is winter here.
Look how white everything is, how quiet, how snowed-in.
I am learning peacefulness, lying by myself quietly
As the light lies on these white walls, this bed, these hands.
5   I am nobody; I have nothing to do with explosions.
I have given my name and my day-clothes up to the nurses
And my history to the anaesthetist and my body to surgeons.

They have propped my head between the pillow and the sheet-cuff
Like an eye between two white lids that will not shut.
10  Stupid pupil, it has to take everything in.
The nurses pass and pass, they are no trouble,
They pass the way gulls pass inland in their white caps,
Doing things with their hands, one just the same as another,
So it is impossible to tell how many there are.

15  My body is a pebble to them, they tend it as water
Tends to the pebbles it must run over, smoothing them gently.
They bring me numbness in their bright needles, they bring me sleep.
Now I have lost myself I am sick of baggage —
My patent leather overnight case like a black pillbox,
20  My husband and child smiling out of the family photo;
Their smiles catch onto my skin, little smiling hooks.

I have let things slip, a thirty-year-old cargo boat
Stubbornly hanging on to my name and address.
They have swabbed me clear of my loving associations.
25  Scared and bare on the green plastic-pillowed trolley
I watched my teaset, my bureaus of linen, my books
Sink out of sight, and the water went over my head.
I am a nun now, I have never been so pure.

I didn't want any flowers, I only wanted
30  To lie with my hands turned up and be utterly empty.
How free it is, you have no idea how free —
The peacefulness is so big it dazes you,
And it asks nothing, a name tag, a few trinkets.

It is what the dead close on, finally; I imagine them
35    Shutting their mouths on it, like a Communion tablet.

The tulips are too red in the first place, they hurt me.
Even through the gift paper I could hear them breathe
Lightly, through their white swaddlings, like an awful baby.
Their redness talks to my wound, it corresponds.
40    They are subtle: they seem to float, though they weigh me down,
Upsetting me with their sudden tongues and their colour,
A dozen red lead sinkers round my neck.

Nobody watched me before, now I am watched.
The tulips turn to me, and the window behind me
45    Where once a day the light slowly widens and slowly thins,
And I see myself, flat, ridiculous, a cut-paper shadow
Between the eye of the sun and the eyes of the tulips,
And I have no face, I have wanted to efface myself.
The vivid tulips eat my oxygen.

50    Before they came the air was calm enough,
Coming and going, breath by breath, without any fuss.
Then the tulips filled it up like a loud noise.
Now the air snags and eddies round them the way a river
Snags and eddies round a sunken rust-red engine.
55    They concentrate my attention, that was happy
Playing and resting without committing itself.

The walls, also, seem to be warming themselves.
The tulips should be behind bars like dangerous animals;
They are opening like the mouth of some great African cat
60    And I am aware of my heart: it opens and closes
Its bowl of red blooms out of sheer love of me.
The water I taste is warm and salt, like the sea,
And comes from a country far away as health.

*(1962)*


# Daddy

You do not do, you do not do
Any more, black shoe
In which I have lived like a foot
For thirty years, poor and white,
5    Barely daring to breathe or Achoo.

Daddy, I have had to kill you.
You died before I had time —

Marble-heavy, a bag full of God,
Ghastly statue with one grey toe
10  Big as a Frisco seal

And a head in the freakish Atlantic
Where it pours bean green over blue
In the waters off beautiful Nauset.°                    *Cape Cod harbour*
I used to pray to recover you.
15  Ach, du.°                                          *Ah, you (German)*

In the German tongue, in the Polish town[1]
Scraped flat by the roller
Of wars, wars, wars.
But the name of the town is common.
20  My Polack friend

Says there are a dozen or two.
So I never could tell where you
Put your foot, your root,
I never could talk to you.
25  The tongue stuck in my jaw.

It stuck in a barb wire snare.
Ich,° ich, ich, ich,                                    *I (German)*
I could hardly speak.
I thought every German was you.
30  And the language obscene

An engine, an engine
Chuffing me off like a Jew.
A Jew to Dachau, Auschwitz, Belsen.°               *[concentration camps]*
I began to talk like a Jew.
35  I think I may well be a Jew.

The snows of the Tyrol, the clear beer of Vienna
Are not very pure or true.
With my gypsy ancestress and my weird luck
And my Taroc° pack and my Taroc pack       *tarot (fortune-telling cards)*
40  I may be a bit of a Jew.

I have always been scared of *you*,
With your Luftwaffe,° your gobbledygoo.                 *Air Force (German)*
And your neat moustache
And your Aryan eye, bright blue.
45  Panzer°-man, panzer-man, O You —                       *tank (German)*

---

1  Granbow, birthplace of her father Otto.

Not God but a swastika
So black no sky could squeak through.
Every woman adores a Fascist,
The boot in the face, the brute
50 Brute heart of a brute like you.

You stand at the blackboard, daddy,
In the picture I have of you,
A cleft in your chin instead of your foot
But no less a devil for that, no not
55 Any less the black man who

Bit my pretty red heart in two.
I was ten when they buried you.
At twenty I tried to die
And get back, back, back to you.
60 I thought even the bones would do.

But they pulled me out of the sack,
And they stuck me together with glue.
And then I knew what to do.
I made a model of you,
65 A man in black with a Meinkampf[1] look

And a love of the rack and the screw.
And I said I do, I do.
So daddy, I'm finally through.
The black telephone's off at the root,
70 The voices just can't worm through.

If I've killed one man, I've killed two —
The vampire who said he was you
And drank my blood for a year,
Seven years, if you want to know.
75 Daddy, you can lie back now.

There's a stake in your fat black heart
And the villagers never liked you.
They are dancing and stamping on you.
They always *knew* it was you.
80 Daddy, Daddy, you bastard, I'm through.

*(1962)*                                    *(1966)*

---

1   Adolf Hitler's autobiography (2 volumes, 1925-27); the title means "my battle" or "my struggle."

# JOHN UPDIKE                                      *American (1932-    )*

## Ex-Basketball Player

Pearl Avenue runs past the high-school lot,
Bends with the trolley tracks, and stops, cut off
Before it has a chance to go two blocks,
At Colonel McComsky Plaza. Berth's Garage
5   Is on the corner facing west, and there,
Most days, you'll find Flick Webb, who helps Berth out.

Flick stands tall among the idiot pumps —
Five on a side, the old bubble-head style,
Their rubber elbows hanging loose and low.
10  One's nostrils are two S's, and his eyes
An E and O. And one is squat, without
A head at all — more of a football type.

Once Flick played for the high-school team, the Wizards.
He was good: in fact, the best. In '46
15  He bucketed three hundred ninety points,
A county record still. The ball loved Flick.
I saw him rack up thirty-eight or forty
In one home game. His hands were like wild birds.

He never learned a trade, he just sells gas,
20  Checks oil, and changes flats. Once in a while,
As a gag, he dribbles an inner tube,
But most of us remember anyway.
His hands are fine and nervous on the lug wrench.
It makes no difference to the lug wrench, though.

25  Off work, he hangs around Mae's luncheonette.
Grease-gray and kind of coiled, he plays pinball,
Smokes those thin cigars, nurses lemon phosphates.°        *a kind of soda*
Flick seldom says a word to Mae, just nods
Beyond her face toward bright applauding tiers
30  Of Necco Wafers, Nibs, and Juju Beads.

*(1958)*

# The Bull Moose

Down from the purple mist of trees on the mountain,
lurching through forests of white spruce and cedar,
stumbling through tamarack swamps,
came the bull moose
5   to be stopped at last by a pole-fenced pasture.

Too tired to turn or, perhaps, aware
there was no place left to go, he stood with the cattle.
They, scenting the musk of death, seeing his great head
like the ritual mask of a blood god, moved to the other end
10   of the field, and waited.

The neighbours heard of it, and by afternoon
cars lined the road. The children teased him
with alder switches and he gazed at them
like an old, tolerant collie. The women asked
15   if he could have escaped from a Fair.

The oldest man in the parish remembered seeing
a gelded moose yoked with an ox for plowing.
The young men snickered and tried to pour beer
down his throat, while their girl friends took their pictures.

20   And the bull moose let them stroke his tick-ravaged flanks,
let them pry open his jaws with bottles, let a giggling girl
plant a little purple cap
of thistles on his head.

When the wardens came, everyone agreed it was a shame
25   to shoot anything so shaggy and cuddlesome.
He looked like the kind of pet
women put to bed with their sons.

So they held their fire. But just as the sun dropped in the river
the bull moose gathered his strength
30   like a scaffolded king, straightened and lifted his horns
so that even the wardens backed away as they raised their rifles.
When he roared, people ran to their cars. All the young men
leaned on their automobile horns as he toppled.

*(1962, 1970)*

# I Have Not Lingered in European Monasteries

I have not lingered in European monasteries
and discovered among the tall grasses tombs of knights
who fell as beautifully as their ballads tell;
I have not parted the grasses
5    or purposefully left them thatched.

I have not released my mind to wander and wait
in those great distances
between the snowy mountains and the fishermen,
like a moon,
10   or a shell beneath the moving water.

I have not held my breath
so that I might hear the breathing of G-d,
or tamed my heartbeat with an exercise,
or starved for visions.
15   Although I have watched him often
I have not become the heron,
leaving my body on the shore,
and I have not become the luminous trout,
leaving my body in the air.

20   I have not worshipped wounds and relics,
or combs of iron,
or bodies wrapped and burnt in scrolls.

I have not been unhappy for ten thousand years.
During the day I laugh and during the night I sleep.
25   My favourite cooks prepare my meals,
my body cleans and repairs itself,
and all my work goes well.

*(1965)*

# Suzanne

Suzanne takes you down
to her place near the river
you can hear the boats go by
you can spend the night beside her
5   And you know that she's half crazy
but that's why you want to be there

and she feeds you tea and oranges
that come all the way from China
And just when you mean to tell her
10  that you have no love to give her
she gets you on her wavelength
and she lets the river answer
that you've always been her lover
        *And you want to travel with her*
15      *you want to travel blind*
        *and you know that she can trust you*
        *for you've touched her perfect body*
        *with your mind*

And Jesus was a sailor
20  when he walked upon the water°                    *[see Matthew 14:22-33]*
and he spent a long time watching
from his lonely wooden tower
and when he knew for certain
only drowning men could see him
25  he said All men will be sailors then
until the sea shall free them
but he himself was broken
long before the sky would open
forsaken, almost human
30  he sank beneath your wisdom like a stone
        *And you want to travel with him*
        *you want to travel blind*
        *and you think maybe you'll trust him*
        *for he's touched your perfect body*
35      *with his mind*

Now Suzanne takes your hand
and she leads you to the river
she is wearing rags and feathers
from Salvation Army counters
40  And the sun pours down like honey
on our lady of the harbour
And she shows you where to look
among the garbage and the flowers
There are heroes in the seaweed
45  there are children in the morning
they are leaning out for love
they will lean that way forever
while Suzanne holds the mirror
        *And you want to travel with her*
50      *you want to travel blind*
        *and you know that you can trust her*
        *for she's touched your perfect body*
        *with her mind*

                    *(1966)*

# DON KERR

Canadian (1936-    )

## Editing the Prairie

Well, it's too long for one thing
and very repetitive.
Remove half the fields.
Then there are far too many fences
5    interrupting the narrative flow.
Get some cattlemen to cut down those fences.
There's not enough incident either,
this story is very flat.
Can't you write in a mountain
10    or at least a decent-sized hill?
And why set it in winter
as if the prairie can grow nothing
but snow? I like the pubic bush
but there's too much even of that,
15    and the empty sky filling all the silences
between paragraphs is really boring.
I think on due consideration
we'll have to return your prairie.
Try us again in a year
20    with a mountain or a sea or a city.

*(1987)*


# MARGE PIERCY

*American (1936-    )*

## A Work of Artifice

The bonsai tree
in the attractive pot
could have grown eighty feet tall
on the side of a mountain
5    till split by lightning.
But a gardener
carefully pruned it.
It is nine inches high.
Every day as he
10    whittles back the branches
the gardener croons,
It is your nature
to be small and cozy,

202

domestic and weak;
15  how lucky, little tree,
to have a pot to grow in.
With living creatures
one must begin very early
to dwarf their growth:
20  the bound feet,
the crippled brain,
the hair in curlers,
the hands you
love to touch.

*(1973)*

# Barbie Doll

This girlchild was born as usual
and presented dolls that did pee-pee
and miniature GE stoves and irons
and wee lipsticks the color of cherry candy.
5   Then in the magic of puberty, a classmate said:
You have a great big nose and fat legs.

She was healthy, tested intelligent,
possessed strong arms and back,
abundant sexual drive and manual dexterity.
10  She went to and fro apologizing.
Everyone saw a fat nose on thick legs.

She was advised to play coy,
exhorted to come on hearty,
exercise, diet, smile and wheedle.
15  Her good nature wore out
like a fan belt.
So she cut off her nose and her legs
and offered them up.

In the casket displayed on satin she lay
20  with the undertaker's cosmetics painted on,
a turned-up putty nose,
dressed in a pink and white nightie.
Doesn't she look pretty? everyone said.
Consummation at last.
25  To every woman a happy ending.

*(1973)*

# ROBERT CURRIE

*Canadian (1937-    )*

## A Day No Pigs Would Die

Instead
the man who killed them
dead
and his son finding him
5    in the barn where he'd exiled himself
because of the cough that wrenched their nights.
The boy was thirteen years old
but his father
who killed for a living
10   had taught him of life and death
so that
he made the arrangements
did the chores
and before sundown
15   the clods of dirt
had turned the wooden box
into a drum echoing briefly
through silent woods.
And then there was
20   nothing to do
but walk away
from the mound of fresh earth.
    Closing the book
I hear Gwen asking
25   *How was It?*
and mumbling *Okay*
I leave the room
so she won't see
the tears that well
30   for a gentle man
whose job was killing pigs
and for a father
I will one day
lower to the earth
35   and for me
with Ryan
looking
down.

*(1975)*

# Postcard from the Center of the Continent

*Rugby, North Dakota*

The big story from out here
is that on the face
of things, the Center Motel
stands just a little

5    off-center, given the cairn
across the road
that marks the true center,
there by the diner

where a newspaper dispenser
10   holds all the clarities
a tired body cares to know,
and wants a rest from.

Even the cement block walls
pictured on the card
15   show what whitewash means
in towns like this,

and in the emptiness of sky
I weigh the lasting creed
of Lutheran churches
20   deserted now on the prairie.

How plain everything looks
here at the center,
except for those ornaments
the size of globes

25   rising over the motel facade
from a decade of cars
with great fins,
all those stalled years

when everybody believed
30   that if you kept up
a good appearance
you could go almost anywhere.

*(1992)*

## GLEN SORESTAD

*Canadian (1937-    )*

# Beer at Cochin

The lazy August fire
              wanted quenching.
Even the slightest breeze
                from the lake
5   could not suppress the knowledge
that Cochin° pub was near            *[Saskatchewan village]*
and cool
       and wet.

Entering the dim-cool
10                    (alive
with beer promises) room is
so good
       you want to stop
              forever
15   the moment
        to hang suspended.

        The Indians and Metis have their own
        section in the pub at Cochin —
        no cordons
20             no signs
                no markers
        of any kind
        no, nothing so blatant.
        But in Cochin
25        they know
           where to sit.
        Everyone in the room knows
                even you
        total stranger
30              even you know too.

But you ignore it and sit down
next to a table of Indians
           and wait
and it doesn't take long
35          no
not long at all

Someone flips a switch
          and conversation
in the room is silenced —

and even the table next to you
is frozen.

And the bartender comes over
                his face pained
and he asks
45           if you wouldn't like to
           move closer to the bar

and you are well aware
that it isn't really a question
                now
50  or ever.

*(1985)*

---

PETER WILLIAMS                       *American (1937-   )*

# [When she was here, Li Bo, she was like cold summer lager]

*Her presence was a roomful of flowers,*
*Her absence is an empty bed*
      Li Bo (701-762)

When she was here, Li Bo, she was like cold summer lager,
Like hot pastrami at Katz's on Houston Street,°        *[N.Y. delicatessen]*
Like a bright nickname on my downtown express,
Like every custardy honey from the old art books:
5  She was quadraphonic Mahler°              *[famous composer]*
And the perfect little gymnast.

Now she's gone, it's like flat Coke on Sunday morning,
Like a melted Velveeta on white, eaten
Listening to Bobby Vinton —
10  Like the Philadelphia Eagles.

*(1978)*

# The Double-Headed Snake

Not to lose the feel of the mountains
while still retaining the prairies
is a difficult thing. What's lovely
is whatever makes the adrenalin run;
5    therefore I count terror and fear among
the greatest beauty. The greatest
beauty is to be alive, forgetting nothing,
although remembrance hurts
like a foolish act, is a foolish act.

10   Beauty's whatever
makes the adrenalin run. Fear
in the mountains at night-time's
not tenuous, it is not the cold
that makes me shiver, civilized man,
15   white, I remember
the stories of the Indians,
Sis-i-utl, the double-headed snake.

Beauty's what makes
the adrenalin run. Fear at night
20   on the level plains, with no horizon
and the stars too bright, wind bitter
even in June, in winter
the snow harsh and blowing,
is what makes me
25   shiver, not the cold air alone.

And one beauty cancels another. The plains
seem secure and comfortable
at Crow's Nest Pass;° in Saskatchewan        *[in the Rocky Mountains]*
the mountains are comforting
30   to think of; among
the eastwardly diminishing hills
both the flatland and the ridge
seem easy to endure.

As one beauty
35   cancels another, remembrance
is a foolish act, a double-headed snake
striking in both directions, but I
remember plains and mountains, places
I come from, places I adhere and live in.

                    *(1968)*

# Running on Empty

As a teenager I would drive Father's
Chevrolet cross-county, given me

reluctantly: "Always keep the tank
half full, boy, half full, ya hear?"

5   The fuel gauge dipping, dipping
toward Empty, hitting Empty, then

— thrilling! — 'way below Empty,
myself driving cross-county

mile after mile, faster and faster,
10  all night long, this crazy kid driving

the earth's rolling surface,
against all laws, defying chemistry,

rules, and time, riding on nothing
but fumes, pushing luck harder

15  than anyone pushed before, the wind
screaming past like the Furies ...

I stranded myself only once, a white
night with no gas station open, ninety miles

from nowhere. Panicked for a while,
20  at standstill, myself stalled.

At dawn the car and I both refilled. But,
Father, I am running on empty still.

*(1981)*

# Margaret Atwood *Canadian (1939-    )*

## Siren song[1]

This is the one song everyone
would like to learn: the song
that is irresistible:

   the song that forces men
5  to leap overboard in squadrons
even though they see the beached skulls

the song nobody knows
because anyone who has heard it
is dead, and the others can't remember.

10  Shall I tell you the secret
and if I do, will you get me
out of this bird suit?

I don't enjoy it here
squatting on this island
15  looking picturesque and mythical

with these two feathery maniacs,
I don't enjoy singing
this trio, fatal and valuable.

I will tell the secret to you,
20  to you, only to you.
Come closer. This song

is a cry for help: Help me!
Only you, only you can,
you are unique

25  at last. Alas
it is a boring song
but it works every time.

*(1974)*

---

1   The Sirens, in Greek myth, were part-human sea nymphs whose sweet singing lured sailors to
destruction on the rocky island upon which they lived.

# All bread

All bread is made of wood,
cow dung, packed brown moss,
the bodies of dead animals, the teeth
and backbones, what is left
5   after the ravens. This dirt
flows through the stems into the grain,
into the arm, nine strokes
of the axe, skin from a tree,
good water which is the first
10  gift, four hours.

Live burial under a moist cloth,
a silver dish, the row
of white famine bellies
swollen and taut in the oven,
15  lungfuls of warm breath stopped
in the heat from an old sun.

Good bread has the salt taste
of your hands after nine
strokes of the axe, the salt
20  taste of your mouth, it smells
of its own small death, of the deaths
before and after.

Lift these ashes
into your mouth, your blood;
25  to know what you devour
is to consecrate it,
almost. All bread must be broken
so it can be shared. Together
we eat this earth.

*(1978)*


# Variations on the word love

This is a word we use to plug
holes with. It's the right size for those warm
blanks in speech, for those red heart-
shaped vacancies on the page that look nothing
5  like real hearts. Add lace
and you can sell
it. We insert it also in the one empty
space on the printed form

that comes with no instructions. There are whole
10 magazines with not much in them
but the word *love*, you can
rub it all over your body and you
can cook with it too. How do we know
it isn't what goes on at the cool
15 debaucheries of slugs under damp
pieces of cardboard? As for the weed-
seedlings nosing their tough snouts up
among the lettuces, they shout it.
Love! Love! sing the soldiers, raising
20 their glittering knives in salute.

Then there's the two
of us. This word
is far too short for us, it has only
four letters, too sparse
25 to fill those deep bare
vacuums between the stars
that press on us with their deafness.
It's not love we don't wish
to fall into, but that fear.
30 This word is not enough but it will
have to do. It's a single
vowel in this metallic
silence, a mouth that says
O again and again in wonder
35 and pain, a breath, a finger
grip on a cliffside. You can
hold on or let go.

*(1981)*

---

## SEAMUS HEANEY                    *Irish (1939-    )*

# Mid-Term Break

I sat all morning in the college sick bay
Counting bells knelling classes to a close.
At two o'clock our neighbours drove me home.

In the porch I met my father crying —
5 He had always taken funerals in his stride —
And Big Jim Evans saying it was a hard blow.

The baby cooed and laughed and rocked the pram
When I came in, and I was embarrassed
By old men standing up to shake my hand

10   And tell me they were "sorry for my trouble,"
Whispers informed strangers I was the eldest,
Away at school, as my mother held my hand

In hers and coughed out angry tearless sighs.
At ten o'clock the ambulance arrived
15   With the corpse, stanched and bandaged by the nurses.

Next morning I went up into the room. Snowdrops
And candles soothed the bedside; I saw him
For the first time in six weeks. Paler now,

Wearing a poppy bruise on his left temple,
20   He lay in the four foot box as in his cot.
No gaudy scars, the bumper knocked him clear.

A four foot box, a foot for every year.
*(1963)*                    *(1963, 1966)*


# Digging

Between my finger and my thumb
The squat pen rests; snug as a gun.

Under my window, a clean rasping sound
When the spade sinks into gravelly ground:
5   My father, digging. I look down

Till his straining rump among the flowerbeds
Bends low, comes up twenty years away
Stooping in rhythm through potato drills°                    *small furrows*
Where he was digging.

10   The coarse boot nestled on the lug, the shaft
Against the inside knee was levered firmly.
He rooted out tall tops, buried the bright edge deep
To scatter new potatoes that we picked
Loving their cool hardness in our hands.

15   By God, the old man could handle a spade.
Just like his old man.

My grandfather cut more turf° in a day                  *peat slabs*
Than any other man on Toner's bog.
Once I carried him milk in a bottle
20   Corked sloppily with paper. He straightened up
To drink it, then fell to right away
Nicking and slicing neatly, heaving sods
Over his shoulder, going down and down
For the good turf. Digging.

25   The cold smell of potato mould, the squelch and slap
Of soggy peat, the curt cuts of an edge
Through living roots awaken in my head.
But I've no spade to follow men like them.

Between my finger and my thumb
30   The squat pen rests.
I'll dig with it.

                                *(1966)*

---

# GARY HYLAND                         *Canadian (1940-    )*

# Out of Habit

They discuss things in the car driving
nowhere up and down the streets so that
if one of them screams or weeps the kids
won't be disturbed. The kids are at home
5   watching a Disney flick in the family room.
She is not sure how much she will tell him
whether to mention the other man or maybe
just the job having to keep her away.

He sits too erect, arms stiff, hands tight.
10   Tonight is different in a way he doesn't know.
What has happened? What is going on?
Everything he says begins with *but.*
It's raining. He can't find the wiper switch.

She wishes she'd brought some cigarettes. Now
15   that she has started she must finish the job.
Somewhere in this purse there are cigarettes.
His rational spiel is almost over. She
breathes deeply, mumbles that she doesn't want
to be married. She has no reasons. Just that.
20   There is no traffic, no one on the sidewalks.

She looks at house lights through wet glass.
How many of them she wonders, how many.

He pulls into a closed service station.
Trying to expel the pain, coughing, crying, he
25   doubles over, slams himself against the door.
She lights a cigarette and takes a slow drag.
He looks like one of those black and white
films, the old ones where nothing much happens.

He gets out, walks a while in the cool rain,
30   over and over slamming wet fist into wet palm.

Her breath mists the windows. He gets in,
turns on the defogger, the headlights, the wipers.
Out of habit the car returns them to the house.

*(1991)*

---

# JAMES WELCH                    *Blackfoot/Gros Ventre/American (1940-    )*

## Surviving

The day-long cold hard rain drove
like sun through all the cedar sky
we had that late fall. We huddled
close as cows before the bellied stove.
5   Told stories. Blackbird cleared his mind,
thought of things he'd left behind, spoke:

"Oftentimes, when sun was easy in my bones,
I dreamed of ways to make this land."
We envied eagles easy in their range.
10   "That thin girl, old cook's kid, stripped naked
for a coke or two and cooked her special stew
round back of the mess tent Sundays."
Sparrows skittered through the black brush.

That night the moon slipped a notch, hung
15   black for just a second, just long enough
for wet black things to sneak away our cache
of meat. To stay alive this way, it's hard....

*(1971)*

# for all my Grandmothers

A hairnet covered her head.
a net
encasing the silver strands.
A cage
5   confining the wildness.
No thread escaped.

(once, your hair coursed down your back
streaming behind
as you ran through the woods.
10   Catching on branches,
the crackling filaments
gathered leaves.
Burrs attached themselves.
A redbird plucked a shiny thread
15   for her nest,
shed a feather that glided
into the black cloud and
became a part of you.
You sang as you ran.
20   Your moccasins
skimmed the earth.
Heh ho oh heh heh)

Prematurely taken
from the woodland.
25   Giving birth
to children that grew
in a world that is white.
Prematurely
you put your hair up and
30   covered it
with a net.
Prematurely grey
they called it.

Hair Binding.

35   Damming the flow.

With no words, quietly
the hair fell out
formed webs on your dresser

on your pillow
40  in your brush.
These tangled strands
pushed to the back of a drawer
wait for me.
To untangle
45  To comb through
To weave together the split fibers
and make a material
Strong enough
to encompass our lives.

*(1988)*

---

# MARIE ANNHARTE BAKER    *Anishinabe/Canadian (1942-    )*

## Pretty Tough Skin Woman

old dried out meat piece
preserved without a museum
missing a few big rips
her skin was guaranteed

5   her bloomers turned grey
outliving the city washing
not enough drinks to keep her
from getting home to the bush

tough she pushed bear fat down
10  squeezed into sally ann° clothes                    *Salvation Army*
she covered up her horny places
they tried sticking her under

soft jelly spots remain in bone
holding up this pretty tough hide
15  useful as a decorated shield for baby
swinging in her sweet little stink

just smell her old memories, gutted fish
baked muskrat — she saw a lady
in a shopping mall with a fur coat
20  told her an Indian must eat such delicacies

her taste was good she just needed a gun
to find a room in the city to put down

her beat-up mattress where her insides fell out
visitors ate up the bannock drank her tea

25 they were good at hocking her radio or tv
everywhere she stopped she told her troubles
if I press my ear down on this trail I bet
I'll be able to hear her laughing and gabbing

*(1990)*

---

MARK VINZ                          *American (1942-    )*

# The Other Side

Hoods were the ones who knew
about wheels, who smoked and shaved
and even got the stuck-up girls
to turn their heads.
5 Like Kenny Liston in his black
leather jacket and motorcycle boots
with those half-moon cleats, years
older than the rest of us 9th graders,
who said he kept a switchblade
10 somewhere up his sleeve. Kenny Liston
under the awning of the little store
across the street, chain-smoking Camels
while we watched amazed from the
windows of our history classroom.
15 Kenny Liston, begging my English
homework and getting it, because
it never hurt to have a friend like him
who kept the others off you in the pool.
Kenny Liston in typing class
20 the day the teacher said he was
hopeless, always jamming the keys.
We watched his throat and ears
turn red, and then he did it —
took the brand-new Smith Corona
25 to the third floor window and
pitched it out.
                    Later, we heard
Kenny robbed the little store and shot
it out with cops over on Clinton Avenue.
30 The rumors grew. He'd stolen a
beer truck and passed out samples
at Central High just up the street.

He'd taken the principal's car and
driven all the way to Florida. Who
35  knows the truth in 9th grade anyway?
All we cared about was that he
terrified us, that he knew what
we didn't and dared to do it.
How we hoped we could forget Kenny,
40  never imagining we'd be meeting him
over and over again, out there
cruising in his stolen wheels with a
back seat full of smashed typewriters,
giving the finger to all the hopeless cases
45  trapped behind the window glass.

*(1992)*

---

MICHAEL ONDAATJE                    *Canadian (1943-    )*

# A House Divided

This midnight breathing
heaves with no sensible rhythm,
is fashioned by no metronome.
Your body, eager
5   for the extra yard of bed,
reconnoitres and outflanks;
I bend in peculiar angles.

This nightly battle is fought with subtleties:
you get pregnant, I'm sure,
10  just for extra ground
— immune from kicks now.

Inside you now's another,
thrashing like a fish,
swinging, fighting
15  for its inch already.

*(1967)*

*how there in the plaid light in broad
daylight she played
with his affections plied them spikes from
his heart
she stood by pliers in hand
he has his pride*

lady lady how you play
with me & my tennis ball heart
the pleas i let loose plop them prop them at your
feet
5          please i say please

how petty it all seems how paltry
you sitting pretty & partly it is
my putty heart flaps
the way poultry flap when a skunk shows up

10         when i go courting your affections
you lob them archly achingly
back to the back of courtesy
right to the very edge of cow pastures
smash my overtures when timidly
15      they approach the net hope for some small return
gentle return is what i go for

& yet you volley my hopefulness
boom it back in thunder
it's lumber you're stacking
20      not that i mind my hesitant serves you slash cross
court your loud & curt returns your backhand
compliments

but
do you really think i deserve this
25      the passing shots you serve me ill madam
the way you take shots at me
stroke after vicious stroke
boy oh boy i don't mind saying i find it hard
to go in for this courting

feel i am somehow
courting disaster
plain & simple

though you stand constant as Thor[1]
at the net you have strung
between us my heart slams
when you slam your racket
when you shout love
at the top of your lungs

*(1992)*

---

TOM WAYMAN                                    *Canadian (1945-    )*

# Did I Miss Anything?

*Question frequently asked by students after missing a class*

Nothing. When we realized you weren't here
we sat with our hands folded on our desks
in silence, for the full two hours

Everything. I gave an exam worth
40 per cent of the grade for this term
and assigned some reading due today
on which I'm about to hand out a quiz
worth 50 per cent

Nothing. None of the content of this course
has value or meaning
Take as many days off as you like:
any activities we undertake as a class
I assure you will not matter either to you or me
and are without purpose

Everything. A few minutes after we began last time
a shaft of light descended and an angel
or other heavenly being appeared
and revealed to us what each woman or man must do
to attain divine wisdom in this life and
the hereafter

---

1 Norse god of war and thunder.

221

This is the last time the class will meet
before we disperse to bring this good news to all people on earth

Nothing. When you are not present
how could something significant occur?

25      Everything. Contained in this classroom
is a microcosm of human existence
assembled for you to query and examine and ponder
This is not the only place such an opportunity has been gathered
but it was one place

30      And you weren't here

*(1993)*

---

## R.L. BARTH                  *American (1947-    )*

# The Insert[1]

Our view of sky, jungle, and fields constricts
Into a sink hole covered with saw-grass

Undulating, soon whipped slant as the chopper
Hovers at four feet. Rapt, boot deep in slime,

5   We deploy ourselves in a loose perimeter,
Listening for incoming rockets above

The thump of rotor blades; edgy for contact,
Junkies of terror impatient to shoot up.

Nothing moves, nothing sounds; then, single file,
10  We move across a stream-bed toward high ground.

The terror of the insert's quickly over.
Too quickly ... and more quickly every time ...

*(1981)*

---

1  The dropping of troops into an area by helicopter. Barth, a United States marine from 1966 to 1969, served in Vietnam.

# Cities Behind Glass

Dusty light falls through windows
where entire families journey together, alone.
Mothers open the sills and shake the old world
from lace tablecloths.

5    Beneath flowered babushkas°             *Russian head scarves*
immigrant women put their faith in city buses.
They take refuge behind glass,
lay their heads against windows.
Behind veined eyelids
10   they journey.

Brussels, perhaps, is their destination
where older women make lace,
wrapping linen around pins
and where the sun lies down in spider webs.

15  On the street
invisible panes of glass are strapped
to the sides of a truck.
The world shows through
filled with people, with red horses
20  making their departures between streets.
Inside that slow horse flesh
behind blinders
the dark animals are running,
shadow horses,
25  horses of light
running across American hills.

Everything is foreign here.
No one sees me.
No one sees this woman walking city streets.
30  No one sees the animals running inside my skin,
the deep forest of southern trees,
the dark grandmothers looking through my eyes,
taking it in, traveling still.

*(1985)*

# Mary Old Owl

The owl
crevice sitter
opens its eyes
only at night
5    to watch
for prey

She awoke one night late. The air, clean and cold, tingled raw edges on her nose. She remembered the bright sunlight that day and how green branches, piled high, suddenly snapped and the snow dust whirled, then slowly settled
10    into all-whiteness. She could trace, in her mind, pencil thin tracks in the snow that squiggled over big ruffle-edged ones.

On chill
nights
little things
15    that feed
on decay
leave tracks

A neighbour, smoking by in an old cattle-feed truck, stopped for a cup of tea. He said we were having a "cold snap." She wondered if that had anything
20    to do with the sound frozen trees made in the still black nights when even three quilts weren't enough. But her poppa liked the snow-cold. He brought home some fool hens along with some of those "smart-ass coyotes." There was a grand meal that night: fire roasted hen, skin-boiled potatoes, bannock, and sweet dried Saskatoons.

25    She wondered if maybe "smart-ass coyotes" were anything like "bad-ass injuns." Her knees still had scabs that bled, from when some kids had pushed her down and called her and her little brother that.

In the dark she heard a soft sound
She could see herself
30    Her body was
old,
her bones like powder
the soft sound
rose
35    from her
bone-powder body

In a whirl
of soft white
dust wings
40    the owl
rose silently

Later, when she left home for Edmonton, nights were sometimes that cold, when she stood outside the beer parlours, waiting. The cold stung her nostrils but there were no more sunlit days, green branches, or roast to remember. Only
45  the snow, the tracks and a scab that still bled.

> Low over moon dust mounds
> the old owl hunts
> Whisper wings brush
> little tracks
50  that scurry legs
> and fur and bones
> which splinter
> easily
> Warm blood trickles

*(1991)*

---

L<small>ORNA</small> C<small>ROZIER</small>                                    *Canadian (1948-    )*

# On the Seventh Day

On the first day God said
*Let there be light.*
And there was light.
On the second day
5  God said, *Let there be light,*
and there was more light.

*What are you doing?* asked God's wife,
knowing he was the dreamy sort.
*You created light yesterday.*

10  *I forgot,* God said. *What can I do
about it now?*

*Nothing,* said his wife.
*But pay attention!*
And in a huff she left
15  to do the many chores
a wife must do in the vast
(though dustless) rooms of heaven.

On the third day God said
*Let there be light.* And
20  on the fourth and the fifth
(his wife off visiting his mother).

When she returned there was only
the sixth day left. The light

225

was so blinding, so dazzling
25 God had to stretch and stretch the sky to hold it
and the sky took up all the room —
it was bigger than anything
even God could imagine.
*Quick*, his wife said,
30 *make something to stand on!*
God cried, *Let there be earth!*
and a thin line of soil
nudged against the sky like a run-over serpent
bearing all the blue in the world on its back.

35 On the seventh day God rested
as he always did. Well, *rest*
wasn't exactly the right word,
his wife had to admit.

On the seventh day God
40 went into his study
and wrote in his journal
in huge curlicues and loops
and large crosses on the *t*'s
changing all the facts, of course,
45 even creating Woman
from a Man's rib, imagine that!
But why be upset? she thought.
Who's going to believe it?

Anyway, she had her work to do.
50 Everything he'd forgotten
she had to create
with only a day left to do it.
Leaf by leaf,
paw by paw, two by two,
55 and now nothing
could be immortal
as in the original plan.

*Go out and multiply*, yes,
she'd have to say it,
60 but there was too little room for
life without end,
forever and ever,
always, eternal, *ad infinitum*
on that thin spit of earth
65 under that huge prairie sky.

                    *(1992)*

# Prayer to the Pacific

I traveled to the ocean
        distant
           from my southwest land of sandrock
           to the moving blue water
5         Big as the myth of origin.

Pale
pale water in the yellow-white light of
         sun    floating west
             to China
10        where ocean herself was born.
Clouds that blow across the sand are wet.

Squat in the wet sand and speak to the Ocean:
        I return to you    turquoise    the red coral you sent us,
            sister spirit of Earth.
15 Four round stones in my pocket    I carry back the ocean
         to suck and to taste.

Thirty thousand years ago
        Indians came riding across the ocean
        carried by giant sea turtles.
20 Waves were high that day
        great sea turtles waded    slowly out
           from the gray sundown sea.
Grandfather Turtle rolled in the sand    four times
        and disappeared
25           swimming into the sun.

And so    from that time
        immemorial,
           as the old people say,
rain clouds drift from the west
30         gift from the ocean.

Green leaves in the wind
Wet earth on my feet
        swallowing raindrops
           clear from China.

*(1981)*

BETH CUTHAND                    *Cree/Canadian (1949-    )*

# Four Songs for the Fifth Generation

*Drums, chants, and rattles*
*pounded earth and*
          *heartbeats*
          *heartbeats*

5      "They were our life     the life
            of the prairies
      We loved them
            and they loved us.
      Sometimes     they were so many
10    they flowed     like a river
      over the hills     into the valleys.

      I saw them.     I knew them.
      I helped my mother
            cut away their skin
15          chop their bones
      and dry their meat
            Many times
            many times.

      Aye, but now     they are gone
20          ghosts     all ghosts.

      The sickness came
            we were hungry
      I saw my children     die
      one by one
25    one by one.

      There was no freedom     then my girl
            They were stronger
            They thought they knew
      what it was     their God wanted.

30    Aye, but now     they are gone
            ghosts     just ghosts.

      Sometimes     I think I hear
      their thunder     smell their dust
      at night my girl
35          at night I dream
      dream of their warm blood

                 their hides covering
Aye, covering          all my children
              in their sleep."

40  *Drums, chants, and rattles*
    *pounded earth and*
              *heartbeats*
              *heartbeats.*

    "That's the old Simmons homestead.
45            He's dead now
    I don't know what happened
              to his wife     and children.

    Back in the thirties
              we cut posts for him
50  10 cents a post       that was good money
              back then.
    Clarence Simmons was his name
              came from England
                 with his skinny little wife
55  and a bunch of pale scrawny little kids.

    Poor Simmons      we felt sorry for him
              so we helped him
                 as much as we could.

    Back in the thirties,
60  things weren't so bad for us
                 as it was for the homesteaders
    We hadn't cut our trees
                 or tore up the land.
                 We still had deer
65                 and fish
                    rabbits
    and gophers and fat dogs
                       heh heh

    But the settlers really suffered.
70            It was pitiful.
    My dad would tell us
                 'take this meat over to the Simmons
                 place. Drop it at the door.'

    So I'd ride over       real quiet
75            and hang it by the house

    Poor Simmons
                 one day he hung himself

                    from a tree
                        in his yard.
80    Couldn't take it no more.
                    Dad found him,
                    cut him down
        and laid him        real gentle
                    on the ground
85                      under the tree.


        That was one of the few times
                    I ever saw him cry.


        I don't know what makes
                    some men
90                      go on living
        while other men
                    give up."


        *Drums, chants and rattles*
        *pounded earth and*
95                      *heartbeats*
                        *heartbeats.*


        "It was 1960
                    when dad and mom
                    got the vote.
100   All us kids got copies of Canada's
                    'Declaration of Human Rights'
        and took them home
                    and put them up
                    all over the walls.
105   Yeah, that was a great day
        for Canada
                    'Oh Canada
                    Our true north strong and free.'


        We moved south when I was ten
110         to a town with sidewalks
                    and running water
        and a playground with a pool
                    not a lake
        'Hey Injuns!        Yer not allowed
115             in the pool.
        You'll get it dirty,
                    dirty.'


        We closed ranks after that
                    spent a lot of time
120             exploring the creek.


230

My brother found an arrowhead
    Some white kid said
      it didn't belong to us,
so my brother beat him up.

125 My brother was always
           fighting
      It seemed
    he had a rage
      that wouldn't go out.
130 Me,       I just retreated
    and retreated
      until I couldn't
      find myself.

There was a boy down the street
135    who had it in
      for my brother
      called him dirty Indian.
He'd sick his dog on him
      every time
140    we'd walk to school.
We took to walking the long way,
    everyone    except my brother.

One time my brother hit that dog
    smack between the eyes
145      with a rock
The old dog tucked his tail
    between his legs and
    went howling off
      behind the house.

150 The boy came to our place
    with a baseball bat
We were all going to go out
    and kick that kid around,
but dad said 'No
155    let your brother
   fight it out.'

They were pretty evenly matched
    the kid with his bat,
    my brother with his stones
160      they fought
    for an hour

kicking
hitting
scratching
165 punching
thwacking
ripping

Mom wanted to stop them
    but Dad said no.
170     'He's got to take a stand.'

Finally it was over
    nobody won.

That kid never sicked
    his dog on my brother again.
175       but
my brother's rage
never did go away."

*Drums, chants and rattles*
*pounded earth and*
180       *heartbeats*
      *heartbeats.*

"I don't want to go
    to a white high school
      Mama.
185 My spirit would die
    in a place like that
I love our little school
    us Indians
    we help each other.
190     We care.
We share smokes Mom

When I grow up
will my kids
have to fight
195 for a place in the neighbourhood
too?"

*Drums, chants and rattles*
*pounded earth and*
      *heartbeats*
200       *heartbeats.*

*(1989)*

# She Had Some Horses

She had some horses.

She had horses who were bodies of sand.
She had horses who were maps drawn of blood.
She had horses who were skins of ocean water.
5   She had horses who were the blue air of sky.
She had horses who were fur and teeth.
She had horses who were clay and would break.
She had horses who were splintered red cliff.

She had some horses.

10   She had horses with long, pointed breasts.
She had horses with full, brown thighs.
She had horses who laughed too much.
She had horses who threw rocks at glass houses.
She had horses who licked razor blades.

15   She had some horses.

She had horses who danced in their mothers' arms.
She had horses who thought they were the sun and their
bodies shone and burned like stars.
She had horses who waltzed nightly on the moon.
20   She had horses who were much too shy, and kept quiet
in stalls of their own making.

She had some horses.

She had horses who liked Creek Stomp Dance songs.
She had horses who cried in their beer.
25   She had horses who spit at male queens who made
them afraid of themselves.
She had horses who said they weren't afraid.
She had horses who lied.
She had horses who told the truth, who were stripped
30   bare of their tongues.

She had some horses.

She had horses who called themselves, "horse."
She had horses who called themselves, "spirit," and kept
their voices secret and to themselves.

She had horses who had no names.
She had horses who had books of names.

She had some horses.

She had horses who whispered in the dark, who were afraid to speak.
She had horses who screamed out of fear of the silence, who
40 carried knives to protect themselves from ghosts.
She had horses who waited for destruction.
She had horses who waited for resurrection.

She had some horses.

She had horses who got down on their knees for any saviour.
45 She had horses who thought their high price had saved them.
She had horses who tried to save her, who climbed in her
bed at night and prayed as they raped her.

She had some horses.

She had some horses she loved.
50 She had some horses she hated.

These were the same horses.

*(1982)*

---

**DI BRANDT**                                   *Canadian (1952-     )*

# [completely seduced]

completely seduced
by motherhood,

this is how you got
through the day

5   without sleep,
without pay,

without help,
words,

companions,
10   a break.

your mind bouncing
off walls,

    & the ceiling
    & the floor,

15    eyes blurred
    with exhaustion.

    you weren't thinking
    about that.

    you weren't thinking
20    about your stretched

    skin.

    you saw yourself
    in the dark pool

    of your baby's eyes,
25    shining,

    a goddess, the source,
    the very planet.

    your breaths flowing
    together,

30    your breasts filled
    with milk & honey.

    all night, you were
    the earth,

    rocking.

35    (later you shrank
    into an ordinary

    middle-aged woman,
    enjoying sleep.

    amused by the ordinary
40    world,

    half mother,
    half not mother.

    bewildered by time
    and place,

45    & wrinkled skin.
    & missing children.)

*(1992)*

# ANITA ENDREZZE-DANIELSON    *Yaqui/American (1952-    )*

## The Stripper

### I

On the stage, mirrored many times,
my body is cubed and squared,
sequined and feathered, bare
and rounded, bright and hot
5   under the lights and sweaty stares;
drum roll, grinding hips, pivot
swing, cupping my warm hands slowly
up to my breast, slipping off
the red laced bra in twenty wet sighs
10   unfastening silk underwear to reveal
skin dark fur, musty stroke of things,
while they grasp their brown bottles
and I groan, opening my mouth,
looking not at the men below
15   but at the luminous green exit sign.

### II

During the intermissions, I walk over
the thrown coins on the floor, mostly dimes,
into the bathroom to replace
my breasts, flick ashes into toilet bowls
20   put back my underwear Newberry pink
and fluff out the black feathers:
I always lose some every time.
These lights show the bones carving
through the finish of my face:
25   Jukebox songs knife years across my lips,
echoing in the hollows of my cheeks,
rattling my tongue dry,
but the only music in here
is the gargle of the toilets
30   and the sound of its blue beat
matching the wine in my veins.

*(1973)*

236

# The Way to the Heart[1]

*Wīhtikōw* travels
with a hatchet, bladder pail
and snares.
His ragged moccasin feet bare
5    to thistles, to rocks, to snow.

He boils robins and sparrows.
The tiny bones stain
necklaces, little skulls on breasts.
He lives a lonely life
10    filled with relatives in his gut,
dreaming of fat Indians
in the deep of winter.

*Wīhtikōw* and *Wīsahkecāhk* meet.
*Wīsahkecāhk* is a laughing fox,
15    coyote, and word-hustler.
Chickadee sings about the time *Wīsahkecāhk*
ate dry meat-scabs that fell off his rump.

*Wīhtikōw* casts a spell.
He thinks.

20    *Wīsahkecāhk* dances,
building fires for *Wīhtikōw*. Dancing the feast of death.
*Sihkos*, slender weasel, little brother
pokes his breath
to watch the dance and feast of bones.
25    Dance, oh dance, little brother,
travel the back hole of
*Wīhtikōw*. Cut the straps
inside his chest. Tomorrow
you will be most celebrated.

30    And when *Wīhtikōw* blew
the fire rose, the back hole
opened, foul wind breathed.
Little brother travelled
up the dark passage
35    to the North
and the heart of *Wīhtikōw* was cut.

---

1   This poem refers to legendary Cree figures: *Wīhtikōw* is a greedy cannibal who terrorizes the
people; *Wīsahkecāhk*, the ambiguous trickster/teacher hero (or antihero); *Sihkos* is the Weasel.

*Wīsahkecāhk*, spirit of vision
*Wīhtīkōw*, spirit of twisted hunger,
they dance, they dance,
40 come alive, come alive. Let
tobacco speak, the spirit
of *sihkos* will free you.

*(1994)*

---

## LOUISE ERDRICH *Chippewa/American (1954-    )*

# Dear John Wayne

August and the drive-in picture is packed.
We lounge on the hood of the Pontiac
surrounded by the slow-burning spirals they sell
at the window, to vanquish the hordes of mosquitoes.
5 Nothing works. They break through the smoke screen for blood.

Always the lookout spots the Indians first,
spread north to south, barring progress.
The Sioux or some other Plains bunch
in spectacular columns, ICBM missiles,
10 feathers bristling in the meaningful sunset.

The drum breaks. There will be no parlance.
Only the arrows whining, a death-cloud of nerves
swarming down on the settlers
who die beautifully, tumbling like dust weeds
15 into the history that brought us all here
together: this wide screen beneath the sign of the bear.

The sky fills, acres of blue squint and eye
that the crowd cheers. His face moves over us,
a thick cloud of vengeance, pitted
20 like the land that was once flesh. Each rut,
each scar makes a promise: *It is*
*not over, this fight, not as long as you resist.*

*Everything we see belongs to us.*

A few laughing Indians fall over the hood
25 slipping in the hot spilled butter.
*The eye sees a lot, John, but the heart is so blind.*
*Death makes us owners of nothing.*
He smiles, a horizon of teeth

the credits reel over, and then the white fields
30  again blowing in the true-to-life dark.
The dark films over everything.
We get into the car
scratching our mosquito bites, speechless and small
as people are when the movie is done.
35  We are back in our skins.

How can we help but keep hearing his voice,
the flip side of the sound track, still playing:
*Come on, boys, we got them*
*where we want them, drunk, running.*
40  *They'll give us what we want, what we need.*
Even his disease was the idea of taking everything.
Those cells, burning, doubling, splitting out of their skins.

                    *(1984)*


# Indian Boarding School: The Runaways

Home's the place we head for in our sleep.
Boxcars stumbling north in dreams
don't wait for us. We catch them on the run.
The rails, old lacerations° that we love,                    *rough tears or cuts*
5   shoot parallel across the face and break
just under Turtle Mountains.° Riding scars                    *[in North Dakota]*
you can't get lost. Home is the place they cross.

The lame guard strikes a match and makes the dark
less tolerant. We watch through cracks in boards
10  as the land starts rolling, rolling till it hurts
to be here, cold in regulation clothes.
We know the sheriff's waiting at midrun
to take us back. His car is dumb and warm.
The highway doesn't rock, it only hums
15  like a wing of long insults. The worn-down welts
of ancient punishments lead back and forth.

All runaways wear dresses, long green ones,
the color you would think shame was. We scrub
the sidewalks down because it's shameful work.
20  Our brushes cut the stone in watered arcs
and in the soak frail outlines shiver clear
a moment, things us kids pressed on the dark
face before it hardened, pale, remembering
delicate old injuries, the spines of names and leaves.

                    *(1984)*

# Jacklight[1]

*The same Chippewa word is used both for flirting and hunting game,*
*while another Chippewa word connotes both using force in intercourse*
*and also killing a bear with one's bare hands.*

R.W. Dunning, *Social and Economic Change*
*Among the Northern Ojibwa (1959)*

We have come to the edge of the woods,
out of brown grass where we slept, unseen,
out of knotted twigs, out of leaves creaked shut,
out of hiding.

5    At first the light wavered, glancing over us.
Then it clenched to a fist of light that pointed,
searched out, divided us.
Each took the beams like direct blows the heart answers.
Each of us moved forward alone.

10  We have come to the edge of the woods,
drawn out of ourselves by this night sun,
this battery of polarized acids,
that outshines the moon.

We smell them behind it
15  but they are faceless, invisible.
We smell the raw steel of their gun barrels,
mink oil on leather, their tongues of sour barley.
We smell their mothers buried chin-deep in wet dirt.
We smell their fathers with scoured knuckles,
20  teeth cracked from hot marrow.
We smell their sisters of crushed dogwood, bruised apples,
of fractured cups and concussions of burnt hooks.

We smell their breath steaming lightly behind the jacklight.
We smell the itch underneath the caked guts on their clothes.
25  We smell their minds like silver hammers

cocked back, held in readiness
for the first of us to step into the open.

We have come to the edge of the woods,
out of brown grass where we slept, unseen,
30  out of leaves creaked shut, out of our hiding.
We have come here too long.

---

1  A light used for hunting or fishing to attract game or fish for easy capture (usually illegal).

It is their turn now,
their turn to follow us. Listen,
they put down their equipment.
35   It is useless in the tall brush.
And now they take the first steps, not knowing
how deep the woods are and lightless.
How deep the woods are.

*(1984)*

ഇരു

# GLOSSARY OF LITERARY TERMS

The following list is selective. It concentrates on critical terms of the greatest use in the study of poetry at an introductory university level, and in discussing works in this anthology. Since all poems involve characters and many have plots, however, some terms relevant to narratives are also included. Cross-referencing has been kept to a minimum, so look for such compounds as *feminine rhyme* under Rhyme or *hexameter* under Metre. Bold roman type within an entry indicates a term defined in the glossary; *bold italic type* indicates an important term not defined elsewhere in the glossary.

**Accent.** The rhythmical alternation of light and heavy (unstressed and stressed) syllables in verse. See **Metre**.

**Action.** Derived from Aristotle, another term for **plot**.

**Alexandrine.** A poetic line of six iambic feet (iambic hexameter). See **Metre**.

**Allegory.** A narrative with at least two parallel levels of meaning, one literal (concrete) and one figurative (abstract); the latter is often moral or political. Fables and parables are simple allegories. "The Castaway" (page 78) is a more complex example.

**Alliteration.** Repetition of the same initial sounds in words close together. For example, see line 4 of Blake's "The Chimney Sweeper" (page 80).

**Allusion.** A reference in a literary work to something outside the work itself (often from literature, history, mythology, or the Bible) which the author expects readers to recognize. Meredith, for example, alludes to the banquet scene in Macbeth in his "At dinner, she is hostess, I am host" (page 114).

**Anapest.** A metrical foot consisting of two unaccented syllables followed by an accented one. See **Metre**.

**Anaphora.** A figure of speech repeating words or phrases. For an example, see Harjo's "She Had Some Horses" (page 233).

**Antagonist.** The opponent of the **protagonist** in a plot. The conflict of the two generates the action of the narrative. A more appropriate term than "villain" in most cases. See **Character**.

**Antistrophe.** The second section of an **ode**.

**Apostrophe.** Address to an absent character or personification: "Death be not proud" (Donne, page 26), "O Rose, thou art sick" (Blake, page 83). See **Figures of Speech**.

**Archetype.** Recurrent characters, narrative patterns, or images that are universal in human experience and literature. Examples include the death and rebirth of the hero, the journey to the underworld, the quest, the cruel mother or temptress. An example of the last is Keats's "La Belle Dame Sans Merci" (page 96).

**Assonance.** Repetition of the same vowel sounds in a series of words close together: "I *ro*se and *to*ld him of my *wo*e."

**Aubade.** A lyric about dawn or the morning, originally about lovers parting. Wordsworth's "Composed Upon Westminster Bridge" (page 87) is a serious example, Swift's "A Description of the Morning" (page 57) a parodic one.

**Ballad.** A narrative poem, originally of folk origin, commonly in quatrains rhyming *abcb* and containing a **refrain**. Ballads frequently also use dialogue. A traditional example is "Edward" (page 4). In the nineteenth and twentieth centuries, many poets have imitated the older examples in *literary* ballads such as Keats's "La Belle Dame Sans Merci" (page 96) or Robinson's "Richard Cory" (page 135). See also **Common Measure**.

**Blank Verse.** Unrhymed iambic pentameter lines. See **Metre.**

**Cacophony.** Harsh and unpleasant sounding language, usually emphasizing consonants such as *b, c, d, g, k, p,* and *t.* For example, the opening stanza of Owen's "Dulce et Decorum" (page 154). Cf. **Euphony.**

**Caesura(e).** An obvious pause in a poetic line, normally indicated by punctuation, as in Pope's

> A needless alexandrine ends the song,
> That, // like a wounded snake, // drags its slow length along.

**Carpe Diem.** "Seize the day" in Latin, from an ode of Horace. A work which stresses the brevity of life, youth, or beauty and therefore urges making the most of time. See Herrick's "To the Virgins" (page 32) or Souster's "The Lilac Poem" (page 180).

**Catastrophe.** Another term for a tragic denouement. See **Plot.**

**Character.** The imaginary "persons" of a literary work. Those who are one-dimensional are usually called *flat* and include *stereotypes* and *stock characters* (the skin-flint miser, pathetic orphan, nagging wife, hard-drinking private eye). *Round* characters are complex and individual. *Dynamic* characters grow and change; *static* ones remain the same. Characters can also be classified as **protagonist** (the main figure in a work) or **antagonist** (the opposing character or force), or as **foils** (a minor character with qualities contrasting with those of the protagonist in order to highlight the latter).

**Chiasmus.** A **figure of speech** in which the order of terms in the first of two parallel clauses is reversed in the second: "Despised, if ugly; if she's fair, betrayed" (Mary Leapor, 1751). The shepherdess in Ralegh's "The Nymph's Reply" (page 14) uses the figure in line 11.

**Climax.** Turning point in an action. See **Plot.**

**Chorus.** See **Ode.**

**Common Measure.** A four-line stanza of alternate iambic tetrameter and trimeter, used often in ballads and hymns. See **Stanza.**

**Complication.** The second stage of a plot.

**Conceit.** An elaborate or bizarre **metaphor.**

**Conflict.** The struggle between opposing forces causing an action. See **Plot** and **Character.**

**Connotation.** The social, personal, and emotional associations a word may carry, which go beyond its literal or denotative meaning. Thus "cat" for many people has connotations of aloofness, independence, stealthiness, and mystery while "dog" suggests familiarity, companionship, dependence, or even inferiority. Cf. **Denotation.**

**Consonance.** The repetition of inner or final consonant sounds when the preceding vowels differ, as in "torn - burn" or "flush - flash." At the ends of lines it creates *imperfect* or *slant* rhyme. Examples occur in Emily Dickinson's "A narrow Fellow in the Grass" (page 117).

**Couplet.** A pair of rhymed lines, either independent as a stanza (as in some **epigrams**) or as a component of a larger unit (as in the Shakespearean **sonnet** or *heroic* verse, composed of a succession of iambic pentameter couplets). See **Metre** and **Stanza.**

**Crisis.** Peak or moment of tension in an action. See **Plot.**

**Dactyl.** A metrical foot consisting of an accented syllable followed by two unaccented ones. See **Metre.**

**Denotation.** The literal dictionary meaning of a word. Cf. **Connotation.**

**Denouement.** The "unknotting" of the threads of an action after the climax. See **Plot.**

**Diction.** An author's word choices and an important element of style. Diction may be *formal (high)*, using elaborate words in complicated sentences, *informal (low)*, using simple colloquial language and sentences, or a combination of the two known as *standard* or *general (middle)*. Diction in verse also tends to use more *concrete* or specific language than *abstract* or general words which describe ideas, qualities or concepts. Consequently, imagery is important in poetry, as are the connotations of words.

**Double Entendre.** A sexual pun.

**Elegy.** A poem lamenting the death of an individual, such as Dryden's "To the Memory of Mr. Oldham" (page 46) or Kroetsch's "Elegy for Wong Toy" (page 186). Gray's "Ode on the Death of a Favourite Cat" (page 70) is a comic version.

**End-Stopped (Line).** A verse line concluding a grammatical sense unit, usually indicated by a semicolon or period. Cf. **Run-On (Line).**

**Enjambment.** Use of run-on lines.

**Envoi (Envoy).** A short concluding stanza, summarizing a poem's theme, repeating a refrain line, or addressing a prince or patron. Chaucer does the last in his "Complaint to His Purse" (page 11).

**Epigram.** A short, pithy (and often witty or satirical) poem or saying. This anthology contains examples by Harington, Donne, Prior, Gay, Pope, Wesley, Byron, Crane, Frost, and Hughes.

**Epigraph.** In literature, a relevant, short quotation or motto placed at the head of the work. Auden's "The Unknown Citizen" provides an example (page 165).

**Epode.** The final section of an ode.

**Euphony.** Pleasing, mellifluous sounds created by numerous vowels and smooth consonants. Cf. **Cacophony.** For an example, see **Onomatopaeia.**

**Exposition.** The opening, informational stage of an action. See **Plot.**

**Fable.** A simple **allegory,** whose characters are usually animals.

**Figures of Speech.** A general term covering forms of language which suggest more than their literal meanings. It commonly applies to comparisons of denotatively dissimilar things in **metaphor** or **simile** or comparisons emphasizing the relation between parts and a whole (**synecdoche**) or a concrete object and a more abstract concept (**metonymy**). Related to these are **personification** and **apostrophe.** This category also includes rhetorical devices such as **anaphora** (repetition of words or phrases); parallelisms and antitheses of various sorts including **chiasmus; hyperbole** (overstatement), **understatement** and other forms of **irony; paradox;** and **pun.**

**Foil.** A character contrasting with a major figure.

**Foot.** A unit of rhythm in verse. See **Metre.**

**Form.** The overall organizing principle of a literary work. In verse, *closed form* refers to poems with obvious **metre,** stanzaic patterns or rhyme schemes. *Open form,* often called **free verse,** has no regular patterns but structures according to the meaning as the poem develops.

**Foreshadowing.** The presentation early in a work of some event, character, atmosphere, or image which anticipates later developments.

**Free Verse.** See **Form.**

**Freytag Pyramid.** The analysis of a narrative action into five parts structured in rising and falling form with a climax at the apex. Devised by the German critic Gustav Freytag (1863). See **Plot.**

**Genre.** Loosely, a type or kind of literature defined by some conventions of literary form. Manner of presentation defines the major genres of fiction, drama, and poetry.

Subgenres of these include the detective novel, sentimental comedy, or confessional lyric. Some subgenres are created by fixed forms, such as the sestina, sonnet, or villanelle.

Haiku. A seventeen-syllable, three-line form of Japanese verse emphasizing concrete images of the natural world. Influential on earlier twentieth-century imagist poetry such as Pound's "In a Station of the Metro" (page 151).

Hyperbole. A figure of speech using overstatement or exaggeration, as in Burns's "A Red, Red Rose" (page 85).

Iamb. A verse foot of an unaccented syllable followed by an accented one. See Metre.

Image, Imagery. Words, usually concrete, which appeal to the physical senses — most often sight (*visual* image) but also the other four (*auditory, tactile, gustatory,* and *olfactory* images). There are also *kinetic* images of movement or change. A *pattern of imagery* is a group of related images in a work. See also Synaesthesia.

Irony. A literary device or situation which depends on differences in understanding or values between characters and the narrator or reader. In *verbal irony,* a character says one thing but means something different; it frequently depends upon overstatement (hyperbole), understatement, or sarcasm (blatantly obvious irony). For example, see Wyatt's use of "kindly" in "They flee from me" (page 12). *Situational irony* occurs when something different from the expected happens as in "Porphyria's Lover" (page 105). If fate plays a part in this, the irony is called *fatal* or *cosmic irony;* for an example, see Hardy's "The Convergence of the Twain" (page 123). *Dramatic irony* depends on the audience knowing more than a character does. The classic case is Sophocles's *Oedipus the King.* A complex exercise in several forms of irony is Hardy's "The Workbox" (page 124).

Jargon. The specialized language of a particular profession or trade. See Diction.

Language. See Diction. For figurative language, see Figures of Speech.

Lyric. Originally in Greek, a song accompanied by lyre. In more recent times, a relatively short poem expressing a speaker's intense, subjective thoughts or feelings. Examples include Swift's "Stella's Birthday" (page 57), Keats's "When I have fears that I may cease to be" (page 98), and Smith's "Not Waving but Drowning" (page 162).

Metaphor. A figure of speech comparing two items which have different denotations but similar connotations. For instance, Jacques in *As You Like It* says, "All the world's a stage,/And all the men and women merely players" (page 21). I.A. Richards describes this metaphorical transfer by using the terms *tenor* (the general idea being expressed) and *vehicle* (the concrete image which conveys the meaning). The tenor in Jacques' comparison is human life; his vehicle is theatrical drama. Metaphors generally say, in other words, that "X is Y." A simile more obviously signals its figurative nature by introducing such a comparison with the terms "like," "as" (also "as if," or "as though"), or "resembles." For example, Burns writes "O my Luve's like a red, red rose" (page 85). Metaphors and similes may be *simple* (occurring in a single, isolated comparison, as is Burns) or *extended* (developed over a whole work, or large portion of a work, for example Bradstreet's "The Author to Her Book" [page 41]). They may also be *explicit* ("He is a pig") or *implicit* ("He bellied up to his trough" or "Time is on the wing"). A conceit is an elaborate, ingenious, even bizarre, metaphor or simile, such as Donne's extended use of the insect in "The Flea" (page 27). In his sonnet "My mistress' eyes are nothing like the sun" (page 20), Shakespeare mocks a set of cliché conceits Elizabethan sonneteers imitated from the fourteenth-century lyricist Petrarch.

**Metaphysical Poets.** The name given to a diverse group of earlier seventeenth-century poets whose themes include physical love, religious devotion, and death. These themes are treated with witty ingenuity, odd **paradox**, erudite **allusion**, and surprising **metaphor** or **conceit**. John Donne is the most famous of them; others represented in this anthology are George Herbert and Andrew Marvell.

**Metonymy.** A **figure of speech** which replaces the word for one thing with a term closely associated with it, for example, "the press" for journalism, "Parliament Hill" for the Canadian legislature, or "cradle" and "grave" for birth and death. See also **Synecdoche**, a related figure.

**Metre.** Recurrent patterns of accented and unaccented syllables in verse. A metrical unit is a **foot**, consisting of two or three syllables, with at least one stressed. *Rising metres* go from unaccented to accented, *falling metres* the opposite. The commonest feet are these:

| | | | |
|---|---|---|---|
| *Rising Metres:* | *iambic* | ∪ — | (the *iamb*) |
| | *anapestic* | ∪∪ — | (the *anapest*) |
| *Falling Metres:* | *trochaic* | — ∪ | (the *trochee*) |
| | *dactylic* | — ∪∪ | (the *dactyl*) |

Iambic metre is by far the commonest in English verse, though poems in the other three (especially anapestic) exist. More commonly, however, the other three provide the occasional foot in an iambic line for variety or emphasis. Other brief interruptions in a line of regular feet may be provided by substitution of one of these:

| | | |
|---|---|---|
| *spondaic* | — — | (the *spondee*) |
| *pyrrhic* | ∪∪ | (the *pyrrhic*) |
| *imperfect* | either ∪ or — | |

A poem's metre is described in terms of the kind of foot (iambic or anapestic, for example) and the number of feet in a line:

*monometer* (one foot)
*dimeter* (two feet)
*trimeter* (three feet)
*tetrameter* (four feet)
*pentameter* (five feet)
*hexameter* (six feet). If iambic also called an *alexandrine*.
*heptameter* (seven feet). If iambic also called a *fourteener*.

Some examples, including substitutions:

Iambic tetrameter:

The grave's | a fine | and priv | ate place,
But none, | I think, | do there | embrace.

(Marvell, "To His Coy Mistress" [page 44])

Close to | the sun | in lone | ly lands,
Ringed with | the az | ure world, | he stands.

(Alfred, Lord Tennyson, "The Eagle")

Anapestic trimeter and dimeter define the perfect *limerick*, but the following illustrates a common substitution of an iambic foot at the start of lines 1, 2, 4, and 5:

> ⏑ — | ⏑ ⏑ — | ⏑ ⏑ — |
> There was | a young man | of Moose Jaw |
> ⏑ — | ⏑ ⏑ — | ⏑ ⏑ — |
> Who want | ed to meet | Bernard Shaw; |
> ⏑ ⏑ — | ⏑ ⏑ — |
> When they ques | tioned him, "Why?" |
> ⏑ — | ⏑ ⏑— |
> He made | no reply, |
> ⏑ — | ⏑ ⏑ — | ⏑⏑ — |
> But sharp | ened his axe | and a saw.
>                    (from *Punch*, 1918)

Iambic pentameter is the most common metrical pattern in English; numerous examples can be found in this anthology. When rhymed in pairs, such lines are called *heroic* couplets; when unrhymed, *blank* verse.

**Monologue.** An extended speech by a single character. A *dramatic* monologue is addressed to a silent listener or *narratee* in the text.

**Narratee.** See Monologue.

**Narrative.** The relation of a sequence of events in an action by a narrator. Many poems, especially ballads, romances, and epics are narratives which recount "stories." See Plot.

**Narrator.** The voice and implied speaker who tells a "story." See Point of View.

**Octave.** An eight-line stanza, or the opening section of an *Italian* sonnet.

**Ode.** Originally a choral lyric in Greek drama, divided into strophe, antistrophe, and epode. This three-part structure was also used by Pindar in his elaborate praises of Olympic heroes; his large-scale formal tone (but not structure) was revived in the seventeenth-century *irregular pindaric* (see, for instance, Dryden's "A Song for St. Cecilia's Day" [page 46]). A more intimate type of ode, with a shorter, repeated stanza form, was practiced by Horace and also imitated after the Renaissance. Examples include Gray's "Ode on the Death of a Favourite Cat" (page 70) and Keats's "To Autumn" (page 97).

**Onomatopoeia.** Words whose sounds suggest their meaning ("buzz," "ding-dong") or lines of verse whose sound conveys much of their meaning, as in these from Tennyson's *The Princess*:

> The moan of doves in immemorial elms,
> And murmuring of innumerable bees.

**Open Form.** See Form.

**Oxymoron.** A condensed form of paradox conveyed by a combination of two contradictory terms: "bittersweet," "jumbo shrimp," "a deafening silence," or Milton's "darkness visible." See also Figures of Speech.

**Paradox.** A seemingly contradictory situation or statement which is nonetheless valid. Donne's "Death thou shalt die" (page 26) is an example. See also Oxymoron and Figures of Speech.

**Pastoral.** From "pastor" (Latin for shepherd), a poem or drama idealizing rustic life. A good example is Marlowe's "The Passionate Shepherd to his Love" (page 17).

**Persona.** From Greek "actor's mask," a first person narrator, usually to be distinguished from the author. See Point of View.

**Personification.** A **figure of speech** attributing human characteristics to nonhuman things or abstractions, as in Waller's "Go, lovely rose!/Tell her that wastes her time and me/...How sweet and fair she seems to be" (page 37).

**Plot.** Traditionally, a causally related series of actions in a literary work. E.M. Forster differentiates a story from a plot because the former has only time-sequence and lacks causal connections; his examples are useful: "The King died, and then the Queen died" is a story, while "The King died, and then the Queen died of grief" is a plot. Larger-scale literary works may intertwine *double* or *triple plots* of equal importance. If one or more actions are less significant than another, they are termed *subplots* and *main plot* respectively.

Plots are generated by a **conflict** between a **protagonist** and an **antagonist** (see **Character**) and, according to the nineteenth-century critic Gustav Freytag, are structured into the following parts: **exposition** (introduction of characters, setting, etc.); **complication** (the conflict and *rising action* begins); **crisis** (the conflict nears the height of its tension leading to the **climax** at which a decisive action takes place); then ensues a *falling action* consisting of **denouement** (the unravelling of the plot threads as a consequence of the protagonist's decision, also called the *catastrophe* in tragedy) and **resolution** (closure of the action).

**Point of View.** The narrative perspective of a literary work. The **narrator** may be a character in the work (*first-person narrator*), or someone not part of the action (*third-person narrator*). In the latter case, he or she may know the actions and thoughts of all the participants (*omniscient narrator*) or focus on one or two only (*limited omniscient narrator*). First-person narrators are limited in what they can know of others' internal doings, and may be *unreliable* because they do not understand what they report, are biased or even insane. Third-person narrators are normally *reliable* but may be uncertain or ambiguous in the information they provide. If the perspective is like that one would get by watching the action unfold on stage — largely through dialogue — the point of view is *dramatic* or *objective.*

**Prosody.** The study of the sounds and rhythms of verse. See **Metre** and **Rhyme**.

**Protagonist.** See **Character** and **Plot**.

**Pun.** A witty word play depending on the fact that some words have multiple **denotations** or that words of different denotations sound the same. Gay's "Let us take the road" (page 63) depends on puns. A sexual pun is usually identified by the French term **double entendre** (double meaning). Pope uses this sort of pun in "Epitaph on the Stanton-Harcourt Lovers" (page 66).

**Pyrrhic.** See **Metre**.

**Quatrain.** A four-line stanza.

**Refrain.** A repeated group of words within a poem or song, as in the **ballad**.

**Resolution.** The final stage of closure in a traditional **plot**.

**Rhyme.** The repetition of the final vowel sound and any following consonants (a syllable) or two or more words produces *perfect* or *exact* rhyme (b<u>orn</u>/h<u>orn</u>). *End rhymes* are most common in verse lines; *internal rhymes* occur within a line. The example above is a *single rhyme*, but multiple pairs of similar-sounding syllables can produce *double rhyme* (prairie sch<u>ooner</u>/piano t<u>uner</u>) or *triple rhyme*, as in Byron's celebrated

> But O ye lords of ladies intellectual,
> Inform us, truly, have they not hen-pecked-you-all.

Such multiple rhymes work best in comic and satiric verse, and depend on *falling* metres which end with unaccented syllables. These are often called *feminine* (or *falling*) rhymes and they produce a lame, anticlimactic feel. The **trochaic** double rhymes in the even-numbered lines of "Miniver Cheevy" (page 135) are as appropriately ridiculous as Robinson's character. *Masculine* (or *rising*) rhymes end on accented syllables produced by iambic or anapestic metre. *Imperfect rhyme* (also called *slant rhyme, near rhyme,* or *off rhyme*) occurs when consonants in two words are the same, but intervening vowels differ (pick/pack). See Consonance.

Rhythm. The regular pattern of sounds in verse. See Metre. Irregular patterns produce free verse. Hopkins uses *sprung rhythm* in which the number of strong accents in a line determines the rhythm, regardless of how many weak accents exist. See his poems in this anthology (pages 126-128).

Rising Action. The developing action of a plot created by conflict and complication.

Run-On (Line). A line of verse with no final punctuation or normal pause. Cf. End-Stopped (Line).

Sarcasm. See Irony.

Satire. An aesthetically-satisfying literary attack on human follies or vices as measured against normative social, religious, or moral standards. How well does Lawrence's "How Beastly the Bourgeois Is" (page 150) fit these criteria? Cf., say, Swift's "A Satirical Elegy on the Death of a Late Famous General" (page 59).

Scansion. The analysis of metre.

Sestet. A six-line stanza, or the concluding section of an *Italian* sonnet.

Setting. The place, atmosphere, and social or cultural ideas of a literary work.

Simile. A form of metaphor, using "like," "as," etc.

Soliloquy. A convention in drama in which a character speaks directly, and honestly, to the audience to reveal inner thoughts and feelings, as Hamlet often does. In poetry, an example is Browning's "Soliloquy of the Spanish Cloister" (page 108).

Sonnet. A poem, normally of fourteen lines and in iambic pentameter (see Metre). Two major types are common: the *Italian*, or Petrarchan, with an octave of two quatrains (rhymed *abba/abba*) and a sestet (most often *cdc/cdc*); and the *English*, or Shakespearean, consisting of three quatrains rhymed *abab/cdcd/efef* and a concluding couplet. Spenser uses interlocking rhymes in the quatrains (pages 15-16). More modern poets continue the tradition of sonnets; see, for example, Poe's "Sonnet: To Science" (page 99), Frost's "The Silken Tent" (page 141) or Cummings' "next to of course god america i" (page 156). Meredith alters the sonnet's standard format (as have others) in his *Modern Love* sonnets of sixteen lines (page 114), just as he alters its traditional romantic content.

Spondee. See Metre.

Stanza. A group of lines in a poem which forms a metrical or thematic unit. Except for *heroic* couplets, these are usually separated by typographical blank space on the page. Common *stanzaic forms* are the couplet (two lines), tercet (three lines), quatrain (four lines), sestet (six lines), and octave (eight lines). *Heroic* couplets are common in epigrams and also in much larger units, such as in the verse of Chaucer, Bradshaw, Dryden, or Pope. Ballad stanzas and common measure alternate tetrameter and trimeter lines (see Metre), but whereas common measure uses an *abab* rhyme scheme, ballads usually rhyme only the even-numbered lines.

Story. The common name for a narrative or action. See Plot.

Stress. Accent or emphasis (strong or weak) on syllables in words:

e.g. (car̄ | pĕt).

Regular patterns of accents create metre.

**Strophe.** The initial section of an ode.

**Symbol.** An object, action, or person whose meaning transcends its **denotation** (literal meaning) in a complex way, as a flag — a piece of coloured cloth — stands for a nation, or as a cross represents a particular religion and theology. Some symbols are *universal* or *cultural*. These are *conventional* symbols and have meanings for a particular group of people: the red rose for love; springtime or morning for new beginnings, hope, and optimism. *Private* or *contextual* symbols are those created by a particular author (as the "gyre" by Yeats) or gain meaning within an individual work (the albatross in Coleridge's "The Rime of the Ancient Mariner" or the white whale in Melville's *Moby Dick*). Sometimes authors build upon universal or conventional symbols, adding meanings appropriate within a particular work, as Blake does in "The Sick Rose" (page 83).

**Synaesthesia.** A kind of image which mixes the experience of the physical senses, in which one type of image-sensation is referred to in terms more appropriate to another. Thus, jazz (auditory) can be described as "hot" or "cool" (tactile or sensational); colours can be "loud"; we can feel "blue." Kipling writes: "The dawn comes up like thunder" and Robert Graves: "How hot the scent is of the summer rose."

**Synecdoche.** A **figure of speech** in which a part stands for the whole ("hired hand" for labourer, "wheels" or "hot rods" for cars, "foot soldiers" for infantry).

**Tercet.** A three-line stanza.

**Theme.** Central or dominant idea of a literary work, made concrete by the details of **plot, character, setting** (and the like) described in the work. A theme makes an assertion about a subject or topic. For instance, that "war is hell," "love conquers all," or that "human wishes are vain."

**Tone.** Attitude of a speaker or author of a literary work to the subject itself and/or the audience, revealed by the **diction** and arrangement of details. The tone of a work may be sad, joyful, solemn, pessimistic, or ironic (see **Irony**). Cf. the sombre tone of Arnold's "Dover Beach (page 112) with the comic exuberance of Denis Cooley's "how there in the plaid light" (page 220).

**Triplet.** A sequence of three rhyming verse lines. See **Rhyme**.

**Trochee.** A metrical foot consisting of an accented syllable followed by an unstressed syllable. See **Metre**.

**Understatement.** A **figure of speech** which, for emphasis, treats a situation as less significant than it really is, hence a form of **irony**.

**Verse.** Used in two senses: as a unit of poetry (a line or a **stanza**); or poetry in general, as distinct from prose. A *verse paragraph* is a group of verse lines forming a subdivision of a long poem, usually indented like a prose paragraph and written in *blank verse* (unrhymed iambic pentameter — see **Metre**), *heroic* couplet, or *free verse* (poetry without regular **metre**, line length, or **rhyme** scheme). For examples, see Marvell's "To His Coy Mistress" (page 44) or Prior's "An Epitaph" (page 55).

**Villanelle.** A medieval French verse form of nineteen lines (of any length) divided into six **stanzas** — five **tercets** and a final **quatrain** — employing two **rhymes** and two **refrains**. The refrains consist of lines 1 (repeated as lines 6, 12, and 18) and 3 (repeated as lines 9, 15, and 19). The final quatrain concludes by repeating both lines 1 and 3. A famous modern example is Dylan Thomas's "Do Not Go Gentle into That Good Night" (page 176). See also Mandel's "City Park Merry-Go-Round" (page 184).

# ACKNOWLEDGEMENTS

IAN ADAM. "Hallowe'en" by Ian Adam is reprinted from *Draft: An Anthology of Prairie Poetry* (Turnstone Press, 1981). Reprinted by permission of the author.

MAYA ANGELOU. "Africa" is reprinted from *Oh Pray My Wings are Gonna Fit Me Well* by Maya Angelou. Copyright © 1975 by Maya Angelou. Reprinted by permission of Random House, Inc.

JEANNETTE ARMSTRONG. "Mary Old Owl" is reprinted from Jeannette Armstrong's poetry collection *Breath Tracks* published by Theytus Books (ISBN 0-919441-39-4, $9.95 retail). Reprinted by permission of Theytus Books Ltd.

MARGARET ATWOOD. "Siren song," "Variations on the word *love*," and "All bread" from *Selected Poems 1966-1984* by Margaret Atwood. Copyright © Margaret Atwood 1990. Reprinted by permission of Oxford University Press Canada.

W.H. AUDEN. "The Unknown Citizen" from *Collected Poems* by W.H. Auden. Copyright © 1940 and renewed 1968 by W.H. Auden. Reprinted by permission of Random House, Inc.

MARIE ANNHARTE BAKER. "Pretty Tough Skin Woman" is reprinted from *Being on the Moon* (Polestar, 1990) by Marie Annharte Baker. Reprinted by permission of Polestar Book Publishers Ltd., 1011 Commercial Drive, Vancouver, BC V5L 3X1.

R. L. BARTH. "The Insert" is reprinted from *Forced Marching in the Styx: Vietnam War Poems* by R.L. Barth by permission of Perivale Press. Copyright by Perivale Press, 1983.

JOHN BETJEMAN. "In Westminster Abbey" reprinted from *John Betjeman: Collected Poems* (John Murray (Publishers) Ltd., 1979) by permission of John Murray (Publishers) Ltd.

EARLE BIRNEY. "Bushed" is from *The Collected Poems of Earle Birney* by Earle Birney. Used by permission of the Canadian Publishers, McClelland & Stewart, Toronto.

DI BRANDT. "completely seduced" by Di Brandt is reprinted from *mother, not mother* (Mercury Press, 1992). Reprinted by permission of the author.

BETH BRANT. "for all my Grandmothers" is reprinted from *Songs from this Earth on Turtle's Back: Contemporary American Indian Poetry* (The Greenfield Review Press, 1983) by permission of the author.

ELIZABETH BREWSTER. "The Night Grandma Died" by Elizabeth Brewster is reprinted from *Selected Poems* by permission of Oberon Press.

LEONARD COHEN. "Suzanne" and "I Have Not Lingered in European Monasteries" are reprinted from *Stranger Music* by Leonard Cohen. Used by permission of the Canadian Publishers, McClelland & Stewart, Toronto.

ELIZABETH COOK-LYNN. "Grandfather at the Indian Health Clinic" is reprinted from *Harper's Anthology of 20th Century Native American Poetry* (Harper & Row, 1988), edited by Duane Niatum. Reprinted by permission of the author.

DENNIS COOLEY. "how there in the plaid" is from *200% Cracked Wheat* (Coteau Books, 1992) edited by Gary Hyland, Barbara Sapergia and Geoffrey Ursell. Reprinted by permission of the author.

LORNA CROZIER. "On the Seventh Day" is reprinted from *Inventing the Hawk* by Lorna Crozier. Used by permission of the Canadian Publishers, McClelland & Stewart, Toronto.

E.E. CUMMINGS. "in Just-," "next to of course god america i," and "anyone lived in a pretty how town" are reprinted from *Complete Poems: 1904-1962* by E.E. Cummings, edited by George J. Firmage, by permission of Liveright Publishing Corporation. Copyright © 1923, 1926, 1940, 1951, 1954, 1968, 1991 by the Trustees for the E.E. Cummings Trust. Copyright © 1976, 1985 by George James Firmage.

ROBERT CURRIE. "A Day No Pigs Would Die" is reprinted from *Moving Out* (Coteau Books, 1975) by permission of the author.

BETH CUTHAND. "Four Songs for the Fifth Generation" is from *Voices in the Waterfall* (1989) by Beth Cuthand. Reprinted by permission of the author.

EMILY DICKINSON. "Much Madness is divinest Sense," "I heard a Fly buzz when I died," "Because I could not stop for Death," "A narrow Fellow in the Grass," and "Tell all the Truth, but tell it slant" reprinted by permission of the publishers and the Trustees of Amherst College from *The Poems of Emily Dickinson*, Thomas H. Johnson, ed., Cambridge, Mass.: The Belknap Press of Harvard University Press, Copyright © 1951, 1955, 1979, 1983 by the President and Fellows of Harvard College.

ANITA ENDREZZE-DANIELSON. "The Stripper" is reprinted from *The Malahat Review* (No. 33, January 1975).

LOUISE ERDRICH. "Dear John Wayne," "Indian Boarding School: The Runaways" and "Jacklight" are reprinted from *Jacklight* by Louise Erdrich. Copyright © 1984 by Louise Erdrich. Reprinted by permission of Henry Holt and Co., Inc.

LAWRENCE FERLINGHETTI. "Constantly risking absurdity" is reprinted from *A Coney Island of the Mind*. Copyright © 1958 by Lawrence Ferlinghetti. Reprinted by permission of New Directions Publishing Corp.

ROBERT FINCH. "Egg-and-Dart" from *Poems* by Robert Finch. Copyright © Oxford University Press Canada 1946. Reprinted by permission of Oxford University Press Canada.

ROBERT FRANCIS. "Pitcher" reprinted from *The Orb Weaver*, © 1960 by Robert Francis, Wesleyan University Press by permission of University Press of New England.

ROBERT FROST. "Fire and Ice," "The Silken Tent," and "Nothing Gold Can Stay" are reprinted from *The Poetry of Robert Frost* edited by Edward Connery Lathem. Copyright 1942, 1951 by Robert Frost. Copyright © 1970 by Lesley Frost Ballantine. Copyright 1923 © 1969 by Henry Holt and Co., Inc. Reprinted by permission of Henry Holt and Co., Inc.

RALPH GUSTAFSON. "The Sun in the Garden" is from *The Moment is All: Selected Poems 1944-83* by Ralph Gustafson. Used by permission of the Canadian Publishers, McClelland & Stewart, Toronto.

LOUISE HALFE. "The Way to the Heart" is excerpted from *Bear Bones & Feathers* by Louise Bernice

252

# Index of Authors, Titles and First Lines of Poems

Authors are indicated by bold uppercase text, poem titles by regular text, first lines of poems by italic text. Poems with no given title are entered only by first line.